ROYAL HISTORICAL SOCIETY
STUDIES IN HISTORY
New Series

DEBATING ENGLAND'S ARISTOCRACY IN THE 1790s

PAMPHLETS, POLEMICS AND POLITICAL IDEAS

Studies in History New Series
Editorial Board

Professor John Morrill (*Convenor*)
Professor Michael Braddick
Dr S. D. Church
Professor Julian Hoppit (*Honorary Treasurer*)
Dr Janet Hunter (*Economic History Society*)
Professor Aled Jones (*Literary Director*)
Dr Rebecca Spang
Professor Miles Taylor
Dr Alexandra Walsham

This series is supported by annual subventions from the Economic History Society and from the Past and Present Society

F. G. Byron, 'The Knight of the Woeful Countenance going to extirpate the National Assembly'. Burke is shown emerging from the publishers, carrying a shield with the motif 'Shield of Aristocracy and Despotism'.
Reproduced by courtesy of the British Museum

DEBATING ENGLAND'S ARISTOCRACY IN THE 1790s

PAMPHLETS, POLEMICS AND POLITICAL IDEAS

Amanda Goodrich

THE ROYAL HISTORICAL SOCIETY
THE BOYDELL PRESS

© Amanda Goodrich 2005

All rights reserved. Except as permitted under current legislation
no part of this work may be photocopied, stored in a retrieval system,
published, performed in public, adapted, broadcast,
transmitted, recorded or reproduced in any form or by any means,
without the prior permission of the copyright owner

The right of Amanda Goodrich to be identified as
the author of this work has been asserted in accordance with
sections 77 and 78 of the Copyright, Designs and Patents Act 1988

First published 2005
The Royal Historical Society, London
in association with
The Boydell Press, Woodbridge
Reprinted in paperback and transferred to digital printing 2011
The Boydell Press, Woodbridge

ISBN 97 0 86193 275 7 hardback
ISBN 978 1 84383 647 6 paperback

The Boydell Press is an imprint of Boydell & Brewer Ltd
PO Box 9, Woodbridge, Suffolk IP12 3DF, UK
and of Boydell & Brewer Inc,
668 Mt Hope Avenue, Rochester, NY 14620, USA
website: www.boydellandbrewer.com

A CIP catalogue record for this book is available
from the British Library

Library of Congress Catalog Card Number 2004025415

This publication is printed on acid-free paper

Contents

		Page
Acknowledgements		ix
Abbreviations		x
Introduction		1
1	Edmund Burke and *Reflections*	29
2	Thomas Paine and Painite radicalism, 1791–1792	56
3	Loyalist responses to Paine, 1791–1792	85
4	Radical debates and diversification, 1793–1796	113
5	Loyalist strategies and synthesis, 1793–1796	139
Conclusion		166
Bibliography		183
Index		205

Publication of this volume was aided by a grant from the Scouloudi Foundation, in association with the Institute of Historical Research.

Acknowledgements

First, I would like to thank all who taught me with such enthusiasm and talent in the History and English Literature departments at Roehampton Institute in the early 1990s. In particular I would like to thank John Seed for his interest as a tutor and for pushing me on to Royal Holloway University of London and a PhD. John has remained a valued friend and referee ever since.

In researching this book I have received funding from Royal Holloway and the AHRB, which has made a break-through in offering part-time awards, for which I am most grateful.

David Eastwood, my advisory editor for the Royal Historical Society's *Studies in History*, deserves thanks for his support and enthusiasm for my work, as does Christine Linehan for all her skill and patience as executive editor. For references, suggestions and general support I would like to thank Mark Philp, Stephen Conway, Frank O'Gorman, Tim Hitchcock, Julian Hoppit and my fellow PhD students and friends Nicky Pullin and Sarah Toulalan. For his early PhD supervision I acknowledge the contribution made by Gregory Claeys.

It is to Penelope Corfield that I owe the greatest debt and offer my heart-felt thanks. Her excellent PhD supervision and good-humoured guidance over the major hurdles to completion of this book could not have been better. She remains a valued referee, reader, advisor, support and friend. Finally, I thank deeply Lenny Goodrich for his enduring support, emotional and financial, without which I could not even have started.

Amanda Goodrich

Abbreviations

Association	Association for Preserving Liberty and Property against Republicans and Levellers
Association papers	Association for Preserving Liberty and Property against Republicans and Levellers, *Association papers, I: Publications printed by special order of the Society for Preserving Liberty and Property Against Republicans and Levellers, at the Crown and Anchor, in the Strand; II: A collection of tracts, printed at the expense of that society, to which are prefixed, a preface, and the proceedings of the society* (1793) [BLPC, shelfmark, 1141.d.6]
BL	British Library
BLPC	British Library Public Catalogue
ECS	*Eighteenth Century Studies*
EHR	*English Historical Review*
HJ	*Historical Journal*
HPT	*History of Political Thought*
JBS	*Journal of British Studies*
JHI	*Journal of the History of Ideas*
LCS	London Corresponding Society
OED	*The new Oxford dictionary of English*, ed. Judy Pearsall, Oxford 1998
P&P	*Past and Present*
Political broadsides	British Library bound collection of tracts, broadsides, poems, songs and other similar material [BLPC, shelfmark, 648.c.26]
PT	*Political Theory*
SH	*Social History*
SCI	Society for Constitutional Information. For regional branches 'SCI' has the region as a prefix, for example 'Birmingham SCI'

Some pamphlet titles have been cited in abbreviated form in the footnotes; full titles are included in the bibliography.

Introduction

> Mr Burke, in a frenzy of passion, has drawn away the veil; and aristocracy, like a decayed prostitute, whom painting and patching will no longer embellish, throws off her covering, to get a livelihood by displaying her ugliness.[1]

This book focuses upon a key debate in modern political ideas. It is not another social history of the aristocracy of the eighteenth century. Nor is it an attempt to engage with the so-called French Revolution debate in conventional terms.[2] It does not set out to answer the question who won the debate: radicals?[3] Or loyalists?[4] And how they went about it. That is ground already well trodden. Rather this book probes the very centre of the debate, that is the representations of aristocracy that were promulgated in the mass of political writings published between 1790 and 1796. It seeks to reveal how contemporary perceptions of the English aristocracy developed in response to the French Revolution and the corresponding debate in England, and to

---

1 Joel Barlow, *Advice to the privileged orders part 2*, London 1793, in Gregory Claeys (ed.), *Political writings of the 1790s: French Revolution debate in Britain*, London 1995, iii. 324–5.
2 For general studies see, for example, Gregory Claeys, 'The French Revolution debate and British political thought', *HPT* xi (1990), 59–80; Ian R. Christie, *Stress and stability in eighteenth-century Britain*, Oxford 1986; H. T. Dickinson, *Liberty and property: political ideology in eighteenth-century Britain*, London 1977; H. T. Dickinson (ed.), *Britain and the French Revolution, 1789–1815*, London 1994; and Albert Goodwin, *The friends of liberty: the English democratic movement in the age of the French Revolution*, London 1979.
3 Major works on radicalism include H. T. Dickinson, *British radicalism and the French Revolution, 1789–1815*, Oxford 1985; Goodwin, *Friends of liberty*; Mark Philp, 'The fragmented ideology of reform', in Mark Philp (ed.), *The French Revolution and British popular politics*, Cambridge 1991, 38–49; E. P. Thompson, *The making of the English working class*, London 1991; and Gwyn Williams, *Artisans and sans-culottes: popular movements in France and Britain during the French Revolution*, London 1981.
4 For major works on loyalism see J. C. D. Clark, *English society, 1688–1832: ideology, social structure and political practice during the ancien regime*, Cambridge 1985; H. T. Dickinson, 'Popular conservatism and militant loyalism, 1789–1815', in Dickinson, *Britain and the French Revolution*, 103–26; Robert Dozier, *For king, constitution and country: the English loyalists and the French Revolution*, Lexington, Ky 1983; David Eastwood, 'Patriotism and the English state in the 1790s', in Philp, *French Revolution*, 118–45; Michael Duffy, 'William Pitt and the origins of the loyalist Association Movement of 1792', *HJ* xxxix (1996), 943–62; Clive Elmsley, 'Repression, "Terror" and the rule of law in England during the decade of the French Revolution', *EHR* c (1985), 801–25; Austin Mitchell, 'The Association Movement of 1792–3', *HJ* iv (1961), 56–77; and Thomas P. Schofield, 'Conservative political thought in Britain in response to the French Revolution', *HJ* xxix (1986), 601–22.

demonstrate how far such representations influenced contemporary political ideas. It also examines in detail the radical attack on aristocracy and the significance of the loyalist response for the survival of the aristocracy into the next century and beyond.

Although much work has been done by historians to uncover histories of the people and the role of the working classes,[5] or to seek out an ever-elusive middle class, no full study has been made of the representations of the aristocracy in the political writings of this period. Here, for the most part, I will give only a somewhat schematic summary of the relevant historiography. Aristocracy has so often appeared, particularly in the twentieth-century historiography, as an adjunct to the central focus of another sector of society, as the anchor holding back progress in the development of another class or interest group. Historians have regularly studied representations of the middle class, but few have focused on the aristocracy.[6] Yet it is clear that a readjustment is necessary and that the centrality of representations of aristocracy in political writings needs to be asserted.

Moreover this book is a history 'of discourse rather than behaviour'.[7] Of course, in a sense discourse is a form of behaviour, but it is not the day-to-day social and political behaviour of the aristocracy which is the prime concern here. Nor is this study about parliamentary politics *per se*. Rather it explores the discourses that developed within extra-parliamentary political writing, the so-called pamphlet war. During the years 1790–6 a profusion of political pamphlets were written, published and devoured by supporters and opponents almost before the author's ink was dry. Responses were published within weeks and responses to responses rapidly followed. The debate was propelled along at lightning speed by a profusion of paper – paper inscribed with the heated political opinions and prejudices, the sentiment and rhetoric of the political writers and propagandists of the day. These were works created for immediate public consumption in the swiftly moving debate; they were not, on the whole, ponderous, planned, cogent treatises. The authors' intentions are often lost in the obscurity of a hastily written text or in the

---

[5] H. T. Dickinson, 'Popular loyalism in Britain in the 1790s', in Eckhart Hellmuth (ed.), *The transformation of political culture: England and Germany in the late eighteenth century*, Oxford 1990; Ian McCalman, *Radical underworld: prophets, revolutionaries, and pornographers in London, 1795–1840*, Oxford 1988; John Stevenson, 'Popular radicalism and popular protest, 1789–1815', in Dickinson, *Britain and the French Revolution*; Thompson, *Making of the English working class*; Roger Wells, *Insurrection: the British experience, 1795–1803*, Gloucester 1983; Williams, *Artisans and sans-culottes*; Alan Booth, 'Popular loyalism and public violence in the north-west of England, 1790–1800', SH viii (1983), 295–313.
[6] See, for example, Dror Wahrman, *Imagining the middle class: the political representation of class in Britain, c. 1780–1840*, Cambridge 1995.
[7] J. G. A. Pocock, *Virtue, commerce, and history: essays on political thought and history, chiefly in the eighteenth century*, Cambridge 1995, 14.

INTRODUCTION

barrage of responses which have so swiftly ransacked and distorted its intentions and integrity.

It is these political pamphlets and the representations they contain that are the subject of discussion. In the French Revolution debate it was the influences of a moment which dictated what became the dominant representations from within the myriad of possibilities. Within the pamphlets models of society were created and rejected, questions about leadership debated, and competing languages were introduced and abandoned. These developments, reflected in the representations of aristocracy, reveal much about contemporary ideas and perceptions of aristocracy and its role in government and society. As Mark Philp has noted, the pamphlet debate had 'considerable significance as a watershed in the development of British liberal and conservative political thought'.[8] Such representations of aristocracy are explored here through three major themes: the centrality of aristocracy to the debate; the emergence of new radical and loyalist models and definitions of society; and the issue of 'representation' and 'reality'.

But before moving on to these themes, the selection of the years 1790 to 1796 as the focus of this book requires some consideration. Certainly, the period does not reflect the absolute beginning or end of any political event or debate. The French Revolution, which forms the backdrop to this book, most famously erupted with the storming of the Bastille on 14 July 1789 and raged until 1815.[9] In England, it was Richard Price's *A discourse on the love of our country* (1789) that triggered the French Revolution debate. The eventual finale of these arguments is often pinpointed as culminating in the Reform Bill of 1832. Yet the pamphlet debate, which developed from 1790, continued in any meaningful sense only until 1796. Indeed pamphlet publication figures reveal that the debate reached its peak in 1793 and declined quite significantly thereafter.[10] Certainly once William Pitt's government took action to suppress radical writings by prosecuting authors and booksellers, it became more difficult for radicals to publish their work.[11] The Two Acts of 1795 against treason and sedition[12] were the final blow to early 1790s radicalism.

---

[8] Philp, *French Revolution*, 5.
[9] The revolution was in fact initiated by a number of smaller, less symbolic events which commenced in February 1787 with the meeting of the Assembly of Notables, and included the convening of the Estates-General on 1 May 1789 and the Third Estate declaring itself to be the National Assembly on 17 June 1789.
[10] For a table of publications and detailed survey of the pamphlet literature see Amanda Goodrich 'Peers or parasites? Debating the English aristocracy in the 1790s', unpubl. PhD diss. London 2001, 217, 216–231. See also Claeys, *Political writings*, i, p. xliii.
[11] Paine was just one of the radical writers convicted for publishing a seditious libel, *Rights of man, part 2*, in December 1792: Goodwin, *Friends of liberty*, 268–306.
[12] Sedition legislation consisted of two royal proclamations against sedition which were issued on 21 May 1792 and 4 November 1795 and the 'Two Acts' which were 'An Act for the safety and Preservation of His Majesty's Person and Government against Treasonable

Consequently, during the second half of the decade, the possibility of free debate about the revolution was severely limited.[13] Radicalism was pushed underground and became a minority movement of hardcore extremists more interested in action than writing pamphlets.[14] Thus the period 1790–6 represents a small section of the encompassing French Revolution debate, but it has been selected for close analysis on the grounds of its central significance in terms of the volume and intensity of political pamphleteering. It was the period during which the vast majority of political pamphlets on the French Revolution debate was produced. Most important for the discussion here, the years 1790–6 also mark the period in which the English aristocracy became the central focus of the debate and was represented in political writings in a number of new ways.

Themes for debate

There is little doubt that the English aristocracy maintained a central role in both government and society throughout the eighteenth century. In reality England was governed by what amounted to an aristocratic oligarchy.[15] Representations suggest, however, that this was not the perception of the majority of English people before 1790. It was widely believed, even by reformers, that England had a 'mixed' government consisting of monarchy, lords and commons, in which, due to the excellence of England's constitution, each of the three branches was, or could be, kept in balance. Indeed a reforming Whig tradition promoted constitutional reform as the means of maintaining that balance: albeit reform that retained aristocratic political and social supremacy. So great was the English faith in its own constitution that many of those, including reform Whigs, who expressed support for the French Revolution in its initial stages, believed that the revolution would be resolved by France adopting a constitution modelled on the English version. Nevertheless, despite the Whig tradition of reform and the Foxite Whig support for the French Revolution in its initial stages, during the early 1790s extra-parliamentary radicalism overtook Whig politics as the locus of reform and took the debate further towards revolution. The French Revolution

and Seditious Practices and Attempts' and 'An Act for the more Effectually Preventing Seditious Meetings and Assemblies', both enacted in 1795. *Habeas corpus* was also suspended in 1794.
[13] Claeys, *Political writings*, i, p. xviii.
[14] Edward Royle, *Revolutionary Britannia? Reflections on the threat of revolution in Britain, 1789–1848*, Manchester 2000, 23.
[15] It should be noted that most disputants in the heat of argument referred interchangeably to either 'England' or 'Britain'. In the discussion that follows, reference is made chiefly to England (unless following contemporary quotations), since it was the English aristocracy that was the prime target for debate; but 'England' is understood throughout to be part of the United Kingdom of Great Britain (since 1707) and of the emergent British empire.

brought into question not only its own discarded form of government but also, by 1790, government in England. But it was the abolition of the French aristocracy that was of most significance.

The French *noblesse* was stripped of its privileges and the order of aristocracy was effectively abolished by the French National Assembly on 4 August 1789. The French absolute monarchy, backed up by 'popery', had always been much hated and despised on the English side of the Channel. However, the fact that the French abolished their aristocracy in 1789, but did not finally decide what to do about their monarchy for another three years was of crucial importance.[16] It shifted the emphasis in political debate away from monarchy and towards aristocracy in both France and England. As Paine said, the English nation's paranoia was no longer focused simply upon French 'arbitrary power, popery and wooden shoes'.[17] The issues of leadership, who should rule and who did rule, became newly central to the political debates in both countries.

This book explores the centrality of aristocracy within the pamphlet war of 1790–6 in England.[18] The pamphlets reveal that radicals increasingly identified government in this country, explicitly or implicitly, as an aristocratic oligarchy. For the first time leadership in England, and in particular aristocracy, was compared to that in France.

The starting points for the debate about aristocracy were Edmund Burke's *Reflections on the revolution in France* (1790) and Thomas Paine's *Rights of man* (1791). Much has been made of Burke's political ideas and his influence as the 'founder of modern conservatism'.[19] A number of historians have reviewed his representations of aristocracy.[20] Much of this attention is focused on Burke's notable inconsistency in such representations and interpretation of the 'natural aristocracy' he defined in a later work.[21] Despite his inconsistencies, however, Burke's *Reflections* brought the English aristocracy into the foreground of the debate, which was of great significance. And his representations of the English aristocracy, in nostalgic terms inherently

---

16 Louis XVI was executed on 21 January 1793.
17 Thomas Paine, *The Rights of man*, 1791, ed. E. Foner, Harmondsworth 1985, 234.
18 Aristocracy and issues of leadership were mentioned in the majority of the pamphlets and took up much pamphlet space. See Goodrich, 'Peers or parasites?', 221, for the prominence of aristocracy.
19 Edmund Burke, *Reflections on the revolution in France*, 1790, ed. J. G. A. Pocock, Indianapolis 1987, p. vii; Claeys, 'French Revolution', 60; Michael Freeman, *Edmund Burke and the critique of political radicalism*, Oxford 1980, 4. For a revisionist view see David Bromwich, *On empire, liberty and reform: speeches and letters: Edmund Burke*, New Haven, Conn. 2000.
20 Francis P. Canavan, *The political reason of Edmund Burke*, Durham, NC 1960, 96–9; Frederick Dreyer, *Burke's politics: a study in Whig orthodoxy*, Waterloo, Ont. 1979, 30–2; Freeman, *Edmund Burke*, 110–13; Ian Harris (ed.), *Burke: pre-revolutionary writings*, Cambridge 1993, pp. xvi–xxxiii; Frank O'Gorman, *Edmund Burke: his political philosophy*, London 1973, 40, 50–4, 121, 128; Burke (ed. Pocock), *Reflections*, pp. xviii–lvi.
21 Edmund Burke, *An appeal from the new to the old Whigs*, 1791, in Daniel Ritchie (ed.), *Further reflections on the revolution in France*, Indianapolis 1992, 168.

gothic, made a considerable impact on the direction of the debate thereafter.[22] Paine then retained the central focus on aristocracy. It is well established that Paine's *Rights of man* heralded a new radicalism in English politics.[23] Paine's denial of the existence of an English constitution and his proposal to abolish aristocracy are generally noted by historians.

Paine proposed republicanism as an acceptable alternative form of government to the English mixed government. And the republicanism he promoted was one without an aristocracy. 'Republicanism' was a term that invoked a number of meanings in eighteenth-century political discussion, identified by historians as including 'classical', 'Whig', 'Harringtonian' and 'democratic' republicanism. In the rapid fire of the pamphlet war of 1790–6, 'republicanism' was both promoted and condemned and constantly shifted in meaning within the flux of the debate. As has been well documented, Paine clearly defined a new democratic republicanism, which excluded monarchy and aristocracy and thus broke from Whig republicanism. Paine admired the American system and advocated a representative, democratic republic, incorporating popular sovereignty.[24]

Yet what has not been fully studied is the significance of Paine, in his condemnation of aristocracy, likening the English aristocracy to its French counterpart.[25] For Paine, the English aristocracy was a class or caste like the French *noblesse*. Correspondingly, Paine's identification of English society as an *ancien régime*, like France, has been under-played by historians but will receive full attention here. These key works, then, triggered the much wider debate that followed, involving writings by many pamphleteers. Radical writers took their cue from Paine and continued to challenge aristocratic hegemony and lambasted the English aristocracy with fierce criticism. Loyalists, who defended the old system, were then forced to respond. This ensured the centrality of aristocracy in the debate until 1796.

The continuing significance of France to the central focus on aristocracy

---

[22] On Burke's medievalism see Roger J. Smith, *The gothic bequest: medieval institutions in British thought, 1688–1863*, Cambridge 1987, 113–26, and Burke (ed. Pocock), *Reflections*, pp. xxxii–iii.

[23] Texts on Paine include Gregory Claeys, *Thomas Paine: social and political thought*, Boston 1989; Mark Philp, *Paine*, Oxford 1989; A. O. Aldridge, *Man of reason: the life of Thomas Paine*, London 1960; A. J. Ayer, *Thomas Paine*, London 1988: David Powell, *Tom Paine: the greatest exile*, New York 1985; Audrey Williamson, *Thomas Paine: his life, work and times*, London 1973; Richard Whatmore, ' "A gigantic manliness": Paine's republicanism in the 1790s', in Stefan Collini, Richard Whatmore and Brian Young (eds), *Economy, polity, and society: British intellectual history, 1750–1950*, Cambridge 2000, 135–57.

[24] In this study, the term 'republicanism' does not invoke one standard definition, but rather reflects the shifts in contemporary definition. For a seminal study of Paine's republicanism see Claeys, *Thomas Paine*, 45, 86–90.

[25] Olivia Smith has suggested that Paine's familiarity with French authors contributed to the development of his new vernacular language, displayed in *Rights of man: The politics of language, 1791–1819*, Oxford 1984, 39. See also Whatmore, ' "Gigantic manliness" ', 135–57.

in the debate which developed in England is also often under-estimated by historians.²⁶ Both *Reflections* and *Rights of man* can, to some extent, be read as commentaries on French political culture, although their interpretations of French history and politics were very different. It was fear of a French invasion, either physical or intellectual, that provoked Burke to leap to the defence of the establishment and, in particular, of the aristocracy. Conversely, in England, Paine and his followers applauded the French revolutionaries and promulgated their ideas of liberty and equality and their condemnation of aristocracy.

There had, of course, been much social intercourse between these two European aristocracies during the eighteenth century. Some English aristocrats continued to travel to France during the 1790s whilst the revolution raged and, conversely, French aristocrats fled to England to escape persecution. Indeed, Richmond-upon-Thames became known as 'Petty France', so over-run was it with French aristocracy. The English aristocracy reputedly openly offered hospitality and aid to the French *émigrés* and Burke even opened a school for their children.²⁷ A number of contemporary observers remarked that the two aristocracies had more in common with each other than either had with those of lower stations in their own country.²⁸ Yet, whilst both Burke and Paine made comparisons between the English and French aristocracies, the former largely positive and the latter entirely negative, neither saw the English aristocracy as merely the political or cultural equivalent of its French counterpart. It is the fact that comparisons were made, and consequently aristocracy was brought into the spotlight of debate, that was significant.

The execution of Louis XVI, and the outbreak of war with France on 1 February 1793, shifted perspectives for both radicals and loyalists. But the ensuing battle in England over the validity of the war and the resulting economic hardships, suffered largely by the poor, kept the focus predominantly on aristocracy and the wealth of the rich. The Terror in France of 1793–4, in which 'aristocrats' were sought out and summarily guillotined, must have caused many delicate hands to flutter to the throats of English aristocrats. But ultimately the Terror was used to the loyalists' advantage in the continuing debate about leadership. Thus events in France ensured that aristocracy remained a central focus of the debate in England.

Moreover, it was particularly in connection with things French that gender issues were raised in England throughout the century.²⁹ Eighteenth-

---

26 But see Philp, 'Fragmented ideology', 65.
27 C. H. Lockitt, *The relations of English and French society, 1763–1793*, London 1920, 10.
28 See Clark, *English society*, 99–102.
29 L. Davidoff and C. Hall, *Family fortunes: men and women of the English middle class, 1780–1850*, London 1987; Amanda Vickery, *The gentleman's daughter: women's lives in Georgian England*, New Haven, Conn. 1998; Amanda Foreman, *Georgiana duchess of Devonshire*, London 1998; H. Barker and E. Chalus (eds), *Gender in eighteenth-century*

century writings on manners and morals and high society, often to be found within the so-called 'luxury debate', reveal much on issues of masculinity and effeminacy. There was a long tradition, well illustrated in satire, of identifying young men of 'high society' as fops and 'macaronis' and effeminate, like the French.[30] There is material in the pamphlets of the 1790s that raised the issue of masculinity. Paine and some of his followers polemically identified 'effeminacy' as a characteristic of both the English and French aristocracies.[31] In response, a few references to manliness can be found in loyalist tracts.[32] Whilst masculinity was by no means a central issue in the French Revolution debate, and such references are rare in the pamphlets, it did form part of the back-drop to political debate. Particularly for those who defended the aristocracy against radical accusations of 'foppery', the assumption was that England had a manly set of rulers. Moreover, it should be noted that the aristocracy as defined here was entirely male, since only noblemen were entitled to a seat in the House of Lords. Secondly, the overwhelming majority of political pamphlets were written by men, with the notable exceptions of Catherine Macaulay, Mary Wollstonecraft, Anna Barbauld and Hannah More

The second theme of this book concerns the dynamics within the debate between radicals and loyalists. The terms 'radical' and 'loyalist' are employed throughout this book to describe loosely the two opposing parties in the French Revolution debate.[33] Nevertheless, there are distinctions to be made between those who may be identified as 'reformers' and 'radicals'. Whilst the former wanted reform of government but not revolution, the latter wished to follow France and to develop a revolutionary ideology.[34] In practice, however, the cut and thrust of debate allowed for a shifting range of ideas, which did not crystallise into a strict division between reformers and radicals. Mark Philp stated that 'reformism or radicalism in the 1790s is protean stuff', which resists a simple definition or classification.[35] As will become apparent in the discussion that follows, the increasingly complex relationship between radical ideology, rhetoric and propaganda muddied the waters of radical iden-

---

England: roles, representations and responsibilities, London 1997; S. Amussen, *An ordered society: class and gender in early modern England*, Oxford 1988.

[30] Paul Langford, *A polite and commercial people: England, 1727–1783*, Oxford 1989, 565–614. See also Hannah Greig, 'The *beau monde* and fashionable life in eighteenth-century London, 1688–1800', unpubl. PhD diss. London 2003.

[31] Paine, *Rights of man*, 80: titles 'mark a kind of foppery'. See also Charles Pigott, *Strictures on the new political tenets of the Rt. Hon. Edmund Burke*, 1791, in Claeys, *Political writings*, ii. 142.

[32] [Thomas Green], *Slight observations upon Paine's pamphlet*, 1791, in Claeys, *Political writings*, v. 229.

[33] It should be noted, however, that contemporaries did not use the term 'radical' during the period 1790–6.

[34] Dickinson, *Liberty and property*, 239.

[35] Philp, 'Fragmented ideology', 56.

tity still further in the years 1790–6. Hence 'radicalism' here describes a diffuse movement, distinguished essentially by commitment, at least, to reform of the English constitution.

Loyalism too was a broad Church, especially after the alarming events of 1793 precipitated the coalition instituted between Pitt's administration and the conservative Whigs led by the duke of Portland in July 1794.[36] Inevitably the coalition broadened the base of loyalist support, as the increase in pamphlet out-put illustrates.[37] Moreover, this book identifies the emergence of a new definition of 'loyalist' that arises from the development of a loyalist commercial model of the English economy and society. Clearly then, there was not one 'loyalism' but a number of 'loyalisms'. So, for the purposes of discussion here, 'radicalism' and 'loyalist' are defined as broad-based positions, distinguished ultimately by attitudes for and against immediate reform of the English constitution in the 1790s. In particular, this book challenges the traditionally held view of loyalism promoted by historians such as Robert Dozier, Jonathan Clark and Thomas Schofield.[38] The majority of historians has identified loyalism as a mass movement in defence of 'Church and King', a conservative defence of the establishment.[39] Clark's identification of a united, conservative, Anglican loyalism surviving intact until 1832 is strongly disputed. Contemporary representations in the pamphlets reveal not just one conservative loyalism but, in particular, a two-fold loyalism, old and new.

Dror Wahrman has argued that in their writings both radicals and loyalists invoked one dominant binary model of 'aristocracy and people' upon which other paradigms were superimposed. Wahrman also claimed that politics, or the representation thereof, became 'painted in black and white' and that 'two political extremes' emerged between radicals' 'all inclusive' language of 'natural rights' and the loyalists' 'exclusivity that is the privileged position of the ruling class'.[40] It is true that Burke defended and Paine attacked what they represented predominantly as an *ancien régime* aristocracy in England. A dual model of aristocracy and people could then be applied by radicals to English society as it was to *ancien régime* France. Consequently, through such representations, England was saddled with an *ancien régime* it did not think it had. Yet, this book contends that loyalists did not merely defend the establishment and the aristocracy by invoking this dual model.

---

[36] Goodwin, *Friends of liberty*, 365–6; Frank O'Gorman, *The Whig party and the French Revolution*, London 1967, 192–208.
[37] See Goodrich, 'Peers or parasites?', 216–18, appendix 2 at pp. 274–97.
[38] Dozier, *King, constitution and country*; Clark, *English society*; Schofield, 'Conservative political thought'.
[39] See, for example, Dozier, *King, constitution and country*, 20–5; Clark, *English society*; Robert Hole, *Pulpits, politics and public order in England, 1760–1832*, Cambridge 1989, and 'English sermons and tracts as media of debate on the French Revolution, 1789–99', in Philp, *French Revolution*, 18–37; and Dickinson, 'Popular conservatism', 112–17.
[40] Wahrman, *Imagining the middle class*, 33–6, 55.

Clearly, the French Revolution provided a model for the destruction of the governing order and Paine's *Rights of man* suggested to Englishmen the possibility of a revolution in England.[41] But historians have not fully investigated the important role played by loyalists in preventing a revolution occurring in England.[42] It was not only defeat of the radicals and government acts of repression which precluded such a revolution, but also the loyalist response, in the form of loyalist representations that provided an alternative picture of English society. As Gregory Claeys has argued, in an attempt to defy Painite republicanism, loyalists promoted a commercial and opulent England.[43] This is true and evidently loyalists in the 1790s had borrowed the basis for their commercial model from the reform Whigs. And, as Pocock has pointed out, Whig social theory always held commercial progress to be perfectly compatible with hereditary monarchy and landed aristocracy.[44] But what Claeys did not go on to say, was that loyalist representations went further than Whig social theory and redefined the English aristocracy to fit in to their new model of England.[45] To counter Painite representations of an exclusive aristocracy, the loyalist model deliberately represented an inclusive society with many gradations and an open elite. As will be seen, loyalist writers argued that England had a progressive society with an appropriately progressive aristocracy, which formed part of an increasingly broad elite.

There is, of course, debate amongst historians as to whether eighteenth-century England actually had an open elite. However, this book is not concerned with the actual openness or otherwise of the elite but only with the representations of aristocracy by radicals and loyalists. It is significant that this question was raised and used in the French Revolution debate by political writers of the 1790s.[46]

Ultimately this process of redefinition and re-modelling was instrumental in moving the focus of the debate away from aristocracy and towards economic issues and a broader elite. Loyalists' readiness to innovate intellectually, and their ability to understand what was at the heart of perceptions of

---

[41] Ibid. 32, 35.
[42] Schofield, 'Conservative political thought', 601–22. On the conservative Anglican response see John Dinwiddy, 'Interpretations of anti-Jacobinism', in Philp, *French Revolution*, 38–50.
[43] Claeys, 'French Revolution', 59–80.
[44] Burke (ed. Pocock), *Reflections*, p. xv.
[45] It should be noted that throughout this book the new loyalist model will be defined as 'the loyalist commercial model'.
[46] See, for example, John Cannon, *Aristocratic century: the peerage of eighteenth-century England*, Cambridge 1984; Christie, *Stress and stability*; Langford, *Polite and commercial people*; G. E. Mingay, *English landed society in the eighteenth century*, London 1963; Peter Laslett, *The world we have lost*, London 1965; Harold Perkin, *The origins of modern English society, 1780–1880*, London 1969; Lawrence Stone and Jeanne C. Fawtier Stone, *An open elite? England, 1540–1880*, Oxford 1984; and Ellis Archer Wasson, 'The crisis of the aristocracy: parliamentary reform, the peerage and the House of Commons, 1750–1914', *Parliamentary History* xiii (1994), 297–311.

English superiority, help to explain why loyalism triumphed politically in the French Revolution debate. As will be shown, loyalism became increasingly a two-fold movement incorporating both a conservative loyalism and the new commercial loyalism. It should be noted, however, that these two loyalisms were not developing in competition with one other but concurrently, converging and diverging in the fast flow of the ever-fluid debate. This confirms, as a number of historians have suggested, that the loyalist reaction was not an orchestrated movement controlled from above but, for the most part, was as spontaneous and individual as the radical attack.[47]

And now to the third theme of this book, 'representation' and 'reality'. Delineation between these two concepts cannot always be clearly identified but, as Dror Wahrman has proposed, there is a 'space of possibilities between social reality and its representation'.[48] The French Revolution debate took place within that space. The battle between radicals and loyalists was fought on the streets, in riots and demonstrations, in the courts in cases of sedition and treason, and through the workings of societies set up to obtain the support of the people. It took place largely outside parliament, although the radical societies did resort to petitioning parliament.[49] But the locus of the debate was undoubtedly the battle waged on paper, in pamphlets, tracts and broadsides. This was a war of representations. As H. T. Dickinson and others have claimed, this pamphlet war was important because it contributed as much to the loyalist victory in the debate as did the forces of law and order.[50]

Yet historians have largely ignored the significance of representations of aristocracy in the pamphlet debate. During the years 1790–6, aristocracy came under constant attack in both England and France but, whilst in England the peerage survived unmolested, in France titles and accompanying privileges were abolished. It was significant that in England the radical attack on the aristocracy remained intellectual, restricted only to written representation, while in France it was fatally and increasingly physical. This book argues that the new loyalist representations of aristocracy helped to ensure the survival of the English aristocracy.

It is also the contention that such representations changed only perceptions of aristocracy amongst English people, rather than the reality of aristocratic hegemony. Indeed, in England no reform of parliament or curtailment of aristocratic power was effected during the years 1790–6. A number of historians have claimed that, in the later eighteenth century, the aristocracy

---

[47] See Dickinson 'Popular conservatism', 120–1, and Philp, 'Fragmented ideology', 54. Gayle Trusdel Pendleton states that, although a few of the pamphlets in her bibliography were 'composed by Treasury hirelings' or 'Whig party writers', the majority were independent: 'Towards a bibliography of the *Reflections* and *Rights of man* controversy', *Bulletin of Research in the Humanities* lxxxv (1982), 70.
[48] Wahrman, *Imagining the middle class*, 7–8.
[49] A number of radical societies united to petition parliament in 1793.
[50] Dickinson, *British radicalism*, 25.

was increasingly pressurised to reform by political agitation from middle and lower classes, including that coming from the radicals of the 1790s. Linda Colley and Paul Langford, in particular, have argued respectively that in response to pressures from below the aristocracy was increasingly obliged to reform its behaviour and adopted middle-class values and culture.[51]

Colley and Wahrman, have proposed that the French Revolution and Painite radicalism presented a direct challenge to the legitimacy of the elite.[52] These historians are correct, but what they and others failed to distinguish was that this was a threat which, during the period 1790-6, was encompassed within, and limited predominantly to writings, to representations. This study of the pamphlet debate raises certain questions. Did such depictions reflect reality and, how, if at all did they affect the reality of aristocratic existence? Indeed, did the aristocracy really reform and conform, as historians have suggested, or was it merely that loyalists' representations gave that impression, whilst enabling the aristocracy in reality to carry on as before? It could indeed be argued that loyalist writings in effect masked continuity with suggestions of change. In fact, this book is not attempting to assert the power of 'perceptions' over 'facts', or *vice versa*, in the manner of Lawrence and Jeanne Stone.[53] It cannot necessarily be assumed that representations and reality interact, formulate cause and effect, or work within the same context, as Linda Colley appears to infer. This book aims to illustrate that within the French Revolution debate 'representations' did not necessarily, or even intentionally, reflect the immediate reality of political or social existence. Instead, they could, and did, distort and mask reality and, to some extent, preclude change within it.

It should be noted here that language had a part to play in this war of representations. The political pamphlets reveal much about the protagonists' choice of language. Whilst language is not a major focus of this book, the fact that the debate involved the development of opposing languages as well as opposing ideas should be noted.[54] In particular, the pamphlets reveal a

---

[51] Linda Colley, *Britons: forging the nation, 1707-1837*, London 1992, 149, 152-3; Paul Langford, *Public life and the propertied Englishman, 1689-1798*, Oxford 1991, 510, 565-6, and *Polite and commercial people*. For the opposing branch of historical opinion see Clark, *English society*, and J. V. Beckett, *The aristocracy in England, 1660-1914*, Oxford 1986, 4-5; Cannon, *Aristocratic century*, 6. A number of historians have pointed out that there was little awareness of class as it is understood today, and there was no identifiable united middle class during the eighteenth century: Asa Briggs: *The age of improvement, 1783-1867*, London 1959, 28-9; Wahrman, *Imagining the middle class*, esp. pp. 2-18

[52] Colley, *Britons*, 152; Wahrman, *Imagining the middle class*, 32.

[53] Stone and Stone, *Open elite?*, 29.

[54] For key studies of language in the writings of the French Revolution debate see Smith, *Politics of language*, and Linda Hunt, *Politics culture and class in the French Revolution*, Berkeley, Ca. 1984, esp. pp. 27, 50. For further studies of language in this period see J. T. Boulton, *The language of politics in the age of Wilkes and Burke*, London 1963, and Steven Blakemore, *Burke and the fall of language: the French Revolution as linguistic event*, Hanover, NH 1988.

'language of aristocracy', defined by Burke's defence of the English aristocracy. Burke introduced a gothic language of an *ancien régime* to embellish and to legitimise his representations of an honourable aristocracy with its roots in a medieval chivalric past.[55] And Burke's medievalism, revealed in *Reflections* through such language, is of significance to the discussion here.

Radicals condemned Burke's aristocratic language as sentimental and out-dated. They presented an alternative aristocratic history of brutality and oppression, of conquest and bloodshed. Moreover, many radicals determinedly avoided aristocratic language and Paine showed the way with his use of the vernacular and his promotion of a language for the people, rather than for the educated elite. Consequently Burke and Paine developed opposing languages within the 'aristocracy and people' paradigm. It took post-Burkean loyalists to break away from that paradigm and create a new model of society and a corresponding new loyalist language. Thus Burke's 'language of aristocracy' had a short reign in the language battle of the French Revolution debate, but its significance was far-reaching. There is little doubt that Burke's representations of aristocracy were instrumental in starting the debate and in focusing attention upon the aristocracy.

The pamphlet debates

In terms of disciplinary approach, the emphasis in this book falls especially upon the immediate development of political ideas within the cut and thrust of the debate.[56] It does not focus on parliamentary politics for this was predominantly an extra-parliamentary debate. It is notable that few of the writers were MPs, with the notable exception of Edmund Burke, and even fewer were members of the House of Lords.[57] Moreover, rather than tracing the effect of great works of political theory, by the likes of Locke, Hobbes and Harrington, on writings of the 1790s, this book examines the set of ideas, old and new, that were promoted and promulgated throughout the numerous and ephemeral political writings of 1790–6. Whilst the debate was undoubtedly stimulated by the self-conscious writings of great thinkers, such as Burke, Paine, Thelwall and Godwin, most of the works were those of ordinary

---

55 See Smith, *Gothic bequest*.
56 For relevant works on political ideas see, for example, Q. R. D. Skinner, *The foundations of modern political thought*, Cambridge 1978; J. G. A. Pocock, *Politics, language and time: essays on political thought and history*, New York 1971, and *Virtue, commerce and history*; Donald R. Kelley, *The descent of ideas: the history of intellectual history*, Aldershot 2002; Richard Tuck, *Natural rights theories: their origin and development*, Cambridge 1979; Joyce Appleby, 'Modernization theory and the formation of modern social theories in England and America', *Comparative Studies in Society and History* xx (1978), 259–85; and Isaac Kramnick, 'Religion and radicalism: English political theory in the age of revolution', *PT* v (1977), 505–34.
57 See Goodrich 'Peers or parasites?', 223.

educated men.[58] Arguments were often fragmented and disconnected, semi-conscious commentaries, which reveal ideas commonly aired and discussed at the time.[59] As John Tosh has argued, 'the diffusion of new ideas through second-rate and ephemeral literature is as important as their genesis in the mind of the great thinker'.[60] This book, therefore, reviews political ideas in the broadest sense, within the context of the pamphlet debates.[61]

It has been established that approximately 4,000 pamphlets on the issues of reform and revolution appeared in England during the period between the fall of the Bastille and the peace of Amiens in 1802.[62] Of these Gregory Claeys has estimated that approximately 600 contributed directly to the French Revolution debate.[63] Gayle Trusdel Pendleton has identified 400 works, which represent the fifty or so relevant works of Price, Burke and Paine, plus 340 pamphlets commenting upon the issues raised by these three.[64] This book was based on a data set of just over 500 pamphlets.[65] It is not possible, however, to calculate precisely the numbers of sources relevant to the French Revolution debate, as there can be no exact demarcation of the field. The aim here is not to assess the contribution the pamphlets made to the French Revolution debate *per se*. Rather, it is to analyse the representations of aristocracy, conscious or otherwise, contained within the pamphlets. Consequently, the main criterion for inclusion in this book was, in the broad sense, reference to aristocracy, to the governing elite. As it happens very few of the works viewed in the research for this book did not refer to aristocracy, a finding which reinforces the claim that the role of 'aristocracy' was central to the French Revolution debate.

Of course, many additional eighteenth-century publications, from private journals and correspondence to published treatises on manners and morals and much else besides, incorporated representations of aristocracy. However, much material that commented upon aristocracy was focused predominantly

---

[58] The pamphlets were written by educated men, clergymen, leaders of radical and loyalist societies and associations, and a variety of others, many anonymous, who felt strongly enough to put pen to paper.

[59] See Wahrman, *Imagining the middle class*, 13.

[60] John Tosh, *The pursuit of history: aims, methods and new directions in the study of modern history*, 2nd edn, London 1991, 85.

[61] The term 'pamphlet' is used loosely here and incorporates political writings that engaged in the debate for and against reform, including, monographs, tracts, treatises and broadsides, published during the years 1790–6. Whilst this book concentrates on documents in the public domain, unpublished or private documents such as minutes of proceedings of radical and loyalist societies, and correspondence have been included where appropriate.

[62] Pendleton, 'Towards a bibliography', 65–103.

[63] Claeys, 'French Revolution', 60.

[64] Pendleton, 'Towards a bibliography', 65–6. It should be noted that Pendleton excluded newspapers and periodicals from her bibliography because 'their extraordinary partisanship and corruption' rendered them too partial (p. 70).

[65] See Goodrich 'Peers or parasites?', appendix 2 at pp. 274–97.

on social behaviour rather than political leadership and can be categorised within the 'luxury debate', which continued throughout the eighteenth century, rather than the French Revolution debate. The luxury debate incorporated wide-ranging social criticism and focused primarily on manners and morals. Complaints of luxury emanating largely from ever-increasing commerce, came from many perspectives, from Dissenters and reformers, to 'country Tories' and Anglican churchmen. The 'country ideology' of the earlier eighteenth century lingered on in such condemnation. Where there is overlap between these two debates and commentary upon aristocratic behaviour has appeared within political pamphlets it is included here.

There is also much material that is relevant to the French Revolution debate, in particular some religious material and works focused upon war with France, which does not engage with the debate centred on aristocracy and which was consequently excluded.[66] Many pamphlets written by Anglican clergymen promoted a conservative defence of Church and State and the social order, stressing obedience and subordination, but without reference to aristocratic social models or issues of political leadership.[67] That is not to say that all religious works were excluded from this book. Religion continued to influence politics throughout the eighteenth century and beyond. Consequently a number of works both by Anglican loyalists and radical Protestant Dissenters can be found amongst those cited. Thus the political writings included in this book were selected on the grounds that they contributed to the French Revolution debate and contained representations of aristocracy, either express or implicit.

'Aristocracy' in context

At this point it is helpful to consider use of the term 'aristocracy' in the eighteenth-century context and how it may be defined for the purposes of this book. In a work devoted to representations, definitions inevitably present problems. Use of the term 'aristocracy' is neither clear nor consistent in the pamphlets themselves – nor indeed in the secondary literature. This is not least because the aristocracy itself was not a clear entity. As a result of the French Revolution, the term developed more than one meaning. Confusion is increased by the fact that, for much of the eighteenth century, the term 'aristocracy' did not denote a social class as it does today. The terms 'aristocracy, 'nobility' and 'peer' are of course all linked, as they were in the eighteenth century, through association with the House of Lords. But, whilst

---

[66] See, for example, Hole, *Pulpits, politics and public order*; Anthony Lincoln, *Some political and social ideas of English dissent, 1763–1800*, Cambridge 1938; W. R. Ward, *Religion and society in England, 1790–1850*, London 1972; and Michael Watts, *The Dissenters: from the Reformation to the French Revolution*, Oxford 1978.
[67] Dinwiddy, 'Interpretations of anti-Jacobinism', 38–50.

the latter two terms have retained a largely consistent meaning, the term 'aristocracy' has proved to be something of a linguistic chameleon.

First, it is helpful to start with clear eighteenth-century definitions. A legal definition of 'nobility' did exist in the eighteenth century in terms of the peerage. As Penelope Corfield has pointed out, there was 'a clear legal distinction between the very few who were titled nobility and the very many who were commoners'.[68] Only the eldest son of a peer was a nobleman, and even he was technically a commoner until he inherited his title.[69] The younger children, unless they held a specific title, were and remained commoners. And, of course, all peers had a seat in the House of Lords. Those non-nobles with titles, such as baronets, were not included in the definition of peers and were not members of the Lords.

For much of the eighteenth century 'aristocracy' was also capable of clear definition. It was predominantly defined, in accordance with the ancient Greek definition, as 'that form of government which places the supreme power in the nobles'.[70] And the enduring existence of the so-called 'mixed' government in England meant that 'aristocracy' had become a negative term allied with concepts of despotism. It is significant that, throughout the eighteenth century, 'aristocracy' in its political meaning retained this negative connotation. Interestingly, the term 'aristocrat', with a specifically socio-political meaning, was introduced into English usage from the French as a direct result of the French Revolution.[71] Contemporary definitions require further investigation, however, in order to understand fully the significance of the changes in the usage of the term 'aristocracy'. During the long Whig hegemony in government between 1714 to 1761, the Old Whig government was often described as an 'aristocracy', the 'Whig aristocracy'. In more general terms, J. G. A. Pocock has suggested that for much of the eighteenth century the term 'aristocracy' was synonymous with the term 'Whig'.[72] When George III came to the throne in 1760 a schism developed between what may loosely be termed 'Whig' factions. 'Aristocracy' then became an accusation made against a Whig faction that had, in the eyes of its opponents, obtained too much power.

---

[68] Penelope J. Corfield, 'The rivals: landed and other gentleman', in Negley Harte and Roland Quinault (eds), *Land and society in Britain, 1700–1914*, Manchester 1996, 4.
[69] See Cannon, *Aristocratic century*, 10.
[70] For eighteenth-century dictionary definitions of 'nobility' see Samuel Johnson's *Dictionary of the English language*, 2nd edn, London 1760. More than 60 items and 14 editions plus a number of miniatures, dated from 1756 to 1866, of Johnson's *Dictionary* are listed on the BLPC. For a discussion of Johnson's definitions see Goodrich 'Peers or parasites?', 17–19.
[71] A full definition of 'aristocrat' was not included in Johnson's *Dictionary* until an 1818 version, edited by Revd H. J. Todd, defined 'aristocrat' as 'A word of modern use imported into this country in the early part of the French democratical revolution'.
[72] J. G. A. Pocock, 'Radical criticisms of the Whig order in the age between revolutions', in Margaret Jacob and James Jacob (eds), *The origins of Anglo-American radicalism*, London 1984, 35–57 at p. 46.

Thus 'aristocracy' did not traditionally define the nobility or the House of Lords *per se* during the eighteenth century. The term defined, in one way or another, government by the few, or the few who have gained too much power within given political parameters. Consequently, 'aristocracy' was not at this stage a social class as such, for it did not necessarily include all or only the nobility. Insofar as eighteenth-century Englishmen and women perceived society in terms of class, clearly it was the nobility rather than 'aristocracy', which was perceived as the elite class.

Paul Langford has suggested that it was during the American War of Independence that the term 'aristocracy' began to be used to describe 'a body of men rather than a system of government'.[73] It is true that concepts of 'aristocracy and people' began to develop in the political debates during the period 1779–85. It was not until the 1790s, however, that the term began to define a class of nobility. Certainly in France, during the revolution, 'aristocracy' became a derogatory term among the revolutionaries, a term of abuse even, denoting the class of *noblesse*. In 1794 Arthur Young noted that in France 'The cry of aristocrate or traitor is followed by immediate imprisonment or death.'[74] It was Paine who introduced the concept of the English 'aristocracy' constituting a class like the French *noblesse*, defined by its unacceptable hereditary rights and privileges. He argued that 'Aristocracy' and 'nobility' were interchangeable terms, and denoted 'all that class . . . which in some countries is called "*aristocracy*" and in others "*nobility*" '.[75] Thus, the term 'aristocracy' had moved on from the traditional identification as a form of despotic government, through definitions as a political faction, to the new radical definition as a political and social class. Certainly, this was not a clear-cut progression. References to the 'Whig aristocracy' can still be found in pamphlets well into the 1790s and the classical definition of aristocracy as a form of government was used alongside other definitions throughout the eighteenth century, by radicals as well as loyalists.

Although, there was much use of the term 'aristocracy' in the radical anti-aristocratic rhetoric, it was used loosely to define an ever-shifting English elite in the years 1791–6. Many radicals followed Paine and used the term 'aristocracy' to describe a class defined by its hereditary rights and privileges. William Vaughan, in a pamphlet published in 1794, provided a clear definition on the Paine model. The 'people at large' consisted of 'the labouring Hand, the industrious Farmer, the useful Artizan, the ingenious Manufacturer, the enterprising Merchant, and the lower, but most virtuous part of the Landholders', whilst the other 'order of the State' consisted of those 'wearing a crown, honored with a title, or adorned with a star and

---

[73] Langford, *Public life*, 535.
[74] Arthur, Young *The example of France a warning to Britain*, London 1793, 4th edn 1794, in Claeys, *Political writings*, viii. 73.
[75] Paine, *Rights of man*, 80.

garter'.⁷⁶ The powerful orator and radical writer, John Thelwall, who wrote much, stated in 1791 that: 'The Nobles of England are a *Senate* of 200.'⁷⁷

Aristocracy also became representative in the radical political discourse, on the Painite aristocracy and people model, of the 'few' opposed to the 'many'. Wahrman has argued that during the early 1790s 'aristocracy' became 'any smaller and more exclusive group that prevented the people from realising their rights'.⁷⁸ Here 'aristocracy' included those with seats in the House of Commons, as well as those in the Lords, but did not differentiate between political parties or factions as had been the case earlier in the eighteenth century. But radicals were not consistent in their use of terms identifying the elite and definitions became broader, particularly during 1793–6, as the focus shifted towards economic equality. Within one pamphlet Henry Redhead Yorke described the elite as 'the institution of privileged orders'⁷⁹ and later as '*noble* lords, wealthy merchants, and large manufactories'.⁸⁰

Definitions of 'aristocracy' took an interesting turn in loyalist hands. Not surprisingly, in view of its increasing use as a term of abuse by radicals, loyalists rarely used it to denote the English nobility. In fact, the term 'aristocracy' was generally used in loyalist pamphlets to describe the French nobility rather than the English.⁸¹ Frederick Hervey referred to the French 'liberal aristocracy' but to 'our nobility' in England.⁸² One loyalist pamphleteer complained in 1793 that 'the word *aristocracy*' had become 'of so indeterminate a signification', that it may be reasonable to reject it.⁸³ Another, in 1792, complained:

> The man . . . who presumes to think for himself concerning the late revolution in France, and refuses to be lead down the stream of popular opinion, is immediately marked and stigmatized as an *aristocrat* . . . Such an appellation may be very fashionable, yet it appears to me to be very vague, and very ill applied to those who ultimately disapprove of it, . . . Those gentlemen

---

76 [William Vaughan], *The catechism of man, pointing out from sound principles, and acknowledged facts, the rights and duties of every rational being*, 1794, in Claeys, *Political writings*, iv. 213.
77 James Mackintosh, *Vindiciae gallicae: defence of the French Revolution and its English admirers against the accusations of the Rt. Hon. Edmund Burke*, 1791, in Claeys, *Political writings*, i. 350–1.
78 Wahrman, *Imagining the middle class*, 76.
79 Henry Redhead Yorke, *Thoughts on civil government addressed to the disenfranchised citizens of Sheffield*, 1794, in Claeys, *Political writings*, iv. 258.
80 Ibid. 264.
81 For example, anon., *A defence of the constitution of England against the libels that have been lately published on it: particularly in Paine's pamphlet on the Rights of man*, 1791, in Claeys, *Political writings*, v. 48.
82 [Frederick Hervey], *An answer to the second part of Rights of man*, 1792, in Claeys, *Political writings*, v. 69, 74.
83 Charles Patton, *An attempt to establish the basis of freedom on simple and unerring principles*, Edinburgh 1793, in Claeys, *Political writings*, vii. 388–9.

however, who are pleased to make use of that epithet, ought previously to define in what sense the word *aristocrat* is to be taken.⁸⁴

Paine's use of the term aristocracy also invoked loyalist criticism. Alexander Dalrymple referred scornfully to the 'aristocracy, as Paine calls them, by which he means sometimes Lords, and sometimes landed gentlemen'.⁸⁵ Sir Brooke Boothby argued that Paine

> did not know the meaning of the word *aristocracy* himself, every dictionary would have told him that it signifies simply (as its original sense imports) *the government of the better sort*; a word never used in a bad sense, to express any tyrannical exercise of abuse of power, before Mr. La Fayette and Paris fish-wives. The Gothic feudal government of France no more resembled an *aristocracy* than the parliament of Paris did the Roman senate.⁸⁶

These early loyalists, then, rejected Paine's adoption of the French meaning for the term 'aristocracy', as a class or caste. Nor did the loyalists, for the most part, accept Burke's representations of aristocracy contained in *Reflections*. In general, 'aristocracy' reverted to its traditional meanings in loyalist pamphlets, in the Aristotelian sense as a form of government and, of course, as an element in the mixed government that loyalists were defending.⁸⁷ When the need to describe the aristocratic elite arose, most loyalists referred to the 'nobility' or the 'peerage'. A common identification was 'our nobility and gentry', as those who own 'the numerous and splendid estates'.⁸⁸ At the same time, a clear identification of a broader elite was emerging in the pamphlets. With the development of the new commercial model came concomitant definitions of the elite. References to an elite of the wealthy or the 'opulent landholder and merchant' together, were becoming more common.⁸⁹ Penelope Corfield has well illustrated that, by the 1790s, England was often represented as having an increasingly broad elite, in which wealth jostled with titles, land and qualifications, in a primarily property-led hierarchy.⁹⁰ But the fact that already a diversity of elites was being increasingly reflected in loyalists' representations is both surprising and suggestive of a sector of loyalism intent on moving away from traditional paradigms.

Moreover, both loyalist and radical writers used a wide variety of terms to

---

84 Anon., *Letters to a friend, on the late revolution in France*, 1792, 1.
85 Alexander Dalrymple, *The poor man's friend*, Edinburgh 1793, 8.
86 Sir Brooke Boothby, *Observations on the appeal from the new to the old Whigs, and on Mr. Paine's Rights of man*, 1792, in Claeys, *Political writings*, vi. 234.
87 See anon., *Defence of the constitution*, 23; Isaac Hunt, *Rights of Englishmen: an antidote to the poison now vending by the transatlantic republican Thomas Paine*, London 1791, 45.
88 Anon., *A letter to Mr Paine, on his late publication*, 1792, in Claeys, *Political writings*, vi. 170.
89 Hunt, *Rights of Englishmen*, 70; anon., *A candid inquiry into the nature of government, and the right of representation*, London 1792, 9.
90 Penelope, J. Corfield, *Power and the professions in Britain, 1700–1850*, London 1995, 1–13.

describe the ruling elite.[91] The Painite 'aristocracy' was certainly invoked by radicals but they also frequently reverted to more familiar expressions. Terms used in 1790s England included the 'nobility', the 'great', the 'rich', the 'higher ranks', the 'superior ranks', 'patricians', the 'great proprietors', the 'landed interest' and more besides. And the increasing difficulty in differentiating rank from wealth was reflected in the terminology used in the debate.[92] Nevertheless, shifts are detectable in the use of definitions of the elite in response to the dynamics of the debate; and it is these shifts that are of significance to this book.

Historians too vary greatly in their definition of aristocracy in eighteenth-century England.[93] Nevertheless, a number of them are clearly in broad agreement, although they may not use precisely the same terminology, in identifying a two-fold elite. One was the legal distinction, which defined nobility, and the other was a less well-defined but more important social definition of an elite few (some with titles, some without), generally landowners, who were identified as the 'gentry' or the 'quality'.[94]

For the purposes of this book, however, which is primarily concerned with representations of political leadership, it is appropriate to define the English aristocracy primarily as the peerage. As Cannon has noted, the English peerage 'is capable of precise legal definition through membership of the House of Lords'.[95] The number of peers in the eighteenth century was, however, remarkably small. There were only 173 peers in 1700, with numbers rising to 220 in 1790 and to 267 by 1800.[96] The increases were due to the creation of new peers and it is notable that 113 peerages were created between 1780 and 1800. These were primarily the result of Pitt's promotions, intended to weaken the dominance of the old Whig aristocracy in the House of Lords.[97] A. S. Turberville justified his decision to close his history of the eighteenth-century House of Lords in 1783 on grounds that 'The days of the Younger Pitt, because of his lavish creation of peerages, open a new era in the

---

[91] However, 'elite', another word of French provenance, was not one of the terms used in the debate, coming as it did into common usage only in the nineteenth century.
[92] See Langford, *Public life*, 529, and Corfield, *Power and the professions*, 1–17.
[93] On the lack of consensus see Wasson, 'Crisis of the aristocracy', 300–1. For a variety of definitions see Langford, *Public life*, 510–22; E. P. Thompson, *Customs in common*, London 1991, 9, 16; and Colley, *Britons*, 154.
[94] Corfield, 'The rivals', 4. See also Stone and Stone, *Open elite?*, 1; Vickery, *Gentleman's daughter*, 14; and Perkin, *Origins of modern society*, 17–19.
[95] Cannon, *Aristocratic century*, 9–10. See also T. H. Hollingsworth, 'The demography of the British peerage', *Population Studies Supplement* xviii (1965), 1–108; M. W. McCahill, *Order and equipoise: the peerage and the House of Lords, 1783–1806*, London 1978, and 'Peerage creations and the changing character of the British nobility, 1750–1830', *EHR* xcvi (1981), 259–84; and A. S. Turberville, *The House of Lords in the eighteenth century*, Oxford 1927.
[96] Cannon, *Aristocratic century*, 10, 15.
[97] Michael J. Turner, *British politics in the age of reform*, Manchester 1999, 42.

history of the Upper House.'⁹⁸ In reality, a number of the newcomers were promotions within the peerage and most of the others were already connected to the nobility.⁹⁹

Nevertheless this comparatively large influx caused some anxiety amongst old aristocratic families and others among the elite. Accusations of degradation of the peerage and the inappropriate rise of 'mushroom men', in response to the creation of new peerages were common throughout the eighteenth century.¹⁰⁰ Significantly, during the 1790s, the issue of new peerages became politicised in the battle over leadership that arose within the French Revolution debate. Whilst loyalists promoted new peerages as evidence of social mobility and an open elite in England, radicals condemned them as contributing to the bulwark of corruption in government.¹⁰¹ In 1795 Thelwall lamented that 'a fresh batch of Borough proprietors has been decorated in the *borrowed plumage* of nobility, that they might increase the *fixed* majority of the Minister, by their *votes* in the house of Peers, and by their *influence*, in the House of Commons'.¹⁰²

Despite using the precise definition of aristocracy as the peerage, the difficulties encountered when relying on any one definition have not been entirely avoided here. For one thing, this definition includes only a small number of what can be identified as a governing elite. For another, this definition remains constant whereas contemporary definitions certainly did not. Ultimately, the use of the term here has rubbed along with that of contemporary writers and sometimes a divergence of definitions must occur. But it is the nature of such definitions to be uncertain. Indeed, as this is a study of representations, it is necessary while retaining a core definition, to incorporate and discuss.

Another term used throughout this book, *ancien régime*, also requires some explanation. Although the term literally describes the old order of government and society in France before 1789, during the 1790s radical pamphleteers commonly identified European societies, including England, as 'old governments', or 'old societies', which were compared unfavourably with the 'new' governments of America and France. Such 'old societies' in radical parlance came to embrace any society, including England, that was domi-

---

98 Turberville, *House of Lords*, 1. Turberville included the 1790s in his subsequent volume: *The House of Lords in the age of reform, 1784–1832: with an epilogue on aristocracy and the advent of democracy, 1837–67*, London 1958.
99 Cannon, *Aristocratic century*, 21. McCahill, however, has argued that as a result of such new creations the main qualification for titles gradually changed from land to distinguished public service: 'Peerage creations', 259–84.
100 James Raven, *Judging new wealth: popular publishing and responses to commerce in England, 1750–1800*, Oxford 1992, 235–6. See also Cannon, *Aristocratic century*, 16–17.
101 Cannon, *Aristocratic century*, 17.
102 John Thelwall, *The natural and constitutional rights of Britons to annual parliaments, universal suffrage, and the freedom of popular association*, London 1795, in Gregory Claeys (ed.), *The politics of English Jacobinism: writings of John Thelwall*, University Park, PA 1995, 59.

nated by monarchy and aristocracy, based on hereditary succession. The *Oxford dictionary* defines '*ancien régime*', not only as pre-Revolutionary France, but also as 'a political or social system that has been displaced, typically by one that is more modern'. And this identifies the very nub of the battle between loyalists and radicals over English government and society. As this book reveals, the loyalists who developed their ideas in contradistinction to those of Edmund Burke, increasingly represented England as a 'modern' state as opposed to the radical representations of it as an *ancien régime*. Consequently, the term '*ancien régime*', is used here to describe the 'old society' in eighteenth-century England, only in terms invoked in contemporary representations. This book does not actually identify 1790s England as an *ancien régime*, but notes this identification, albeit in different terms, in the representations of the period. It is important to point out that it is not the intention here to enter into the debate, initiated by Jonathan Clark, about whether eighteenth-century English society actually was, or was not, an *ancien régime*. The focus instead is upon the polemics of the 1790s.[103]

The French Revolution debate

A review of the historical context of the French Revolution debate reveals many connections with the past. Political ideas from the past were certainly much discussed within the pamphlets. The failure of the Roman republic and the emergence of a corrupt empire were incorporated within enduring eighteenth-century debates about corruption, luxury, commerce and civilisation. Democracy was much debated, from the democracy of the ancient Athenian city states to that of North America. Whether democracy was appropriate to the larger more complex societies of eighteenth-century Europe was a common theme. Moreover radicals in particular made much of the Norman Conquest and its detrimental effect upon government in England. The loss of a Saxon 'Golden Age', and the accompanying liberty and equality were lamented.[104] The source and nature of the English constitution and the constitutional implications of the Glorious Revolution of 1688–9 were also recurring themes in the pamphlets of the French Revolution debate.

Furthermore, it is clear that an anti-aristocratic discourse had arisen from time to time at least in the 150 years which preceded the French Revolution. Such comment, and calls for reform of political rights, can be traced back to

---

[103] For this debate see Clark, *English society*, and reviews thereof by John Cannon in *British Journal for Eighteenth Century Studies* x (1987), 74–7; Joanna Innes in *P&P* cxv (1987), 165–200; and Clark's riposte in *P&P* cxvii (1987), 195–207. See also William Doyle, *The ancien régime*, London 1986.
[104] Christopher Hill, 'The Norman yoke', in his *Puritanism and revolution: studies in interpretation of the English Revolution of the seventeenth century*, London 1958, 50–122; Smith, *Gothic bequest*.

the radical movements of the English civil wars.[105] Parallels may be drawn between the criticisms and demands of the Levellers and the Diggers and those of radicals of the 1790s.[106] During the eighteenth century, but before the 1790s, what may be loosely defined as anti-aristocratic discourse was common, although it was not generally a burgeoning issue. Criticisms of aristocracy centred predominantly around the long-standing debates about corruption in government and luxury in society. At the other end of the time-scale it is generally agreed by historians that the French Revolution debate was laid to rest in its most direct form by the passing of the Great Reform Act of 1832. However, in a broader sense, the French Revolution debate was also the trailblazer of later movements.[107] It is commonly stated that Burke's *Reflections* was the founding text of conservatism. Moreover, E. P. Thompson has famously identified 1790s radicalism as fundamental in the 'making of the English working class', the precursor to Chartism and the trades unions.[108] There is, at the same time, much debate amongst historians as to the effect of the Great Reform Act on aristocratic hegemony itself. The widely-held assumption that the passing of the Great Reform Act heralded the end of an earlier aristocratic hegemony, is now being questioned. Historians differ greatly in their identification of the point at which aristocratic dominance was finally overthrown.[109]

A number of political events during the eighteenth century had invoked anti-aristocratic discourses relevant to this book. In particular, the American War of Independence (1776–83), the ensuing attempts to gain constitutional and administrative reform in the years 1779–85, the East India debate (1783–4) and the Regency Crisis (1788–9). It is clear that there was no direct connection between such events and the French Revolution debate. Most significantly, the criticisms of aristocracy used during these earlier events were not for the most part directed at aristocracy as a class. Nevertheless, the debates which emerged from these events did introduce questions and concepts which were taken up once again, and with more force, in the 1790s.

The loss of the American colonies as a result of the American War of Independence was a great blow to the English establishment. It was an emotive moment for England. As one address put it, 'the splendour' of 'meridian glory was indeed past, the dream of greatness dissipated, and the pageantry of

---

[105] See Christopher Hill, *The world turned upside down: radical ideas during the English Revolution*, London 1991.
[106] See F. K. Donnelly, 'The Levellers and early nineteenth–century radicalism', *Bulletin of the Society for the Study of Labour History* xlix (1984), 24–8.
[107] For a discussion of the long-term impact see conclusion.
[108] Thompson, *Making of the English working class*. Thompon's argument has, however, been disputed by a number of historians.
[109] For useful surveys of this debate see Wahrman, *Imagining the middle class*, 409–20, and Wasson, 'Crisis of the aristocracy'.

empire lost'.[110] A number of historians have argued that the English elite were held responsible for the loss of North America.[111] Certainly there is anti-aristocratic rhetoric to be found in the political writings of the period.[112] In particular the traditional role of the aristocracy as defenders of the state was held up for ridicule.[113]

Yet this debate about America did not develop into a full-scale challenge to aristocracy *per se*. In general neither pro-American reformers nor Christopher Wyvill's Yorkshire Association and related county movements represented political divisions as reflecting social class but loose party political affiliations.[114] The term 'aristocracy' here was used primarily in traditional terms to define a political faction, which it was implied had gained, or was attempting to gain, too much power and was consequently destabilising the English constitution. In 1782, for example, David Williams accused the Whig aristocracy of 'always surrounding the throne; draining the whole country of immense treasures' and gaining undue influence. Indeed, he declared, 'aristocratic factions, . . . have usurped the government'.[115] Criticisms of aristocracy were aimed primarily at their control of parliamentary boroughs.[116] But even on the issue of the 'rotten' boroughs, condemnations of aristocracy can rarely be found in the public documents of the county movement, although the private correspondence, subsequently published, contains a number of such condemnations.[117] Moreover, during the 1780s,

---

[110] SCI, *Second address to the public from the Society for Constitutional Information*, n.d., in Christopher Wyvill, *Political papers*, York 1794–1804, ii. 497–8.
[111] Colley, *Britons*, 148–9; Langford, *Polite and commercial people*, 691–2.
[112] Richard Price, *Observations on the importance of the American Revolution*, 1785, in D. O. Thomas (ed.), *Richard Price: political writings*, London 1991, 116, 145–6.
[113] See, for example, anon., *The modern Atlantis: or, the devil in an air balloon*, 1784, in Gregory Claeys (ed.), *Modern British utopias, 1700–1850*, London 1997, iv. 259–60.
[114] For histories of the reform movement see Eugene C. Black, *The Association: British extraparliamentary political organization, 1769–93*, Cambridge, Mass. 1963; John Brewer, *Party ideology and popular politics at the accession of George III*, Cambridge 1976; John Cannon, *The Fox–North coalition: crisis of the constitution, 1782–1784*, Cambridge 1969, and *Parliamentary reform, 1640–1832*, Cambridge 1973; Ian R. Christie, *Wilkes, Wyvill and reform: the parliamentary reform movement in British politics, 1760–1785*, London 1962, and *Myth and reality in late eighteenth-century British politics*, London 1970; Lincoln, *Some political and social ideas*; Leslie G. Mitchell, *Charles James Fox and the disintegration of the Whig party, 1782–1784*, Oxford 1971; Caroline Robbins, *The eighteenth-century commonwealthman*, Cambridge, Mass. 1959; Pocock 'Radical criticisms', and *Virtue, commerce and history*; George Veitch, *The genesis of parliamentary reform*, London 1913; and Watts, *The Dissenters*.
[115] David Williams, *Letters on political liberty*, London 1782, 43–4, 72.
[116] Pocock, 'Radical criticisms', 46. See also John Cartwright, *Take your choice*, 1776, 38, and anon., *A report of the proceedings of the Committee of Association presented to a meeting of 19 Dec. 1782*, in Charles Lennox, 3rd duke of Richmond, *Sound reason and solid argument for a reform in parliament*, c. 1795, 127–9.
[117] See Christopher Wyvill, *The correspondence of the Revd C. Wyvill with Rt. Hon. William Pitt, concerning parliamentary reform*, 2nd edn, 2 pts, Newcastle-upon-Tyne 1796, i. 3, and Wyvill, *Political papers*, ii. 115; iii. 51–2, 261.

there was as much concern expressed about parliamentary boroughs being controlled by the 'new' rich and Asian 'nabobs' as by the old aristocracy. One correspondent wrote to Wyvill that 'venal ministerial boroughs' were more 'injurious to the public' than 'noble and property boroughs'.[118]

In fact it was largely the economic repercussions of the loss of America which formulated English people's response. Commerce was 'gradually diminished' as a result of the war and 'universal poverty seemed to pervade the land'.[119] Corruption and luxury were identified by critics of the government as the cause of the war and its economic consequences. England and Europe as a whole were measured against a virtuous America and found wanting.[120] America was represented by reformers as a land with a more liberal government and better manners and morals.[121] Whilst European states had progressed beyond the peak of civilisation into luxury, America was at an earlier stage of development, of more equal and simple agrarian living.[122] Luxury and corruption in English government and society were represented as the by-products of a corrupt European system, a system of 'old governments'.[123] This dynamic may be viewed as a precursor to the 1790s radical identification of England with *ancien régime* France.

Moreover, the bulk of the political writings of the county movement reflected the reforming Whig position and identified corruption with 'government' but more often with the 'crown', rather than with the aristocracy. Indeed, Whig tradition saw reform of the constitution as perfectly compatible with the preservation of a dominant landed aristocracy. Political writings declared that it was 'THE ENORMOUS, THE COMPACTLY ACCUMULATED, THE ALL-DEVOURING INFLUENCE OF THE CROWN' that posed the greatest threat to the constitutional balance, as a petition urged in 1779.[124] Many reformers identified a politically ambitious George III and his cohorts as the source of corruption. Perhaps not surprisingly, at this stage a number of leading Whig aristocrats were generally recognised as reformers. The county movement clearly valued such aristocratic support for reform. A letter published in the *York Courant* in 1783 by 'A Freeholder of Yorkshire', praised aristocrats who consistently supported reform: 'Richmond, Rutland, Stanhope, Harcourt, Shelburne, Camden and Lord Mahon, Surrey and

---

118 Wyvill, *Political papers*, iii. 317.
119 SCI, *Second address to the public*, ii. 497–8.
120 James Burgh, *Political disquisitions*, 1774–5, i. 30–1.
121 See anon., *Proceedings relative to the Ulster Assembly of Volunteer Delegates on the subject of more equal representation of the people in the parliament of Ireland to which are annexed letters from the duke of Richmond, Dr Price, Mr Wyvill and others*, 1783, 39.
122 See, for example, Richard Price, *Observations on the nature of civil liberty*, 1776, in Thomas, *Richard Price*, 56.
123 Anon., *Proceedings relative to the Ulster Assembly*, 39; Burgh, *Political disquistions*, i. 30.
124 Anon., *Meeting of the deputies of all the committees and associations, 20 March 1780*, in Lennox, *Sound reason*, 21.

Effingham'.[125] Rudely manoeuvred out of government by a king who disliked Whigs, such Whig aristocrats generally advocated reform that would reduce the undue influence of the crown and re-balance the constitution.

However, even those Whigs who supported reform were not a united force. The Rockingham Whigs, a group of which Edmund Burke was a leading member, had supported the initial economic reforms promoted by the county movement but would not go so far as to support Wyvill's parliamentary reform.[126] They viewed economic reforms as a means of limiting corruption and the influence of the king. The earl of Shelburne, on the other hand, supported parliamentary reform and in particular reform of the representative system. And Charles Lennox, the 3rd duke of Richmond, in 1780 proposed some of the most radical reforms of parliament, which included annual parliaments, increased representation and what he termed universal suffrage,[127] although Pocock has claimed that Richmond was not as radical as such reforms suggest. Rather than seeking a democracy in England Richmond merely hoped that an increase of the franchise would result in a re-balancing of the constitution away from the crown and in favour of the aristocracy.[128] But most reform Whigs, in the Whig tradition of Locke, Harrington and Sydney, continued to support only a limited reform of the franchise to include property-holders.

Despite such differences in Whig commitment to reform, the county movement actively sought support from amongst the Whig aristocracy.[129] Wyvill was anxious to obtain 'a more perfect union with the Nobles who have supported the oeconomical petition' in later reform activity.[130] Indeed, once the county movement had lost Rockingham Whig support, the movement declined and it had largely disbanded by 1785. Evidently their belief in the political status of land linked the largely gentry and/or land-owning leaders of the county movement more closely with aristocracy than with the working people. Moreover, for the county movement of the 1780s, which sought reform from within the establishment, it was important to be seen to be led from 'above' rather than 'below'. In this respect, the reform movement was quite different from the radicalism of the 1790s, with its much greater levels of lower-class involvement and activism.

Unlike the county movement, the East India debate of 1783–4 and the Regency Crisis of 1788–9 arose within parliament rather than as a challenge to it from outside. The East India debate was instigated by Charles James

---

[125] Christie, *Wilkes, Wyvill and reform*, 194.
[126] See Frank O'Gorman, *The rise of party in England: the Rockingham Whigs, 1760–1782*, London 1975.
[127] Charles Lennox, 3rd duke of Richmond. For a biography, see A. G. Olson, *The radical duke: career and correspondence of Charles Lennox, third duke of Richmond*, Oxford 1961.
[128] Burke (ed. Pocock), *Reflections*, pp. xxiii–xxiv.
[129] See, for example, Wyvill, *Political papers*, iii. 115, 149; Lennox, *Sound reason*, 19.
[130] Wyvill, *Political papers*, iii. 300.

Fox's proposal to appoint a board of commissioners, consisting primarily of noblemen, to run the East India Company rather than to place it under the control of the crown, as William Pitt had proposed. The Regency Crisis found the Foxite Whigs attempting to empower the profligate prince of Wales as regent during his father's mental illness.[131] Again, these events reflected political faction or party rather than class divisions and it was the Foxite Whig aristocracy that came in for criticism. Fears that it would form an 'Oligarchical Junto in the two Houses of Parliament' or create a 'fourth estate' were commonly expressed by Fox's opponents.[132] The fact that some of the greatest criticisms of Fox's East India bill came from the House of Lords confirms the extent to which the debate was perceived by contemporaries as a debate within the existing political system. Certainly there was extensive hostility to Fox, who was viewed as an aristocratic demagogue. That lay behind the intense, though unsuccessful, government attempt to defeat him in the 1784 Westminster election.[133] It also brought the downfall of the Fox/North coalition and the rise of William Pitt to position of prime minister. Pitt, unlike Fox, presented himself as an untarnished, non-party leader.[134]

However, while the parliamentary rhetoric incorporated direct and savage criticism of the Foxite Whigs, much of it, in both debates, was focused on behaviour. The issue of private luxury, as well as public corruption, became central to political debate. The alleged profligacy, dissipation and extravagance of the Foxite Whig aristocracy, which supported the certainly profligate prince of Wales and was led by the notorious Fox, were the focus of much attention. A direct link between public corruption and private luxury was established. Members of the Whig aristocracy were accused of wanting to get their hands on the spoils of office to support their extravagant private lives.[135] The excessive lives of the Foxite Whig aristocracy, including the prince of Wales and Fox, were brutally used in the political propaganda of the Pittites. Much satire was published and many Pittite pamphlets depicted Fox's private life of gambling, horse-racing and debt.[136] Pitt was represented as the virtuous man to Fox's gamester.[137] Moreover, this condemnation of the

---

131 In fact the king recovered and reigned until 1811 when a permanent relapse resulted in the prince of Wales acting as regent until George III's death in 1820.
132 Lord Abingdon, *Speech in parliament*, 15 December 1783, in *The parliamentary register*, London 1784, xxx–xxxi. 40; Lord Thurlow, *Speech in parliament*, 9 December 1783, in *The parliamentary register*, London 1775–1813, 1784, xxx–xxxi. 19.
133 Penelope J. Corfield, Edmund M. Green and Charles Harvey, 'Westminster man: Charles James Fox and his electorate, 1780–1806', *Parliamentary History* xx (2001), 168–72.
134 Turner, *British politics*, 30.
135 Phyllis Deutsch, 'Moral trespass in Georgian London: gaming, gender and electoral politics in the age of George III', *HJ* xxxix (1996), 637–56.
136 Mitchell, *Fox and the distintegration of the Whig party*, 149.
137 Duetsch, 'Moral trespass'.

Whig aristocracy for luxury, which infiltrated all the above events, reflects the wider luxury debate. It was within this context that the reformation of manners movement emerged at the end of the 1780s.[138] This was a conservative Anglican evangelical movement, led by William Wilberforce and supported by Pittites, rather than a radical reform movement. It called for reformation of manners at all levels of society, but did focus to some extent on the manners of the aristocracy. Hannah More published the first work, *Thoughts on the importance of the manners of the great to general society* (1788). But, although this tract contained some strong criticism of aristocracy, it stood alone in that the reformation of manners movement remained largely dormant for much of the 1790s and did not fully re-emerge until the early nineteenth century.[139]

Events and debates earlier in the eighteenth century thus gave a taste of what was to follow in the 1790s. But, whilst much attention was paid during the earlier eighteenth century to the behaviour of the elite, this did not turn into a full-scale attack on their leadership until the 1790s. Thus the French Revolution debate is important in its own right. It greatly sharpened and focused the disjointed rumble of discourse on aristocracy. Where earlier criticisms had focused upon aristocratic behaviour or upon aristocratic political factions, radicals in the French Revolution debate, for the first time, represented aristocracy as one political class. The debate brought aristocratic hegemony fully into the forefront of political debate and exposed it to direct and sustained attack.

Three main questions form the central themes to this book and are explored in the following chapters. How and why did representations of aristocracy become central to the French Revolution debate? Thereafter, how did radical and loyalist models of society emerge and affect representations of aristocracy? Finally, what was the significance of the radical attack and loyalist defence, both taking the form largely of written 'representations'? The starting point for this discussion must be Edmund Burke and his writings on the French Revolution.

---

[138] See Joanna Innes, 'Politics and morals: the reformation of manners movement in later eighteenth-century England', in Hellmuth, *Transformation of political culture*, 59–118, and F. K. Brown, *Fathers of the Victorians: the age of Wilberforce*, Cambridge 1961.
[139] Brown, *Fathers of the Victorians*, 4.

1

Edmund Burke and Reflections

'Aristocracy! – Aristocracy! – every thing is to be for Aristocracy'.[1]

The historiography is awash with commentary on Burke. Historians disagree loudly about his political ideas, his allegiances and intentions.[2] One reason for this lack of consensus must be, as Pocock has stressed, that there is no unified view in Burke's writings.[3] Roger Smith warned that 'the political critic trying his tools on Burke soon finds their edges turned' and Burke himself 'distrusted intellectual abstraction'.[4] And Jonathan Clark has declared that Burke wrote no 'systematic treatise on political theory' and consequently that historians have been 'drawn into the unhistorical enterprise of writing one for him'.[5] This book accepts Burke's florid diversity. But relevant here is Burke's representations of aristocracy; and the impact of such representations on the ensuing pamphlet debate.

A number of historians have reviewed, although generally briefly, Burke's representations of aristocracy.[6] Here too Burke displayed a notable inconsistency. Pocock has argued that *Reflections* reveals an ambivalence towards the

---

[1] John Thelwall on Burke: *The rights of nature against the usurpations of establishments*, 1796, in Claeys, *Politics of English Jacobinism*, 445.
[2] On Burke's inconsistency see O'Gorman, *Edmund Burke*; on Burke's Anglican defence of the state see Clark, *English society*, 247–58, and Frederick Dreyer, 'Burke's religion', *Studies in Burke and his time*, xvii, London 1976, 199–212. See also Canavan, *Political reason*; Dreyer, *Burke's politics*; Freeman, *Edmund Burke*; and J. G. A. Pocock, 'Burke and the ancient constitution', in his *Politics, language and time*. The introduction to Harris, *Burke: pre-revolutionary writings*, is also useful. Other notable works on Burke include Blakemore, *Burke and the fall of language*; Alfred Cobban, *Edmund Burke and the revolt against the eighteenth century*, London 1929; Carl Cone, *Burke and the nature of politics*, Lexington, Ky 1957; Isaac Kramnick, *The rage of Edmund Burke: the conscience of an ambivalent Conservative*, New York 1977; David McNally, 'Political economy to the fore: Burke, Malthus and the Whig response to popular radicalism in the age of the French Revolution', *HPT* xxi (2000), 427–47; Conor Cruise O'Brien, *The great melody: a thematic biography of Edmund Burke*, London 1992; Daniel Ritchie (ed.), *Edmund Burke: appraisals and applications*, Princeton, NJ 1990; and Peter Stanlis, *Edmund Burke and the natural law*, Michigan 1958.
[3] Pocock, 'Burke and the ancient constitution', 231.
[4] Smith, *Gothic bequest*, 13.
[5] Clark, *English society*, 250.
[6] Canavan, *Political reason*, 96–9; Dreyer, *Burke's politics*, 30–2; Freeman, *Edmund Burke*, 110–13; Harris, *Burke: pre-revolutionary writings*, pp. xvi–xxxiii; O'Gorman, *Edmund Burke*, 40, 50–4, 121, 128; Burke (ed. Pocock), *Reflections*, pp. xviii–lvi.

Whig aristocracy that Burke served and defended.[7] Burke had been allied with Lord Rockingham, a supporter of economic reforms in the early 1780s and also a close friend of Charles James Fox, a voluble supporter of the French Revolution in 1789. But Rockingham died in 1782 and Burke split with Fox in the House of Commons in 1791 over the French Revolution. Thereafter Burke no longer held a place within the Whig aristocracy. Moreover, Burke clearly felt betrayed by those members of that Whig aristocracy who supported the revolution as his attacks on Fox and later on the duke of Bedford illustrate.[8] In Burke's view the Whig aristocracy did not always behave as it should. Consequently examples of Burke both lauding and criticising the aristocracy may be found in his works. Despite his preoccupation with aristocracy in his writings, much of the historiography is focused predominantly on interpreting Burke's definition of a 'natural aristocracy' contained in the *Appeal from the new to the old Whigs* (1791).

However, it is *Reflections on the revolution in France* (1790) that is the focus of this chapter and the starting point for the present discussions. It was that work which triggered a dialogue about aristocracy within the French Revolution debate. In the terms of the French Revolution controversy *Reflections* is often interpreted by historians as a defence of aristocracy, or of aristocratic government.[9] Yet *Reflections* was clearly not intended to represent a defence of aristocracy *per se*. Had it done so the book would have come as less of a surprise to many of Burke's contemporaries who, at that time, perceived Burke as a supporter of the reforming Whigs. Indeed Burke was well known for his Whiggish opposition to the undue influence of the king.[10] And Whig reformers had never seen any contradiction between constitutional reform and the maintenance of aristocratic supremacy.

But in 1790 Burke could be found doing something quite different. Fearful of the spread of an uncontrollable French democracy he defended, in *Reflections*, not just the aristocracy but also the monarchy and the role of the Anglican Church as part of the ruling order. He stressed order and stability,

---

[7] Burke (ed. Pocock), *Reflections*, p. x.
[8] See Edmund Burke, *A letter from the Rt. Hon. Edmund Burke to a noble lord, on the attacks made upon him and his pension in the House of Lords, by the duke of Bedford and the earl of Lauderdale*, 1796, in Paul Langford and others (eds), *The writings and speeches of Edmund Burke*, Oxford 1913–91, x, for Burke's condemnation of the duke of Bedford and also the earl of Lauderdale.
[9] O'Gorman stated that Burke's 'French thought was an even more vigorous defence of elitism than his earlier thought had been' and, whilst he 'made a few gestures in the direction of merit', his main concern was to preserve the system of privilege in Europe: *Edmund Burke*, 120. Clark similarly claimed that Burke emerged in the early 1790s as 'a champion of the Anglican aristocratic-monarchical regime': *English society*, 250. David Bromwich has termed the *Reflections* 'a work of aristocratic propaganda': 'Wollstonecraft as a critic of Burke', *PT* xxiii (1995), 617–34, esp. p. 617. See also Marilyn Butler (ed.), *Burke, Paine, Godwin, and the revolution controversy*, Cambridge 1984, 1.
[10] See Edmund Burke, *Thoughts on the cause of the present discontents*, 1770, in Harris, *Burke: pre-revolutionary writings*.

declaring that all reforms should be anchored in tradition and that liberty under the English constitution was rooted in ancient prescriptive rights and linked to property. Burke had moved away from Whig reform and towards an altogether more conservative position.[11] As Pocock has said, Burke was defending a governing order, which was 'monarchic, clerical, aristocratic, commercial' against the invasion of the 'revolutionary intellect'.[12] Nevertheless, the fact that Burke had much to say about the French aristocracy and brought the English aristocracy into the debate was significant for introducing a new issue into the French Revolution debate. Moreover Burke's representations of England as an *ancien régime* and the 'medievalism' inherent in *Reflections*, clearly influenced the focus of the early responses and the debate that ensued.

Burke's definitions of aristocracy

Burke's apparent ambivalence towards aristocracy, displayed throughout his writings, may be better understood by reviewing his use of the term. In his earlier writings,[13] he took the standard view of his time and identified 'aristocracy' in the classical sense.[14] In 1768 he termed 'aristocracy', 'the most oppressive of absolute governments'.[15] In 1770, however, in support of the Rockingham Whig position Burke focused upon the dangerous increase in royal influence and the need to redress the balance of the constitution in favour of the aristocracy. Consequently he differentiated between such an 'aristocracy' and the members of the English House of Lords:

> If any particular Peers, by their uniform, upright, constitutional conduct, by their public and their private virtues have acquired an influence in the country; the people, on whose favour that influence depends, and from whom it arose, will never be duped into an opinion, that such greatness in a Peer is the despotism of an aristocracy.[16]

And in 1781 Burke identified 'aristocracy' more closely with the peerage and as an order:

---

[11] Clark identified this shift in religious terms from a Whig position of self-conscious libertarianism to one championing the Anglican aristocratic-monarchical regime within which Church and State were not merely allied but were one: *English society*, 250.
[12] Burke (ed. Pocock), *Reflections*, p. xxxviii.
[13] To avoid confusion, in this chapter references to Burke's 'earlier writings' means those published before 1789, his 'revolutionary writings' to the *Reflections* and other works of the same year, and 'later' writings those published in 1792 or thereafter.
[14] See Edmund Burke, *A vindication of natural society*, 1757, in Harris, *Burke: pre-revolutionary writings*, 33.
[15] Idem, *Annual register*, 1768, 272 (2nd pagination), as quoted in Harris, *Burke: pre-revolutionary writings*, 134.
[16] Idem, *Thoughts on the cause*, 134.

> I am accused... of being a man of aristocratic principles. If by aristocracy they mean the peers, I have no vulgar admiration, nor any vulgar antipathy, towards them. I hold their order in cold and decent respect. I hold them to be of an absolute necessity in the constitution; but I think they are only good when kept within proper bounds.[17]

In a letter to Earl Fitzwilliam of 1791, Burke defined those essentially aristocratic attributes that the Whig party had in the past displayed. The Whig party had 'the Estimation of being an Aristocratick party' in 'the true sense of the word; that is to say, a party grave and moral' of 'honest and wise men'.[18] Aristocracy was here for Burke essential to government and society, as historians are fond of saying, both as 'a bulwark of good rulership',[19] and 'a bulwark of the social order'.[20] But he condemned those members of the aristocracy who did not behave as they should as leaders.[21] And it was the issue of aristocracy being kept 'within proper bounds' that presented a problem for Burke from time to time during his political life. It is here that his ambiguities about aristocracy, are revealed.

In *Reflections* Burke accused 'individuals' amongst the French nobility of betraying that order and leading the revolution. These were 'Turbulent, discontented men of quality... puffed up with personal pride and arrogance', who 'generally despise their own order'.[22] In the *Appeal*, Burke lamented that the Foxite Whig party had 'coined to themselves Whig principles from a French die'.[23] The Foxite Whigs had strayed from their former course and were now involved in this new species of French democracy and it was their intention 'to root out that thing called an Aristocrate, or Nobleman and Gentleman'.[24] Similarly, in *A letter to a noble lord* (1796), Burke condemned the duke of Bedford and the earl of Lauderdale, Foxite Whigs who supported the French Revolution. That work was written in terms so vitriolic that it was almost echoing Paine. The duke of Bedford had made a jibe at Burke's pension and this, coupled with the duke's support for the revolution, was for Burke an example of a nobleman not behaving as he should.

Burke again, in *Reflections*, defined 'aristocracy' primarily as a political

---

[17] Idem, *Speech on Mr Fox's bill for the repeal of the Marriage Act, 15 June 1781*, in *The speeches of the Right Honourable Edmund Burke in the House of Commons and in Westminster Hall*, 1816, ii. 279.
[18] Idem, *Letter to Earl Fitzwilliam, 21 November 1791*, in T. W. Copeland and others (eds), *The correspondence of Edmund Burke*, Cambridge 1958–78, vi. 450.
[19] Harris, *Burke: pre-revolutionary writings*, p. xxx.
[20] Canavan, *Political reason*, 99.
[21] Burke (ed. Pocock), *Reflections*, p. x.
[22] Idem, *Reflections on the revolution in France*, 1790, ed. Conor Cruise O'Brien, London 1986, 135–6.
[23] Idem, *An appeal from the new to the old Whigs*, 2nd edn 1791, in *The works of the Right Honourable Edmund Burke*, 1808, vi. 267.
[24] Idem, *Letter to Earl Fitzwilliam, 21 November 1791*, in *Correspondence of Edmund Burke*, vi. 450.

term for a sector of government. 'We are resolved to keep', he confirmed, 'an established monarchy, an established aristocracy, and an established democracy, each in the degree it exists.'[25] None the less the fact that in *Reflections* Burke was defending the French as well as the English nobility affected such definitions. The French *noblesse* was generally recognised by the English as a separate order with excessive rights and privileges, unlike its English counterpart. Burke did not actually identify the English aristocracy simply as the political counterpart of the French aristocracy. But his identification of the English aristocracy with the French, and as an 'order', and his use of the term 'nobility' to describe them both, often together, undoubtedly assisted in shifting contemporary interpretations of the term.[26]

Certainly Paine was swift, in response, to identify the English aristocracy as a separate class or order like the *noblesse*. Moreover *Reflections* also reveals another delineation of the elite into 'monied interest' and the 'landed interest'. Here the differentiating factor was wealth, movable and propertied. In *Reflections*, Burke set a new French 'monied interest' against a dismissed *noblesse*, demagogues against legitimate rulers.[27] The 'landed interest' had become the antithesis to 'the monied interest' in France, although not, for Burke, in England. And the defence of a traditional landed aristocracy, which Burke saw as a bulwark against an unstable monied interest in politics, was an essential focus of *Reflections*.

In the *Appeal*, Burke described 'our house of lords', as 'the chief virtual representative of our aristocracy, the great ground pillar of security to the landed interest, and that main link by which it is connected with the law and the crown'.[28] This brings together Burke's definitions and suggests that he viewed 'aristocracy' as interchangeable with 'nobility' and, loosely, as a class of the 'landed interest'. Nevertheless Burke's ambiguous definition of a 'natural aristocracy' in the *Appeal* has left historians divided as to whether Burke was advocating a hereditary aristocracy or a meritocracy.[29] But to view Burke's 'natural aristocracy' in such terms is to miss the point. In fact Burke's definition of a 'natural aristocracy' incorporates both a hereditary aristocracy and a meritocracy. What Burke was defining here was not 'aristocracy' in terms of the peerage or the nobility but a broader category. Burke's 'natural aristocracy' incorporated all those best suited to govern, in both the House of Lords and the House of Commons. That is the nobility and the gentry, together 'gentlemen', the governing elite, the primary landowners in the nation. Burke's 'natural aristocracy', can loosely be described as comprising

---

25 Idem (ed. O'Brien), *Reflections*, 188.
26 Ibid. 245.
27 Ibid. 209–14.
28 Idem, *Appeal from the new*, 188.
29 Ibid. 217–18. For the meritocracy interpretation see, for example, Ritchie, *Further reflections*, p. xv; Dreyer, *Burke's politics*, 30–2; and Freeman, *Edmund Burke*, 108. For the hereditary aristocracy interpretation see, for example, Canavan, *Political reason*, 97–8, and O'Gorman, *Edmund Burke*, 121.

'virtuous gentlemen',[30] with all the problems of definition that term might bring with it.[31] Clearly hereditary rights, property and merit all played a role in Burke's consideration of who should rule in a mixed government.

Burke's central focus on aristocracy

That Burke's *Reflections* was a response to Richard Price's *Discourse on the love of our country* (1789) is well established. As such, Burke's tract was a defence of the existing political system in England, which was in line with the mainstream of English political thought.[32] He defended the hereditary right of the monarchy and aristocracy to rule under the ancient constitution against Price's claim that the people had the right to remove, replace and select their governors. The hereditary rights of the monarch were, Burke argued, confirmed at the Glorious Revolution of 1688–9 and he dismissed any idea that William III and Mary had been appointed by the will of the people. It is clear, then, that Burke had moved some way from Whig reform. Moreover, against Price's calls for religious toleration, Burke defended the Anglican Church and its established position as part of the civil order.[33] At this early stage in the debate a major focus was religious toleration and the main protagonists were the Anglican Church and Dissenters. French Dissenters had been granted equal citizenship on the eve of the revolution.[34] This fact no doubt encouraged many English Dissenters to join the radicalism that developed in response to Paine's *Rights of man*. Turning to the main focus of this book, it is important to note Price did not focus on aristocracy in his *Discourse*; indeed, he hardly mentioned it. It is necessary, therefore, to turn elsewhere to find the reason for Burke's vehement defence of aristocracy: to France. Burke's condemnation of the membership of the French National Assembly is well documented and will only be briefly discussed here. But historians have for the most part ignored Burke's defence of the French aristocracy. It was Burke's focus on the French as well as the English aristocracy, which helped formulate the foundations of the ensuing debate and maintain the focus on aristocracy.

It should be remembered that *Reflections* was written as a reply to a young Parisian gentleman, who had asked for Burke's opinion upon the French Revolution. Burke began with a statement of his major concern:

> I do most heartily wish that France may be animated by a spirit of rational liberty, and that I think you bound, in all honest policy, to provide a permanent

---

[30] See Ritchie, *Further reflections*, p. xvi.
[31] Corfield, 'The rivals', has a useful discussion of definitions of 'the gentleman'.
[32] Burke (ed. Pocock), *Reflections*, p. xii.
[33] See ibid. p. xxviii.
[34] Royle, *Revolutionary Britannia?*, 14.

body, in which that spirit may reside, and an effectual organ, by which it may act, it is my misfortune to entertain great doubts concerning several material points in your late transactions.[35]

In other words, Burke was hoping that the French would adopt a constitution like the English version, but doubted that they would. Fearful of French revolutionary violence spreading to England, he pledged his 'zeal for maintaining' the constitution and principles enshrined at the 'glorious Revolution', 'in their utmost purity and vigour'.[36] The *Reflections* was no simple 'polemic against democracy'.[37] Burke later explained that he had supported the French monarchy, not because 'he thought it better than the aristocracy or the democracy', but because 'it was attacked and endeavoured to be run down'.[38] Evidently Burke's primary, underlying concern was the preservation of the English constitution, but also, more controversially, the restitution of *ancien régime* France, albeit with reform.[39] It may be, as Bromwich has claimed, that Burke intended *Reflections* as a warning to England more than to France.[40] But there is much notable comment on, and advice to, France in both *Reflections* and his other writings.

Burke advised his French correspondent that 'You might, if you pleased, have profited of our example, and have given your recovered freedom a correspondent dignity':

> Your constitution, it is true, whilst you were out of possession suffered waste and dilapidation; but you possessed in some parts the walls, and in all the foundations of a noble and venerable castle. You might have repaired those walls; you might have built on those foundations . . . you had the elements of a constitution very nearly as good as could be wished.[41]

Whilst the French had 'all these advantages' in their 'antient states' they now chose to act as if they 'had never been moulded into civil society'.[42] And in a speech in parliament when *Reflections* was being written Burke accused the French, after destroying their 'oldest constitution', of laying 'the axe to the root of all property, and consequently of all national prosperity'. They 'made and recorded a sort of *institute* and *digest* of anarchy, called the rights of man . . . By this mad declaration they subverted the state'.[43] The French

---

35 Burke (ed. O'Brien), *Reflections*, 85.
36 Ibid. 86.
37 See Freeman, *Edmund Burke*, 108; Canavan, *Political reason*, 164.
38 Burke, *Speech on the Quebec government bill, 11 May 1791*, in *Burke's speeches*, iv. 36.
39 Burke was, of course, no supporter of absolute monarchy.
40 Bromwich, 'Wollstonecraft as a critic', 617.
41 Burke (ed. O'Brien), *Reflections*, 121–2.
42 Ibid. 122.
43 Idem, *Substance of the speech of the Right Honourable Edmund Burke, in the debate on the army estimates, in the House of Commons, 9 February 1790*, 3rd edn 1790, in Harris, *Burke: pre-revolutionary writings*, 313–14.

aristocracy and their families had been 'driven to seek refuge in every nation throughout Europe, for no other reason than this; that without any fault of theirs, they were born gentlemen, and men of property'. The professed principle of the revolutionaries was:

> an implacable hostility to nobility and gentry, and whose savage war-whoop was '*a l'Aristocrate*', by which senseless, bloody cry, they animated one another to rapine and murder, whilst abetted by ambitious men of another class, they were crushing every thing respectable and virtuous in their nation, and ... disgracing almost every name, by which we formerly knew there was such a country in the world as France.[44]

Just as the French had a constitution suitable for repair, Burke claimed that they had also, before the revolution, an acceptable aristocracy: 'I found your nobility for the greater part composed of men of an high spirit, and of a delicate sense of honour ... They were tolerably well bred; very officious, humane, and hospitable; in their conversation frank and open; with a good military tone; and reasonably tinctured with literature.'[45]

Burke also approved of the French aristocracy's 'behaviour to the inferior classes', which he identified as good-natured and suitably familiar. He admitted that they were 'not without considerable faults'. In particular some of the French aristocracy had developed a licentiousness, a 'habitual dissoluteness of manners', which 'continued beyond the pardonable period of life'. And although such manners had originated in England they had become more common in France and the French aristocracy had failed to copy the finer attributes of the English aristocracy. Most important, Burke lamented that the French nobility was closed to commoners of great wealth, when 'good policy' in every country ought to bestow the appropriate 'rank and estimation'. They had failed to harness wealth to land like their English counterparts. Moreover for Burke it was not the French aristocracy that was the sector of government responsible for the revolution, it was 'the revenue, the system and collection of which were the most grievous parts of the French government'. The monied men and *philosophes* were the leaders of the National Assembly. Indeed, 'all this violent cry against the nobility', Burke took to be 'a mere work of art' and he confirmed that 'to be honoured and even privileged by the laws, opinions, and inveterate usages of our country, growing out of the prejudice of ages, has nothing to provoke horror and indignation in any man'. Significantly it was in this passage on the French aristocracy that Burke declared that 'Nobility is a graceful ornament to the civil order. It is the Corinthian capital of polished society.'[46]

Burke confirmed, 'I do not like to see any thing destroyed; any void

---

[44] Ibid. 315.
[45] Burke (ed. O'Brien), *Reflections*, 242–3.
[46] Ibid. 243–5.

produced in society.' There were no 'incorrigible vices in the noblesse of France, or any abuse that could not be removed by a reform short of abolition'.[47] In his *Letter to a member of the National Assembly* (1791), Burke said, 'I do not advise an House of Lords to you. Your antient course by representatives of the noblesse (in your circumstances) appears to me rather a better institution' and your 'constitution by estates, was the natural and only just representation of France'.[48] Thus, just as Burke believed the French constitution could be restored with reform, so too could the French *noblesse*. Burke's aim remained to put 'every thing without exception as nearly as possible upon its former basis'.[49]

Moreover Burke expressed sorrow at the fate of the French aristocracy. It is, he said, 'a sour, malignant, envious disposition, without taste for the reality, or for any image or representation of virtue, that sees with joy the unmerited fall of what had long flourished in splendour and honour'. The French Revolution had resulted in the 'degradation of the whole noblesse of France; and the suppression of the very idea of a gentleman'.[50] Such an 'attempt to oppress, degrade, impoverish, confiscate, and extinguish the original gentlemen, and landed property of an whole nation, cannot be justified under any form it may assume'.[51] In 1790 Burke declared: 'I never will be persuaded that because people have lived under an absolute Monarchy' they have a right to 'destroy all the credit, power and influence of the gentry of a Country and a great deal of their property', and leave it to the administration of 'Mechanicks'.[52] And Burke's support for the French aristocracy remained constant.[53] Later, in 1795, he said that

> Their Nobility and their men of property, in a mass, had the very same virtues and the very same vices, and in the very same proportions, with the same description of men in this and in other nations. I must do justice to suffering honour, generosity and integrity. I do not know that any time or any country has furnished more splendid examples of every virtue, domestick and publick.[54]

What particularly disturbed Burke was that the French had made a 'great departure from the antient course' and placed the 'whole power of the state'

---

47 Ibid. 245–6.
48 Idem, *Letter to a Member of the National Assembly*, 1791, in Langford, *Writings of Edmund Burke*, iii. 329–32.
49 Burke, *Correspondence*, vii. 389.
50 Idem (ed. O'Brien), *Reflections*, 245, 334.
51 Langford, *Writings of Edmund Burke*, iii. 296.
52 Edmund Burke, *Letter to Philip Francis*, 19 Nov. 1790, in *Correspondence*, vi. 173.
53 It is well documented that Burke supported the French aristocracy in England and even set up a school for their children near his home in Beaconsfield: Lockitt, *Relations of French and English society*, 106.
54 Edmund Burke, *Fourth letter on a regicide peace*, 1795, in Langford, *Writings of Edmund Burke*, x. 67.

in one body, the National Assembly. The 'three orders' had been 'melted down into one'.[55] He warned that 'Considerate people . . . will observe the use which is made of *power*; and particularly of so trying a thing as *new* power in *new* persons, of whose principles, tempers, and dispositions, they have little or no experience.'[56] All the evil that had befallen France would, he declared, 'appear perfectly unaccountable if we do not consider the composition of the National Assembly'. And by this Burke meant its membership. It was here that Burke turned to the issue of qualities of leadership, which was to become central to the radical argument in the French Revolution debate.

Burke's views on the issue of inheritance versus merit, in *Reflections*, are as complex as those contained in the *Appeal*, and the same conclusions may be reached. 'You do not imagine', Burke declared in *Reflections*, 'that I wish to confine power, authority, and distinction to blood, and names, and titles.' The only legitimate qualification for government, was 'virtue and wisdom, actual or presumptive. Wherever they are actually found they have, in whatever state, condition, profession or trade, the passport of Heaven to human place and honour'.[57] Burke was not, however, promoting a pure meritocracy here, but was saying that leadership should conform to the constitution and to the social order. It should not be entirely monarchical, aristocratic or democratic. As he asked of the French, had they

> never heard . . . of anything between the despotism of the monarch and the despotism of the multitude? Have they never heard of a monarchy directed by laws, controlled and balanced by the great hereditary wealth and hereditary dignity of a nation; and both again controlled by a judicious check from the reason and feeling of the people at large acting by a suitable and permanent organ.[58]

Burke was concerned that the leaders in France, who had replaced the 'landed interest', were now a combination of 'a great monied interest' and 'the political Men of Letters' who 'became a sort of demagogues'.[59] They were the source, indeed 'a *cause* of the general fury' aimed at the French nobility and clergy. Moreover the French National Assembly was largely made up of men of no talents, 'mere country curates', 'inferior, unlearned . . . obscure provincial advocates . . . an handful of country clowns' and 'a greater number of traders' and 'dealers in stocks and funds'. Such men did not represent the 'super-eminent authority' necessary to awe the populace, because they did not have the necessary character or knowledge.[60] And evidently it was their lack of qualifications that concerned Burke. Much of Burke's anxiety about

---

[55] Idem (ed. O'Brien), *Reflections*, 129.
[56] Ibid. 91.
[57] Ibid. 127, 139.
[58] Ibid. 227.
[59] Ibid. 209–14.
[60] Ibid. 129–34.

the National Assembly was about the correct formation of representative assemblies. Burke confirmed that

> [the] British house of commons, without shutting its doors to any merit in any class, is . . . filled with every thing illustrious in rank, in descent, in hereditary and in acquired opulence, in cultivated talents, in military, civil, naval and politic distinction, that the country can afford.[61]

Consequently the House of Commons was a body of men who might loosely be termed 'gentlemen', of hereditary position or acquired wealth. This combination of land and money was clearly the composition that Burke considered appropriate for representative assemblies.

Moreover Burke confirmed that he believed, albeit with limitations, in an open elite:

> every thing ought to be open; but not indifferently to every man. I do not hesitate to say that the road to eminence and power, from obscure condition, ought not to be made too easy, nor a thing too much of course . . . The temple of honour ought to be seated on an eminence.[62]

It must be stressed here that Burke's promotion of an 'open elite' did not extend to the hereditary aristocracy. A significant limitation on an 'open elite' for Burke was the natural social order. He warned that the real object of the revolutionary cause in France was to destroy the social order, to 'level all those institutions, and to break all those connections, natural and civil, that regulate and hold together the community by a chain of subordination'.[63] For Burke, 'those who attempt to level, never equalize', because in all societies some citizens 'must be uppermost'. Those with such occupations as 'hairdressers' and 'tallow-handlers' were not fit to rule, not just because they were not qualified but because to permit such men to rule would be 'at war with nature'; it would subvert the natural order.[64] Indeed property was the ultimate source of power for Burke as he had stated in 1770.[65] In *Reflections*, he confirmed that the 'characteristic essence of property . . . is to be *unequal*' as it forms a 'natural rampart' against 'envy' and 'rapacity'. The French had 'strayed out of the high road of nature' for the 'property of France does not govern it'.[66] Property for Burke was also the source of liberty: 'from Magna Charta to the Declaration of Right, it has been the uniform policy of our constitution to claim and assert our liberties, as an *entailed inheritance* derived to us from our forefathers, and to be transmitted to our posterity'.[67]

---

61 Ibid. 132.
62 Ibid. 139–40.
63 Idem, *Substance of the speech*, 315.
64 Idem (ed. O'Brien), *Reflections*, 138.
65 Idem, *Thoughts on the cause*, 134.
66 Idem (ed. O'Brien), *Reflections*, 140–1.
67 Ibid. 111, 119.

Thus with a legal term applicable to the landed interest, Burke linked an aristocratic concept of inheritance to the English constitution and liberties. In England, he declared, all benefited from inheritance:

> We have an inheritable crown; an inheritable peerage; and an house of commons and a people inheriting privileges, franchises, and liberties from a long line of ancestors... Besides the people of England well know, that the idea of inheritance furnishes a sure principle of conservation, and... of transmission; without at all excluding a principle of improvement.[68]

This concept of a universal inheritance was later adopted and adapted by loyalists. Moreover, for Burke, inheritance ensured that property remained in the right place and that consequently the *status quo* was not upset. Pocock has argued that Burke saw the social order as an alliance between heaven and earth, and property as the means by which men assumed a place in this natural order.[69] It was their ownership of great and hereditary property that placed the aristocracy at the pinnacle. Burke stressed the importance of ensuring that property was inherited within families and stated that the House of Lords was formed 'upon this principle'. As it was 'wholly composed of hereditary property and hereditary distinction' and comprised 'a third of the legislature', it was 'the sole judge of all property in all its subdivisions'. This was acceptable to Burke for 'some decent regulated pre-eminence, some preference (not exclusive appropriation) given to birth, is neither unnatural, nor unjust, nor impolitic'.[70]

Thus Burke promoted the English landed aristocracy as the natural leaders in government and the social order. But this did not exclude non-noble gentlemen from obtaining a position in government, albeit overwhelmingly in the House of Commons. Somewhat appropriately Burke ended one of his last works, *A letter to a noble lord*, with a statement on aristocracy which confirmed his position:

> Nobility forms the chain that connects the ages of a nation,... no political fabrick could be well made without some such order of things as might, through a series of time afford a rational hope of securing unity, coherence, consistency and stability to the state... nothing else can protect it against the levity of courts, and the greater levity of the multitude... to talk of hereditary monarchy without any thing else of hereditary reverence in the Commonwealth, was a low-minded absurdity... this nobility, in fact does not exist in wrong of other orders of the state, but by them, and for them.[71]

It was the balance within the constitution and compliance with a natural

---

[68] Ibid. 119–20.
[69] Pocock also points out that Harrington was a source of this view: Burke (ed. Pocock), *Reflections*, p. xxxvi.
[70] Burke (ed. O'Brien), *Reflections*, 140–1.
[71] Idem, *A letter to a noble lord*, in Langford, *Writings of Edmund Burke*, x. 177.

social order that Burke wanted to maintain. Thus *Reflections* brought aristocracy and issues of leadership to the forefront of the French Revolution debate. Radicals then took up the issues Burke had raised.

England as an *ancien régime*

Burke's representations of English society are still the subject of debate. Frank O'Gorman has stated that the French Revolution gave Burke 'a new object: to defend the *ancien régime* in France and in Europe'. Burke could not see that 'a new commercial and industrial society was already emerging. The central feature of Burke's revolutionary thought was his concern to preserve the old society'.[72] Pocock, on the other hand, argued that Burke was a Whig and in tune with Whig social theory that promoted a commercial society. Whig England was 'consciously post-feudal; its cardinal belief was in the natural harmony between landed and commercial wealth'.[73] Consequently, Pocock stated, Burke held commercial progress to be 'part of the science of human nature and perfectly compatible with hereditary monarchy and landed aristocracy'. Land and money were perfectly compatible for Burke.[74] One way to understand this apparent contradiction manifested in *Reflections* is to view Burke's political allegiances as multi-layered. Fundamentally he was and remained a Whig, but in response to the French Revolution he also became first and foremost a loyalist, defending the establishment. And fear of the spread of revolutionary violence from France and an unstable political culture, led by monied rather than landed men, rendered him a conservative loyalist.

Burke certainly celebrated England's commercial achievements, as illustrated in his 1790 comment that since the Glorious Revolution, 'Great Britain rose above the standard, even of her former self. An era of improved domestic prosperity then commenced, and still continues.'[75] In *Reflections*, Burke claimed that England's form of government had contributed to its being wealthier than France.[76] He also argued that before the Revolution France had been an opulent, commercial and industrial country with 'all the arts that beautify and polish life'. It was second only to England 'in the excellence of her manufactures and fabrics'.[77] But the French had 'found their punishment' in the Revolution: 'industry without vigour; commerce expiring; the revenue unpaid, yet the people impoverished ... civil and military anarchy'. Indeed in revolutionary France, a new '*Oligarchy*' of the

---

72 O'Gorman, *Edmund Burke*, 107.
73 Burke (ed. Pocock), *Reflections*, pp. xix–xx.
74 Ibid. pp. xv, xxxi.
75 Burke, *Substance of the speech*, 318.
76 Idem (ed. O'Brien), *Reflections*, 234.
77 Ibid. 235–6.

'monied interest' had so mismanaged the nation's finances that they had 'founded a commonwealth upon gaming' and the 'great object in these politics is to metamorphose France, from a great kingdom into one great play-table . . . a nation of gamesters'.[78]

Burke blamed the French Revolution on the *philosophes* of the enlightenment and the 'monied interest', which, in France, had remained separate and distant from the 'landed interest'.[79] Burke lamented that 'the owners of the two distinct species of property' were 'not so well disposed to each other as they are in this country'. Indeed in France there was a state of real 'warfare between the noble ancient landed interest, and the new monied interest' and the 'strength was in the hands of the latter'.[80] Burke was particularly concerned that the 'monied interest' had seized control of the finances of France in 1789 and appropriated the lands of the Church, to extend their power and that of the new revolutionary state.[81] This was a violation of the property rights of the Church and, Burke believed, would lead to instability. He took the traditional view, shared by conservatives and Old Whigs alike, that landed property was the source of stability in Britain. Hence the aristocracy as hereditary landed proprietors had an important part to play in government. It was, therefore, the combination of the dismissal of the French monarchy and aristocracy and the exploitation of Church property, plus the inevitable consequences thereof, that formulated Burke's response.

Consequently in *Reflections* Burke took a conservative loyalist position and his primary aim was, as O'Gorman stated, to defend the European *ancien régimes* against radicalism and the horrors of revolutionary France. Reform, even limited Whig reform, was out of the question in such a political climate. Burke emphasised that in England it 'is our old settled maxim, never entirely nor at once to depart from antiquity'.[82] Burke may have invoked Whig social theory but he also represented England in terms that identified it as an *ancien régime*. This is significant because clearly English majority opinion did not consider England to be an old regime like its European neighbours. Such 'old governments' were to be found overseas in European 'popish', absolutist states such as France. The English 'mixed' form of government and its commercial and colonial prowess set England apart. Moreover it was the abiding intention of majority opinion in eighteenth-century England to differentiate specifically between England and France and indeed all other European *ancien régimes*. By contrast, it had traditionally been those on the 'left', radicals and reformers, who had identified England as one of the European 'old governments'. During the 1770s and 1780s, and particularly during the debate on the American War of Independence, radicals and reformers

---

78 Ibid. 123, 126, 307–10.
79 See Wahrman, *Imagining the middle class*, 22.
80 Burke (ed. O'Brien), *Reflections*, 210–11.
81 Idem (ed. Pocock), *Reflections*, pp. xxviii–xxix.
82 Idem (ed. O'Brien), *Reflections*, 198.

classed England as one of the old governments of Europe, which had tipped over the edge of civilisation and into corruption and luxury, as opposed to the new America.[83] It has been little noted by historians that in *Reflections* Burke identified European 'old governments' together and included England with them.

Burke confirmed that 'Old establishments are tried by their effects. If the people are happy, united, wealthy, and powerful, we presume the rest. We conclude that to be good from whence good is derived.' Reforms may be necessary when 'errors and deviations' are found, but 'the ship proceeds on her course'. The 'French builders', however, had cleared away 'as mere rubbish whatever they found and, like their ornamental gardeners', had formed 'every thing into an exact level'.[84] Burke argued that the French should have 'resumed their ancient privileges' or looked to their 'neighbours in this land who had kept alive the ancient principles and models of the old common law of Europe meliorated and adapted to its present state'.[85] *Ancien régime* France was not for Burke an absolutist, papist despotism, as the English had customarily described their old enemy. France had not only a 'mild and lawful monarch' and a clergy 'of moderate minds and decorous manners' but also a perfectly acceptable *noblesse*.[86] Ironically, probably the only English people who would have agreed wholeheartedly with Burke's analysis were England's aristocrats. Thus whilst Burke certainly pioneered the conservative loyalist movement most succeeding loyalists avoided both identifying England as an *ancien régime* and associating the country with France.[87]

As David McNally has stressed, Burke's rhetoric was a 'polarizing one'; it divided society into 'civilized gentleman and barbarian rabble'.[88] This is illustrated by Burke's well-known statement on mob rule. If England were to follow the French example, Burke warned, 'learning will be cast into the mire, and trodden down under the hoofs of a swinish multitude'.[89] This reference to the 'swinish multitude' certainly brought forth an angry response from radicals, and a number of pamphlets included the phrase, or related euphemisms, in their title.[90] Most important, this inflammatory rhetoric implied a polarised society in England on the 'aristocracy and people' model, later promoted by Paine. Radicals associated this model with decrepit *ancien régime* societies such as pre-Revolutionary France. Burke only served to promote such a view in his famous oration on chivalry.

Chivalry was a significant European medieval concept to invade the pages

---

[83] Price, *Observations on the nature*, 56, 69.
[84] Burke (ed. O'Brien), *Reflections*, 285.
[85] Ibid. 123.
[86] Ibid. 126, 242, 253.
[87] See chapters 3 and 5 below.
[88] McNally, 'Political economy to the fore', 435.
[89] Burke (ed. O'Brien), *Reflections*, 173.
[90] Daniel Isaac Eaton's *Politics for the people*, 1794, contained a series of tracts entitled 'Hog's wash or a salmagundy for swine' (BLPC, shelfmark T.139).

of *Reflections*. Burke's 'medievalism', this predilection for a romantic, medieval past, enhanced his preoccupation with the ethos of an *ancien régime*.[91] Notably it was in connection with the fate of the French Queen Marie Antoinette at the hands of the French revolutionaries that Burke famously invoked chivalric concepts in sentimental terms:

> I saw her just above the horizon, decorating and cheering the elevated sphere she just began to move in, – glittering like the morning star, full of life, and splendor, and joy. Oh! What a revolution! And what an heart must I have, to contemplate without emotion that elevation and that fall![92]

Moreover, it was the chivalric knights of *ancien régime* France who had failed to defend their queen:

> little did I dream that I should see such disasters fallen upon her in a nation of gallant men, in a nation of men of honour and of cavaliers. I thought ten thousand swords must have leaped from their scabbards to avenge even a look that threatened her with insult. – But the age of chivalry is gone ... and the glory of Europe is extinguished for ever.[93]

Thus Burke depicted the aristocracy in its traditional role as defender of the state. This was not the first time that Burke had used such emotive language to promote the role of the ruling class. In 1790, describing the Glorious Revolution of 1688–9, Burke declared that 'the Prince of Orange, a prince of the blood royal in England, was called in by the flower of the English aristocracy to defend its ancient constitution'.[94] Certainly, the ebullient language Burke invoked to describe the past enhanced its significance to his respondents.

Burke's focus on chivalry also increased the central focus on aristocracy in the debate. Chivalry invoked ideals and codes from the past that were essentially aristocratic.[95] Moreover, in defending his much-criticised oration on Marie Antoinette, Burke claimed that it was natural to feel greater sympathy for the hardships of the great than for those of the lower sort. Here Burke reflected Adam Smith's *Theory of moral sentiments*, in which Smith asserted that a rich man's death is viewed by the populace as far more tragic than a poor man's death, which is hardly noticed.[96] Burke demanded: 'are not high

---

[91] Roger Smith has suggested that the *Reflections* owes something to the gothic revival, although Burke was not a 'fully fledged Romantic': *Gothic bequest*, 114. For Burke and the Gothic see also Boulton, *Language of politics*, 97–133.
[92] Burke (ed. O'Brien), *Reflections*, 169–70.
[93] Ibid.
[94] Idem, *Substance of the speech*, 316–17.
[95] The word 'chivalry' is defined in the *Oxford dictionary* as 'the medieval knightly system with its religious, moral and social code'. 'Chivalrous' is an adjective to describe 'a man or his behaviour', 'courteous and gallant, especially towards women': *OED, s.v.* chivalry.
[96] Adam Smith, *The theory of moral sentiments*, 5th edn 1781, 84–5.

Rank, great Splendour of descent, great personal Elegance and outward accomplishments ingredients of moment in forming the interest we take in the Misfortunes of Men?'[97] Chivalry, then, was an aristocratic ideal, a higher feeling, applicable to those of higher feeling, the aristocracy.

Moreover for Burke chivalry was not a 'mere emotive term, but the name of a complex historical phenomenon'. It marked a 'civilising moment' amongst the nobility when they had acquired a code of manners with which to justify their elevated position in Europe.[98] As Burke said:

> Is it absurd in me, to think that the Chivalrous Spirit which dictated veneration for Women of condition and of Beauty, without any consideration whatsoever of enjoying them, was the great Source of those manners which have been the Pride and ornament of Europe for so many ages?[99]

He confirmed that it was chivalry 'which has given its character to modern Europe' and manners were based upon aristocratic and Anglican codes and ideals. 'Our manners, our civilization' have in Europe 'depended for ages upon two principles; and were indeed the result of both combined; I mean the spirit of a gentleman, and the spirit of religion'. Indeed 'the nobility and the clergy, the one by profession, the other by patronage', have 'kept learning in existence'.[100] For learning was part of England's inheritance and the main reason for England's improvements in science, the arts and literature was 'our not despising the patrimony of knowledge which was left us by our forefathers'.[101] Burke claimed that in England 'Even commerce, and trade, and manufacture, the gods of our oeconomical politicians . . . certainly grew under the same shade in which learning flourished.'[102] Thus Burke suggested that England's cultural and commercial supremacy were due to chivalric concepts, retained in English society. And manners were the source of commerce and civilisation, rather than the converse as Whig social theory generally dictated.

Burke further commented that 'in England we are said to learn manners at second-hand from your side of the water . . . If so we are still in the old cut; and have not so far conformed to the new Parisian mode of good breeding'.[103] The French now relied on a 'barbarous philosophy', which was 'destitute of all taste and elegance'.[104] Indeed the French Revolution had brought with it 'a considerable revolution of the ideas of politeness', and had resulted in 'a ferocious dissoluteness in manners'.[105] He warned that in France all the

---

97 Burke, *Letter to Philip Francis*, 73.
98 Idem (ed. Pocock), *Reflections*, pp. **xxxii–i**. See also Smith, *Gothic bequest*, 120.
99 Burke, *Letter to Philip Francis*, 90–1.
100 Idem (ed. O'Brien), *Reflections*, 173.
101 Ibid. 199.
102 Ibid. 173, 199, 174.
103 Ibid. 163.
104 Ibid. 171.
105 Ibid. 125.

elements of civilised society 'threaten to disappear together' and 'if commerce and the arts should be lost' then the nation will deteriorate into 'gross, stupid, ferocious . . . poor and sordid barbarians, destitute of religion, honour or manly pride'.[106] The French would revert to uncivilised barbarism once again. It is significant that the revolution was retrogressive rather than progressive for Burke. As he said, 'People will not look forward to posterity, who never look backward to their ancestors.'[107] Progress, then, was possible through retention of what Burke represented as *ancien régime* societies but not in a new republic. This identification of revolutionary France as barbaric and uncivilised was one adopted by loyalists.

Early responses to Burke

The early responses to Burke reveal how his representations of aristocracy in *Reflections* were first received. Only those published before Paine's *Rights of man*, or in the same year, are included here.[108] Historians have commonly noted that many English onlookers initially believed that the French would adopt a constitution along the lines of the English version. Consequently the tone of the early debate in England remained, as Claeys put it, 'parliamentary and genteel'.[109] Certainly, the pamphlets reveal that the majority of early 'radical' responses to Burke were by no means as radical as the *Rights of man*. Nevertheless a number of the issues raised in the early pamphlets clearly influenced the course of the subsequent debate.

Mary Wollstonecraft's *Vindication of the rights of men* (1790) was the first response to Burke to appear and was published less than a month after *Reflections*.[110] The *Vindication* has not received much attention from historians, partly because Wollstonecraft is generally viewed within the canon of women's literature, but also because her first pamphlet received little contemporary attention. Claeys has identified Wollstonecraft as 'much more a moderate than a Painite'.[111] Yet the *Vindication* was, at least in tone, the

---

[106] Ibid. 174.
[107] Ibid. 119.
[108] The radical writings of Paine and his followers, 1791–2, are analysed in chapter 2 below.
[109] Claeys, *Political writing*, i, pp. xviii, xix. Jenny Graham has, however, disputed this claim, arguing that the French Revolution was radical from the start and that the 'debate which took place in both England and America on the revolution in France acknowledged as its starting point that France had effectively rejected the constitutional forms of England'. Moreover, she identified Joseph Towers, Joseph Priestley, Capel Lofft and Catherine Macaulay as all having 'the republican spirit', whatever that means. Graham did concede, however, in accordance with Claeys, that 'above all' it was the 'writings of Paine which transformed the English political scene': *The nation, the law and the king: reform politics in England, 1789–99*, Washington, DC 2000, 69–71, 73–4.
[110] Bromwich, 'Wollstonecraft as a critic', 618.
[111] Claeys, 'French Revolution', 79.

tract most premonitory of *Rights of man*. Indeed Wollstonecraft stated right at the beginning 'I contend for the *rights of men*'.[112] As a result this tract did contribute some new ideas to the debate that suggested the arrival of a new current of thought in radical circles.

Unlike other early respondents to Burke, Wollstonecraft rejected the very foundations of Burke's argument; his representation of English society as rooted in the past and protected by its admirable constitution. Wollstonecraft disputed the existence of an English constitution with its roots in Magna Carta. It was not, she said, in 'the dark days of ignorance, when the minds of men were shackled by the grossest prejudices and most immoral superstition' that the source of liberties could be found.[113] The rise of the aristocracy, 'so many petty tyrants', in past society reflected only a brutal domination of the weak by the strong.[114] Correspondingly the English *ancien régime* of the present retained too much from the past and was dominated by laws and customs that benefited the rich at the expense of the poor. She rebuked Burke: 'your respect for rank', for 'hereditary nobility', 'has swallowed up the common feelings of humanity . . . you have so little respect for the silent majority of misery'.[115] Wollstonecraft focused much of this work on the economic and social chasms between 'rich and the poor'. In this respect her work was most premonitory of John Thelwall's writings of the mid-1790s.[116] Furthermore Wollstonecraft accused Burke of being 'the champion of property' rather than a 'friend of liberty'.[117] The ancient systems of prescription, hereditary property and hereditary titles so revered by Burke, were the tools of the aristocracy used only to halt the natural progress of mankind.[118] Thus Wollstonecraft, with her refusal to view government from the past, was the first to move the debate into the present and future and to raise the possibility of a new government and society being formulated outside the English constitutional model.

Unlike other early respondents Wollstonecraft was not much concerned with the French aristocracy and she paused in her condemnation of *ancien régimes* in general only to ridicule Burke's oration on Marie Antoinette. She thus moved the focus of the debate away from France and towards England, and its aristocracy. Her *Vindication* includes much comment on the luxury and greed of the rich, perhaps more familiar from the eighteenth-century luxury debate. It was, in that respect, largely a criticism of behaviour. For Wollstonecraft only greed and ambition motivated the rich and now, steeped

---

112 Mary Wollstonecraft, *A vindication of the rights of men*, 1790, in Janet Todd (ed.), *Mary Wollstonecraft: political writings*, Oxford 1994, 5.
113 Ibid. 10–11.
114 Ibid. 10.
115 Ibid. 8, 16.
116 For Thelwall's works see chapter 4 below.
117 Wollstonecraft, *Vindication of the rights of men*, 11–12.
118 Ibid. 51–2.

in luxury, they were pathetic unmanly creatures.[119] Even their education had served only to warp rather than to cultivate their minds. She retorted that 'Luxury and effeminacy' had introduced 'so much idiotism into the noble families which form one of the pillars of our state'.[120]

Wollstonecraft also challenged Burke's defence of aristocratic manners and inverted his interpretation of progress. The 'civilization which has taken place in Europe has been very partial', because 'hereditary property' and 'hereditary honour' have 'stopped its progress'. Moreover, civilisation 'refines the manners at the expense of morals'. Primogeniture and the game laws, the bastions of aristocratic privilege in England, also came under attack.[121] It was constantly Wollstonecraft's point that the systems Burke promoted actually repressed talent, merit and virtue and prevented merit from succeeding. In contrast, in terms generally associated with Paine, she said:

> Men of some abilities play on the follies of the rich, and mounting to fortune as they degrade themselves, they stand in the way of men of superior talents, who cannot advance in such crooked paths, or wade through the filth which *parasites* never boggle at. Pursuing their way straight forward, their spirit is either bent or broken by the rich man's contumelies, or the difficulties they have to encounter.[122]

For Wollstonecraft the ills of society spread from the top down and started with the distribution of property in accordance with primogeniture and the rules of inheritance, Burke's 'entailed interests'. Wollstonecraft advocated the abolition of such a system and promoted a radical agrarian reform which would give the poor man greater access to the land. She proposed that 'large estates be divided into small farms'.[123] Wollstonecraft was iconoclastic in her approach to the English establishment. She had no respect for 'kings, parliaments, magistrates, priests and nobility'. The alliance between Church and State was formed by 'faction and private interest' rather than by piety and parliament had become stultified by corruption. What Wollstonecraft promoted above all was a meritocracy but she lamented that the social order of *ancien régime* England prevented the operation of such a system.[124]

The majority of the early respondents to Burke did not, however, take up Wollstonecraft's radical ideas. Whilst Burke was accused of having a 'predilection for aristocracy' by James Mackintosh,[125] for the most part the respondents did not directly condemn the English aristocracy and constitution. They took Burke's lead and focused on the French aristocracy and a rather

---

[119] Ibid. 14–15.
[120] Ibid. 23.
[121] Ibid. 8, 21, 37.
[122] Ibid. 23.
[123] Ibid. 23–4, 58–9.
[124] Ibid. 20, 33, 38.
[125] Mackintosh, *Vindiciae gallicae*, 271–2.

vague European *ancien régime*. Whilst their intention was to defend the French Revolution it was predominantly also, in common with Burke, to promote the English constitution. As one respondent noted, in terms similar to Burke's own, 'An aristocracy is generally considered by politicians as a vicious form of government; yet aristocracy properly blended and tempered with limited monarchy and democracy are the constituent parts of our form of Government.'[126] At this early stage in the French Revolution the majority of respondents to Burke expressed the expectation that the French would follow the example of England at the Glorious Revolution and would adopt a constitution similar to the English version.[127]

The respondents made much of Burke's 'medievalism' and *Reflections* was frequently identified as 'gothic'. Such references indicated the impact of the late eighteenth-century gothic revival.[128] Although, as Smith suggested, Burke may not have subscribed to the gothic revival's idealisation of medieval chivalry itself, the respondents attacked Burke for 'what they thought' he had said, for his representations.[129] They focused on Burke's apparent attachment to a medieval and chivalric past. Wollstonecraft scoffed that Burke's suggestion that 'we should reverence the rust of antiquity' and revere an ancient aristocracy, were 'gothic notions of beauty'.[130] Burke's sentiments were 'neither more nor less than the exploded doctrine of the old school revived in a new dress', the 'offspring of superstition confounding all human reason'.[131] She confirmed that 'I have never made my humanity give place to gothic gallantry'.[132] Thomas Christie accused Burke of cherishing 'the principles of gothic feudality', and condemned him:

> As the apologist of ancient prejudice, he is without a rival . . . With majestic grace, worthy of a nobler office, he conducts us to the Temple of Superstition, and the magic of his language soothes our hearts into holy reverence and sacred awe. But when we enter the consecrated portal, and behold a miserable deformed gothic idol in the corner of the temple . . . we turn with disgust from the false splendor of the mansion of Idolatry, and hasten with chearful steps to the humble abode of unadorned Truth.[133]

---

126 Anon., *Strictures on the letter of the Rt. Hon. Mr Burke, on the revolution in France*, 1791, in Claeys, *Political writings*, ii. 186.
127 See Charles Stanhope, *A letter from the earl Stanhope to the Rt. Hon. Edmund Burke: containing a short answer to his late speech on the French Revolution*, 3rd edn 1790, in Claeys, *Political writings*, i. 8.
128 Smith, *Gothic bequest*, 11, 80.
129 Ibid. 120, 125.
130 Wollstonecraft, *Vindication of the rights of men*, 8.
131 George Rous, *Thoughts on government: occasioned by Mr Burke's Reflections, &c., in a letter to a friend to which is added a postscript, in reply to Mr Burke's Reflections*, 4th edn 1791, in Claeys, *Political writings*, ii. 3.
132 Wollstonecraft, *Vindication of the rights of men*, 37.
133 Thomas Christie, *Letters on the revolution of France and on the new constitution established by the National Assembly: occasioned by the publications of the Rt. Hon. Edmund Burke, M.P. and Alexander de Calonne, late minister of state*, 1791, in Claeys, *Political writings*, i. 157–8.

There was also much outrage at Burke's defence of Marie Antoinette. Joseph Priestley said it was as 'if you were her *knight*, pledged to defend her honour... But, is the liberty and happiness of a whole nation to be sacrificed to female beauty and complaisance?'.[134] Similarly, Catherine Macaulay dismissed the miseries of one queen when the revolution had 'secured the *present and future happiness of twenty-four millions of people, with their posterity,* emancipated by their *manly* exertions, from all that is *degrading and afflicting* to the sensible mind'.[135] George Rous ridiculed Burke's extravagant gesture in defence of 'a Queen of France, who is not famed for *all* the virtues which, in times of chivalry, inflamed the imagination of a true knight'. Burke's eulogy was no more than a 'fable'.[136] And Mackintosh condemned Burke's partial 'sensibility' which 'agonizes at the slenderest pang that assails the heart of sottishness or prostitution, if they are placed by fortune on a throne'.[137]

The respondents also attacked Burke's recourse to chivalry. To Benjamin Bousfield, 'chivalry' was no more than a 'wandering spirit'.[138] A number argued that chivalry was now an out-dated concept. Mackintosh confirmed: 'In Government, commerce has overthrown that feudal and chivalrous system under whose shade it first grew.'[139] Wollstonecraft claimed that 'the spirit of romance and chivalry is in the wane; and reason will gain by its extinction'.[140] And to Towers, Burke's ideas of religion seemed closer to the 'Church of Rome' than to Protestantism. He remarked:

> commerce and diffused knowledge have, in fact, so completely assumed the ascendant in polished nations, that it will be difficult to discover any relics of *Gothic manners*, but in a fantastic exterior, which has survived the generous illusions that made these manners splendid and seductive. Their *direct* influence has long ceased in Europe.[141]

Thus some at least of these respondents identified chivalric concepts and the manners they engendered as out-dated and nothing more than a form of show and display. Rous argued that 'These are modern times' when the 'true principles of government are investigated in the abstract, and consequently

---

[134] Joseph Priestley, *Letters to the Rt. Hon. Edmund Burke: occasioned by his Reflections on the revolution in France &c.*, 1791, in Claeys, *Political writings*, ii. 328.

[135] [Catherine Macaulay], *Observations on the reflection of the Rt. Hon. Edmund Burke, on the revolution in France: in a letter to the Rt. Hon. the earl of Stanhope*, 1790, in Claeys, *Political writings*, i. 126.

[136] Rous, *Thoughts on government*, 4.

[137] Mackintosh, *Vindiciae gallicae*, 272.

[138] Benjamin Bousfield, *Observations on the Rt. Hon. Edmund Burke's pamphlet on the subject of the French Revolution*, 1791, in Claeys, *Political writings*, ii. 102.

[139] Mackintosh, *Vindiciae gallicae*, 330.

[140] Wollstonecraft, *Vindication of the rights of men*, 28.

[141] Joseph Towers, *Thoughts on the commencement of a new parliament: with an appendix containing remarks on the letter of the Rt. Hon. Edmund Burke on the revolution in France*, 1790, in Claeys, *Political writings*, i. 114–19.

without passion'.[142] Paradoxically, in this, the respondents were premonitory of later arguments of loyalists, who also rejected Burke's medievalism.

Nevertheless the early respondents reserved their greatest and most vitriolic condemnation for the French nobility. Much of this criticism was of behaviour, similar to criticisms of the English Whig aristocracy earlier in the eighteenth century. But here, significantly, criticism was applied to the French aristocracy as a whole, as an order of *noblesse*. One anonymous respondent claimed that the French aristocracy lived in 'the lap of indolence' and was taken by surprise by the revolution.[143] The French *noblesse* lived in 'a splendour above their means, and yet had substituted the most incoherent haughtiness to that affability which is one of the characteristics of a true nobleness of soul'.[144] Indeed the French aristocracy who had fled to England were

> defaulters escaped from punishment, they consist of statesmen who were unfaithful to their trust – pensioners who plundered the people – titled prostitutes, and monsters of every description – all that disgraced France, and rendered it a country odious to the wise and virtuous of every nation in Europe.[145]

Du Fresnoy traced the source of the French aristocracy's dissipation and profligacy to the French court, which 'under the reign of Lewis the fourteenth became the seat of luxury, pomp and grandeur', where his heirs were 'brought up in an almost Asiatic effeminacy'. The throne was surrounded by 'nobles whose stately merit was too often confined to the length of an ostentatious list of ancestors and whose only remains of the illustrious stock from whom they sprung was a name they shamelessly disgraced'. Consequently most French nobles were motivated by ambition and self-interest and were 'void of the manly virtues which so eminently distinguished their progenitors'.[146]

Much was made of the privileges of the French aristocracy, which English opinion had traditionally used to differentiate between the English and French aristocracies. Sir Brooke Boothby declared that it was to be expected that the French aristocracy would 'employ every expedient either of stratagem or force to defend those darling privileges which they had been accustomed to believe interwoven with nature itself; their hereditary birth-right'.[147] And for Mackintosh it was 'those immense and magnificent

---

142 Rous, *Thoughts on government*, 5.
143 Anon., *Short observations on the Rt. Hon. Edmund Burke's Reflections*, 1790, in Claeys, *Political writings*, i. 67.
144 [du Fresnoy], *An address to the National Assembly of France: containing strictures on Mr Burke's Reflections on the revolution in France*, 1791, in Claeys, *Political writings*, ii. 46.
145 Bousfield, *Observations on the Rt. Hon. Edmund Burke's pamphlet*, 110.
146 [du Fresnoy], *Address to the National Assembly*, 31–2.
147 [Sir Brooke Boothby], *A letter to the Rt. Hon. Edmund Burke*, 2nd edn 1791, in Claeys, *Political writings*, ii. 70.

privileges, which divided France into distinct nations'.¹⁴⁸ Rous stated that the despotic French monarch was supported by

> a numerous body of Nobility, the political Janisaries of the Crown, who prescriptively held all military command – who were favoured as a distinct race with peculiar immunities by law, and yet greater privileges by the habitual superiority they assumed; whose pride was pampered and whose indolence was fed with the spoils of the People; who, besides engrossing all the military and most of the civil appointments under the Crown, divided annually one million and a half sterling of the public money under the denomination of Pensions.¹⁴⁹

Du Fresnoy went so far as to claim that the French aristocracy controlled government. They had become an aristocratic '*junto*', 'an unbounded power' which oppressed the king and the people. The 'whole aristocracy' tried to dispel the 'extravagant spirit of reform' and to squash the revolution.¹⁵⁰ And Depont agreed that there had existed in *ancien régime* France, from time to time, 'an aristocracy of despots'.¹⁵¹ Indeed, ' "the feudal and chivalrous spirit of fealty", so long the prevailing passion of Europe, was still nourished in their bosoms by the military sentiments from which it first arose'. Consequently, by 1789, 'the majority of them had still no profession but war, no hope but in Royal favour'.¹⁵² The French aristocracy, then, still adhered to an ancient chivalric role as defenders of the king.

It was, respondents claimed, the *ancien régime* government of monarchy and aristocracy that was at the root of the French Revolution. As Charles Stanhope said, the poverty suffered by the majority of the French was 'produced by their former detestable and arbitrary Government, and by their mad wars'. Governed 'one hour by a Mistress, and the next by an artful Sycophant at Court, their Administration could be but capricious', for 'it was guided by Intrigue'.¹⁵³ Indeed an anonymous pamphleteer claimed that 'while the court rioted in luxury, government let loose the reigns of cruelty'.¹⁵⁴ It was the oppression of the poor and corrupt government that rendered the French Revolution necessary. The aristocracy was motivated only by self-interest, the 'gratification of their own pride and ambition'.¹⁵⁵ It is significant that here criticism was focused predominantly on the French aristocracy and it was not until the *Rights of man* that the full force of such criticism was aimed

---

148 Mackintosh, *Vindiciae gallicae*, 292.
149 Rous, *Thoughts on government*, 5.
150 [du Fresnoy], *Address to the National Assembly*, 34–6, 49.
151 M. Depont, *Answer to the reflections of the Rt. Hon. Edmund Burke*, 1791, in Claeys, *Political writings*, ii. 266.
152 Mackintosh, *Vindiciae gallicae*, 292.
153 Stanhope, *Letter from the earl Stanhope*, 4.
154 Anon., *Strictures on the letter*, 198.
155 Towers, *Thoughts on the commencement*, 107.

directly at the English aristocracy. Nevertheless the early respondents clearly identified aristocracy as central to the French Revolution debate.

A number of respondents took the opportunity to condemn hereditary titles.[156] A 'titled Nobility' was 'the most undisputed progeny of feudal barbarism', and it was 'Gothic Europe' that attached titles 'to *ranks*'.[157] But the respondents did not extend this criticism to launch a full-scale attack upon titles of the English aristocracy. Indeed not all approved of the abolition of titles in France.[158] Some differentiated between the significance of titles in the two countries. In England, Rous argued, 'the hereditary nobles are a distinct order with distinctive privileges, necessary to the form of our Government'.[159] Boothby concurred that in France titles represented 'no respectable public character' unlike the English 'judicial or legislative peerage', but served only to 'separate the nation into two foolish and unnatural classes of *gentilhomme* and *roturier*, (a division which our language has not even terms to describe)'.[160]

Thus to some respondents the English aristocracy could be differentiated from their French counterparts because the English lords fulfilled a valuable role in government. Significantly this was an argument made later by loyalists.[161] Du Fresnoy claimed that England was the example of how government should be structured. The English were 'blessed with the best constitutions, and protected by the most equitable laws'.[162] Boothby agreed that the 'fabric of the English constitution exists in unimpaired beauty and strength'.[163] And Mackintosh said of the French nobility:

> Their existence, as a member of the Legislature, is a question distinct from their preservations as a separate Order, or great corporation in the State. A senate of Nobles might have been established, though the Order of the Nobility had been destroyed, and England would then have been exactly copied.[164]

Moreover in general the respondents were far from radical on the question of who should rule. Macaulay, one of the more radical of them, implied a preference for 'truly popular government', but did not specifically advocate it for England.[165] Priestley suggested that, as the result of the American and French

---

156 See, for example, [Macaulay], *Observations on the reflection*, 139, and Priestley, *Letters to the Rt. Hon. Edmund Burke*, 333.
157 Mackintosh, *Vindiciae gallicae*, 294.
158 See Capel Lofft, *Remarks on the letter of the Rt. Hon. Edmund Burke, concerning the revolution in France and on the proceedings in certain societies in London, relative to that event*, 1790, 2nd edn 1791, in Claeys, *Political writing*, ii. 290–301.
159 Rous, *Thoughts on government*, 24.
160 [Boothby], *Letter to the Rt. Hon. Edmund Burke*, 68.
161 See chapter 3 below.
162 [du Fresnoy], *Address to the National Assembly*, 38.
163 [Boothby], *Letter to the Rt. Hon. Edmund Burke*, 67.
164 Mackintosh, *Vindiciae gallicae*, 293.
165 [Macaulay], *Observations on the reflection*, 149.

revolutions, 'we may now expect to see' government 'calculated for the general good'. In this government there might be kings but they would not be 'sovereigns', the aristocracy would be replaced with paid '*magistrates*' who would be '*servants of the people*', and there would be no episcopacy.[166] But this was clearly something of a theoretical ideal for him. Priestley's response to Burke was primarily concerned with the alliance between Church and State and contained no concrete proposals for revolutionary change or the introduction of a republic in England.[167] Few other respondents were more specific. Indeed a number suggested that the nobility were natural leaders. Rous claimed that the abolition in France of 'invidious distinctions' was 'the wise means of effectually blending' the aristocracy with 'the great body of the people', because possibly 'when heats have a little subsided', this would prove 'beneficial to the individuals themselves, by enabling them to take that lead in the National Councils which their fortune and talents may claim'.[168] Boothby also suggested that perhaps 'when the storm subsides, landed property and hereditary rank will flow back' into the hands of the noble families. Then 'these patricians will find themselves among the leading representatives of a free people and legislators of a great nation'.[169] Capel Lofft considered financial independence a necessary qualification for the franchise and representation. He agreed with Burke that the qualifications proposed by the National Assembly were too low to ensure such independence.[170]

Furthermore, a number, whilst advocating elevation only on the grounds of virtue and merit as an ideal, accepted the inevitability of a social order based on other criteria. Mackintosh stated that an inequality of property was necessary because '*property* alone' stimulated labour. And those of great property 'necessarily in all countries, administer government, for they alone have skill and leisure for its functions'.[171] John Scott claimed that he would vote in parliament for any plan that would ensure that wiser, or more virtuous, men became representatives. But he went on to confirm that, because of the need for independence, 'I would have no man a member of the House of Commons who did not, *bona fide*, possess ten thousand pounds in money or land.'[172]

---

[166] Priestley, *Letters to the Rt. Hon. Edmund Burke*, 381, 384.
[167] Ibid. 318.
[168] Rous, *Thoughts on government*, 24.
[169] [Boothby], *Letter to the Rt. Hon. Edmund Burke*, 68.
[170] Capel Lofft, *Remarks on the letter*, 301.
[171] Mackintosh, *Vindiciae gallicae*, 191–2.
[172] [John Scott], *A letter to the Rt. Hon. Edmund Burke: in reply to his 'Reflections on the revolution in France', &c. by a member of the Revolution Society*, Dublin 1791, in Claeys, *Political writings*, ii. 163.

Burke's legacy

What was important about Burke's early respondents was not their radicalism, or their condemnation of the English aristocracy. It was their focus upon the French aristocracy and Burke's inherent 'medievalism'. This shaped the direction of the French Revolution debate and has contributed to the interpretation and classification of Burke to this day. Above all Burke opened the door to fresh debate. As Olivia Smith has stated, by 'writing about politics in an unusual manner, Burke made the radical position more capable of being articulated'.[173] Certainly Burke's representations provoked intense responses. In the meantime Burke's concerns were and remained grandly expressed:

> As long as our Sovereign Lord the king, and his faithful subjects, the Lords and Commons of this realm – the triple cord, which no man can break; the solemn, sworn, constitutional frank-pledge of this nation; the firm guarantees of each others being, and each others rights; the joint and several securities, each in it's place and order, for every kind and every quality, of property and of dignity – As long as these endure, ... we are all safe together – the high from the blights of envy and the spoilations of rapacity; the low from the iron hand of oppression and the insolent spurn of contempt. Amen![174]

---

173 Smith, *Politics of language*, 37.
174 Burke, *Letter to a noble lord*, 171–3.

2

Thomas Paine and Painite Radicalism, 1791–1792

> In the superior ranks of life how seldom do we meet with a man of superior abilities, or even common acquirements? The reason appears to me clear, the state they are born in was an unnatural one.[1]

The years 1791–2 saw much activity in France and, as Edmund Burke had predicted, the violence escalated. Monarchy and aristocracy came under increasing attack. In 1791 Louis XVI made his ill-fated attempt to flee to Varennes and Paris witnessed the massacre on the Champ de Mars on 17 July. In April 1792 France declared war on Austria. The storming of the Tuileries in August led to the suspension of the king, the imprisonment of the entire royal family and the declaration of the republic. The bloody September massacres saw a revolutionary crowd murder hundreds of 'aristocrats' and priests in the Paris prisons. On 9 October a decree was issued ordering the death penalty for returned *emigrés*, many of who were aristocrats. The revolution in France was becoming increasingly fanatical.[2]

Meanwhile the debate in England also took a more radical turn with the publication of Thomas Paine's *Rights of man, part 1* in 1791. This work ensured that radicalism remained very firmly outside parliament. Even Charles James Fox, who supported the French Revolution in its initial stages, viewing it as a French version of the Glorious Revolution of 1688, could not support Paine's work which he termed 'a libel upon the constitution'.[3] Fox's alliance with the conservative Portland Whigs was weakening and Whig reform was pushed into the shadows by a new burgeoning extraparliamentary radicalism. Charles Grey's speech on parliamentary reform in April 1792 fell on deaf years and the subsequent motion in May 1793 was heavily defeated.[4] Outside parliament many radicals responded to the *Rights of man* by putting pen to paper, and the pamphlet debate escalated.

---

[1] Mary Wollstonecraft, A *vindication of the rights of woman*, 1792, in Todd, *Wollstonecraft*, 119.
[2] Alan Forrest, *The French Revolution*, Oxford 1999, pp. ix, 43, 49–50, 53–4.
[3] Claeys, *Thomas Paine*, 127. See also O'Gorman, *Whig party*, 32–69.
[4] Turner, *British politics*, 64–6.

Paine and the *Rights of man*

Paine's work is familiar territory for historians and it is well established that his text heralded a new radicalism in English politics and transformed the *Reflections* debate.[5] Within analyses of the *Rights of man*, in both parts 1 and 2, Paine's demand for equality of political rights, his promotion of republican government and his condemnation of hereditary government, aristocracy and economic inequality have also frequently been noted. A number of historians have identified the *Rights of man* as a wholesale attack upon England's power structure and constitution.[6] This is true. As Paine stated, 'when we survey the wretched condition of man under the monarchical and hereditary systems of Government . . . it becomes evident that . . . a general revolution in the principle and constructions of Governments is necessary'.[7] But in fact Paine reserved his most vitriolic condemnation for aristocracy.[8] This book highlights Paine's representations of aristocracy as the starting point of 1790s radicalism. The *Rights of man* constituted the most radical condemnation of aristocracy published within the French Revolution debate. What Paine wanted was to abolish aristocracy altogether and to introduce equality of rank. He strongly centralised aristocracy within the debate.

It was not just that Paine identified the English aristocracy as descending from the invading Normans of the eleventh century, as Christopher Hill in particular has noted.[9] Paine went further and identified the contemporary aristocracy with the French. It was Paine's identification of the English aristocracy as an idle, parasitic elite like the French, then taken up and entrenched by other radicals, that changed representations and, no doubt, perceptions of aristocracy in England. Moreover, at a time when for the majority of the English congratulating themselves on their admirable mixed government, so much preferable to absolutist France, was a well-established habit, Paine redrew the political and cultural map. It was now Revolutionary France that had the admirable constitution whilst England had no constitution at all. Furthermore Paine represented England as an *ancien régime*, divided on a model of aristocracy and people like France before the revolution. That is not to say that Paine actually identified the political structure or the order of nobility in England as the same as that in *ancien régime* France. He recognised in the *Rights of man* that French absolutism had not provided the aristocracy with the legitimate role in government that was allotted to

---

[5] See, for example, Claeys, *Thomas Paine*; Philp, *Paine*; Claeys, 'French Revolution'; Dickinson, *Liberty and property*; Thompson, *Making of the English working class*; and Whatmore, 'Gigantic manliness'.
[6] Wahrman, *Imagining the middle class*, 35; Whatmore, 'Gigantic manliness', 137.
[7] Paine, *Rights of man*, 143.
[8] Whatmore has argued that it was Paine's desire to abolish the rank of aristocracy that distinguished his republicanism from that of his English contemporaries: 'Gigantic manliness', 137–40.
[9] See Hill, 'Norman yoke', 50–122.

England's aristocracy within the mixed constitution. But he made crucial links and connections between the two countries and in particular between their aristocracies.

Paine's aristocracy

During the revolution the term 'aristocrat' became a common term of abuse in France, applied disparagingly to the French *noblesse* and increasingly to all and any who were perceived to be the enemies of the revolution. Correspondingly Paine adopted the term 'aristocracy' to describe the English nobility. He was the first of the political writers of the 1790s to use the term consistently to describe what the majority had previously termed the 'nobility'. Paine also made the point that 'aristocracy' was a negative term and defined a class, like the French *noblesse*, 'separated from the general stock of society' by unacceptable privileges.[10] In political terms he accused this whole class of English nobility of being an 'aristocracy' in the classical sense of a despotic government. Thus Paine moved away from the familiar contemporary use of 'aristocracy' to describe, generally, an over-bearing Whig party or faction and introduced a new interpretation of the term into the debate. It is well established that the French Revolution politicised social class and it was the *Rights of man* that brought about this change in England.[11]

Paine launched a damning attack against aristocracy, challenging both its political hegemony and competence as a ruling class. His criticisms were expressed in an innovative language, devoid of the deference which was an accepted convention governing political writers of the time.[12] Most important, Paine made much of France in the *Rights of man*, a point few historians have noted.[13] He made a lengthy comparison, much of which focused on aristocracy, between England and France under its new constitution. Paine highlighted the fact that the French had now swept away all aristocratic privileges, many of which still existed in England. Whilst all game laws had been abolished in France, they still flourished in England. Titles, which Paine dismissed as 'the baby-clothes of *Count or Duke*', mere 'gewgaws', had also been abolished.[14] The French had recognised the importance of merit over birth and that

---

[10] Paine, *Rights of man*, 82–3.
[11] Wahrman, *Imagining the middle class*, 35–6; McNally, 'Political economy to the fore', 430.
[12] For a useful study of Paine and language see Smith, *Politics of language*, 35–67.
[13] Whatmore noted that most historians 'have refused to examine Paine's political ideas from a French perspective': 'Gigantic manliness', 137. Graham stated that 'much of the attraction of the first part of Paine's work lay in his claim to speak with authority of events in France': *The nation, the law and the king*, 75.
[14] Paine, *Rights of man*, 74–5, 80.

rank and dignity in society must take a new ground. The old one has fallen through. – It must now take the substantial ground of character, instead of the chimerical ground of titles and they have brought their titles to the altar, and made of them a burnt offering to Reason.[15]

Paine took the radical step of recommending the total abolition of titles in England. He warned that when the people of England saw what was occurring in France they too will 'annihilate those badges of ancient oppression'.[16] He declared that it was 'necessary to inquire farther into the nature and character of aristocracy'. He identified: 'That, then, which is called aristocracy in some countries, and nobility in others, arouse out of the governments founded upon conquest. It was originally a military order ... and to keep up a succession of this order ... the law of *primogenitureship* was set up.'

For Paine, as for Wollstonecraft, in England the aristocratic privilege of primogeniture was at the root of aristocratic supremacy. The French, in order to 'exterminate' aristocracy, had 'destroyed the law of PRIMOGENITURESHIP'. This law, which was enacted to maintain aristocratic power, was 'a law against every law of nature' and 'family justice'. Indeed it rendered aristocracy unfit to rule. Moreover Paine contended that primogeniture increased corruption. For it was the necessity of finding roles and positions in public service for the younger 'disinherited' children of the aristocracy that led to the creation of 'unnecessary offices and places in governments and courts', maintained at great public expense.[17] In an attempt to stamp out such corruption the National Assembly had decreed that no member 'shall be an officer of the government, a place-man, or a pensioner'. But in England, whilst parliament was '*supposed* to hold the national purse in *trust* for the nation', in reality 'those who vote the supplies are the same persons who receive the supplies when voted'.[18]

Paine accused the aristocracy in both France and England of being a parasitic elite at the source of corruption. He declared that in 1789 the French *tiers état* began to consider 'aristocracy as a kind of fungus growing out of the corruption of society' and consequently 'disowned any knowledge of artificial Orders and artificial privileges'. The National Assembly also 'saw into the folly, mischief, and injustice of artificial privileges'. Paine argued that the French 'Nation' increasingly despised the aristocracy for its 'visible imbecility and want of intellects ... that while it affected to be more than citizen, was less than man'. The aristocracy 'lost ground from contempt more than hatred; and was rather jeered at as an ass, than dreaded as a lion'. And he confirmed that 'This is the general character of aristocracy, or what are called Nobles or Nobility, or rather No-ability, in all countries.'[19] Indeed Paine challenged the

---

[15] Ibid. 81.
[16] Ibid. 75.
[17] Ibid. 82.
[18] Ibid. 76.
[19] Ibid. 104–6.

very attribution of the term 'nobility', to a class he would only identify by the negative term 'aristocracy'. He scoffed 'Mr Burke talks of nobility; let him show what it is. The greatest characters the world have known, have risen on the democratic floor . . . The artificial Noble shrinks into a dwarf before the NOBLE of Nature.'[20] And, he declared that the courts of Europe, primarily aristocratic institutions, were closer to each other than to their own nations:

> Whether it be the Court of Versailles, or the Court of St James or Carlton House . . . They form a common policy throughout Europe, detached and separate from the interest of Nations; and while they appear to quarrel, they agree to plunder. Nothing can be more terrible to a Court or a Courtier than the Revolution in France.[21]

Thus Paine invoked that long-standing eighteenth-century accusation of corruption and levied it at both the English and French aristocracies as a class.

Although in part 2 of *Rights of man* Paine declared 'certain it is, that . . . monarchy, always appears to me a silly, contemptible thing', it was not the king that in part 1 Paine held primarily responsible for France's decline.[22] Indeed Louis XVI was 'little disposed to the exercise of that species of power' of 'an absolute King', and he was 'known to be the friend of the nation'. But when 'despotism has established itself for ages in a country as in France, it is not in the person of the King only that it resides'. It was 'the hereditary despotism of the established government', and that 'augean stable of parasites and plunderers too abominably filthy to be cleansed, by anything short of a complete and universal revolution' who had necessitated the revolution. In France such government had amounted to not one, but 'a thousand despotisms', in the 'monarchy' (as distinguished from the monarch himself), 'the parliament, and the church' and local fuedal despotisms. And Paine identified these as essentially despotisms of aristocracy. A traditional defence of the English aristocracy, one adopted by Burke, proposed that in England the aristocracy had a legitimate role in government, whilst in *ancien régime* France it did not. Paine inverted this defence. The French aristocracy, he argued, 'had one feature less in its countenance' than in England 'It did not compose a body of hereditary legislators'. The House of Lords, on the other hand, was 'beyond the control of the Nation', it was 'an hereditary aristocracy, assuming and asserting indefeasible, irrevocable rights and authority, wholly independent of the Nation'.[23] Indeed it was more powerful than the French aristocracy of the *ancien régime*, for it was, as M. de Lafayette declared, '*a corporation of aristocracy*'.[24]

[20] Ibid. 83–4.
[21] Ibid. 138–9.
[22] Ibid. 182.
[23] Ibid. 47–8, 130.
[24] Ibid. 83.

The French had now resolved against having such a body as the 'English House of Peers' in their new constitution. This was because, Paine explained, the 'idea of hereditary legislation is as inconsistent as that of hereditary judges, or hereditary juries; and as absurd as an hereditary mathematician, or an hereditary wise man'. To have an aristocracy was to continue 'the uncivilized principle of governments found in conquest'.[25] In part 2 of *Rights of man* Paine challenged the very existence of the House of Lords and questioned the English system, which ensured that a third of the legislature was placed in the hands of one class of men, namely the 'landed interest'. Paine deplored a system that imposed a property qualification on political participation. 'It is difficult to discover what is meant by the *landed interest*', he stated, 'if it does not mean a combination of aristocratical land-holders, opposing their own pecuniary interest to that of the farmer, and every branch of trade, commerce, and manufacture.'[26] Paine asserted that 'All hereditary government is in its nature tyranny.'[27] Government should be founded '*on the indefeasible hereditary Rights of man*'.[28] Universal male suffrage was one such right.

What was most damaging here was Paine's condemnation of the English aristocracy in terms previously reserved for its French counterpart. It has been noted that Paine was influenced by French authors on rank as well as republicanism.[29] Yet the fact that Paine identified the English aristocracy with the French has provoked little comment from historians. Paine accused the aristocracy of making no valuable contribution to society. He asked

> Why then does Mr Burke talk of his house of peers, as the pillar of the landed interest? Were that pillar to sink into the earth, the same landed property would continue, and the same ploughing, sowing, and reaping would go on. The aristocracy are not the farmers who work the land, and raise the produce but are the mere consumers of the rent; and when compared with the active world are the drones, a seraglio of males, who neither collect the honey nor form the hive, but exist only for lazy enjoyment.[30]

The English aristocracy, then, was an idle, parasitic elite like the French before the revolution. The aristocracy was nothing more than 'a band of parasites living in luxurious indolence out of the public taxes'. 'In short', Paine declared, 'the evils of the aristocratical system are so great and numerous so inconsistent with everything that is just, wise, natural and beneficent', that many 'will wish to see such a system abolished'.[31] Paine wanted equality of

---

25 Ibid.
26 Ibid. 226.
27 Ibid. 172.
28 Ibid. 161-2.
29 Smith, *Politics of language*, 39-40; Whatmore, 'Gigantic manliness', 136.
30 Paine, *Rights of man*, 227.
31 Ibid. 203, 257.

rank, the 'peer' to be 'exalted into MAN'.³² It was necessary, therefore, to 'exterminate the monster Aristocracy, root and branch'.³³

England an *ancien régime*

For Paine the identification of England as an *ancien régime* on a par with France was not, however, a favourable development. As Christopher Hill has illustrated, Paine invoked the 'Norman yoke' theory and claimed that England's government had been imposed by the Norman Conquest.³⁴ The 'conqueror' with a 'banditti of ruffians' had 'over-run the country' and tyrannical Norman rule, French rule, was imposed in England.³⁵ Analysis of the *Rights of man* reveals that Paine represented contemporary English society as polarised into a dual paradigm of 'aristocracy and people' like *ancien régime* France.³⁶ Paine claimed that 'Old governments in Europe' needed such a polarised society to survive. It was necessary to maintain 'vast classes of mankind' known as 'the vulgar, or the ignorant mob', for 'It is by distortedly exalting some men, that others are distortedly debased, till the whole is out of nature. A vast mass of mankind are degradedly thrown into the background of the human picture, to bring forward with greater glare, the puppet-show of state and aristocracy.'³⁷ Indeed such old governments had created an 'artificial chasm', a series of barriers to man in the form of manners, language and precepts such as 'awe of kings', 'respect to nobility' and '*chivalry*'.³⁸ To Paine, as a result of the French Revolution, 'the Quixote age of chivalry nonsense is gone' and he redefined heroism as an act of the people. The Bastille was attacked 'with an enthusiasm of heroism, such only as the highest animation of liberty could inspire'. Moreover, because the members of the French National Assembly had been democratically elected from amongst the people, they could act freely rather than as dictated by an aristocratic code. They had 'sprung not from the filth of rotten boroughs, nor are they the vassal representatives of aristocratical ones' and hence they felt 'the proper dignity of their character'. Their 'parliamentary language' was always 'free, bold, and manly'.³⁹ The members of the National Assembly were in the 'happy situation' that 'their moral duty and their political interests [are] united. They have not to hold out a language which they do not themselves believe . . . Their station requires no artifice to support it, and can only be

---

³² Ibid. 80.
³³ Ibid. 82.
³⁴ Hill, 'Norman yoke', 100–3.
³⁵ Paine, *Rights of man*, 168.
³⁶ On this point see Wahrman, *Imagining the middle class*, 35–6.
³⁷ Paine, *Rights of man*, 59.
³⁸ Ibid. 67.
³⁹ Ibid. 50–1, 90.

maintained by enlightening mankind. It is not their interest to cherish ignorance, but to dispel it'.[40]

Conversely Paine claimed that the English House of Commons was dominated by 'the vassalage class of manners', which marked 'the prostrate distance that exists . . . between the conqueror and the conquered'. The Glorious Revolution had not destroyed 'this vassalage idea' as testified by the language of submission used in the declaration of parliament to William and Mary. Paine asserted that 'Submission is wholly a vassalage term, repugnant to the dignity of freedom, and an echo of the language used at the conquest.'[41] This confirms the point made by Olivia Smith, that Paine believed that 'the language of Parliament . . . was corrupted by its origins, that English political language was a remnant of the Norman Conquest'. Smith identified this as a 'linguistic version of the Norman yoke myth'.[42] For Paine the language of *ancien régime* England was the language of aristocracy.

Correspondingly, rather than the French adopting the English constitution, as the majority of Englishmen had advocated, Paine suggested that the reverse should and would happen. Whilst even most reformers and respondents to Burke still viewed the English constitution and mixed government as the source of England's modernity, Paine dismissed both. 'A mixed Government is an imperfect everything, cementing and soldering the discordance parts together by corruption' and England had no constitution.[43] This was not a new point, the radical David Williams had been saying, for nearly twenty years, that England had no constitution.[44] But it was the clarity and timing of Paine's statement, against the back-drop of a turbulent revolution across the Channel, which made it so significant. Paine plainly stated that

> the English government is one of those which arose out of a conquest, and not out of society, and, consequently it arose over the people; and though it has been much modified . . . since the time of William the Conqueror, the country has never yet regenerated itself, and is therefore without a constitution.[45]

Here Paine swept away not only the bedrock of English government but also the justification for the very existence of aristocracy. At a time when the revolution had rendered the French aristocracy redundant, the erstwhile accepted role of the English aristocracy as an essential and legitimate sector of government was now openly challenged. Aristocracy was then released by Paine from the confines of the constitution where, politically, the English had always placed it.

---

40 Ibid. 92.
41 Ibid. 91.
42 Smith, *Politics of language*, 51.
43 Paine, *Rights of man*, 141.
44 J. A. W. Gunn, *Beyond liberty and property: the process of self-recognition in eighteenth-century political thought*, Montreal 1983, 206.
45 Paine, *Rights of man*, 72.

Thus *ancien régime* England was not for Paine the Pockockian Whig 'modern and progressive' England in which there was a 'natural harmony between landed and commercial wealth'.[46] Indeed Paine argued that in England 'the improvements in agriculture, useful arts, manufactures, and commerce, have been in opposition to the genius of its government'. It was from 'the enterprise and industry of the individuals, and their numerous associations... that these improvements have proceeded'.[47] Nor was it members of the English aristocracy who were the enterprising individuals promoting commerce. For Paine aristocrats were only the idle 'drones' in the hive of society. Even their landed estates were 'a waste of national property', for 'a considerable part of the land of the country is rendered unproductive by the great extent of parks and chases'.[48] Indeed Paine wondered how in England's 'continual system of war and extortion', 'this miserable scene of governments', there could have been 'the progress which the peaceful arts of agriculture, manufacture and commerce had made'.[49] It was in America that 'the generality of the people' live in 'a style of plenty unknown in monarchical countries'. And in America, 'the increase of commerce is greater in proportion than in England'.[50] Paine's message was clear: *ancien régime* governments were out of date in this 'age of revolutions'.

In common with Wollstonecraft, Paine moved the debate into the present and the future. But unlike the *Vindication*, Paine's *Rights of man* had an immediate and dramatic impact. Massive sales are frequently quoted by historians and apparently astounded contemporaries. Contemporary printers and distributors commonly boasted sales of 10–12,000 copies per week during 1791–2.[51] One reason for Paine's popularity was that, unlike Wollstonecraft's somewhat hurried and emotional writing, the *Rights of man* was clear and the message was forceful. Ordinary people could understand Paine's written language. Consequently the *Rights of man* was adopted and distributed free or at a cheap rate by the radical popular societies.[52]

Painite radicalism, 1791–2

It is clear that Paine had a great influence on the radicalism that followed closely on his heels. Nevertheless not all radicals were republicans or as radical as Paine.[53] In fact the radical movement incorporated a broad spec-

---

[46] Burke (ed. Pocock), *Reflections*, pp. xix–xx; see also p. 41 above.
[47] Paine, *Rights of man*, 197n.
[48] Ibid. 256.
[49] Ibid. 169–70.
[50] Ibid. 125, 214.
[51] Claeys, *Thomas Paine*, 111–12.
[52] Ibid. 114–17
[53] Idem, *Political writings*, i, p. xxxiv.

trum of views as to what England needed; and a great number of radicals still advocated reform within the English constitution.[54] Most important, however, many of those pamphleteers who did not declare themselves Painite republicans or commit to any specific radical reform, still expressed clear condemnation of aristocracy. In fact the majority of radical texts mentioned aristocracy and many focused upon it.[55] Burke and then Paine had placed the aristocracy in the forefront of the debate and the radicals kept it there.[56]

It must not be forgotten that the term 'aristocracy', as used by Paine, carried a new meaning in England. Correspondingly, during 1791–2, radicals adopted the term with all its French connotations, invoked by him, and applied it liberally to the governing elite as a class of aristocracy.[57] These trends were focused and politicised by Paine and taken up by succeeding radicals. In so doing radicals, perhaps in some cases inadvertently, defined England on the bipolar 'aristocracy and people' model of *ancien régime* France. Moreover in part 2 of the *Rights of man*, Paine fused his political critique with an economic critique of the social order.[58] Consequently for radicals the political divisions of 'aristocracy and people' were becoming closely equated with a social division of 'rich and poor'.[59] This clearly broadened the scope for radical condemnation of aristocracy but also broadened the delineation of 'aristocracy'. From 1792 onwards accusations of economic, as well as political, inequality were levied by radicals against a class of aristocracy, both political and social.

Radical criticisms of aristocracy

Aristocracy was loudly and directly criticised in radical pamphlets in a language devoid of the customary deference. As the radical pamphleteer John Butler confirmed reformers were now the 'foe to aristocracy' rather than to the monarchy.[60] It was 'the exertions of an Aristocracy', which had retarded

---

54 Dickinson, *Liberty and property*, 259–69; Goodwin, *Friends of liberty*, 171–207; Philp, 'Fragmented ideology', 50–77.
55 For radical pamphlets which were not concerned with aristocracy see, for example, William Cuninghame, *The rights of kings*, 2nd edn 1791, in Claeys, *Political writings*, iii; anon., *The confederacy of kings against the freedom of the world*, 1792, in Claeys, *Political writings*, iii.
56 E. P. Thompson went so far as to assert that the 'great landed aristocracy' was and remained the main target of radicalism until the 1880s: *Making of the English working class*, 104–5.
57 Wahrman has stated that for radicals 'aristocracy' came to define 'any smaller and more exclusive group that prevented the people from realizing' their rights: *Imagining the middle class*, 76.
58 McNally, 'Political economy to the fore', 430.
59 Wahrman, *Imagining the middle class*, 36.
60 John Butler, *Brief reflections upon the liberty of the British subject*, Canterbury, c. 1792, in Claeys, *Political writings*, iii. 351.

the progress of 'democratic principles' and perpetuated 'Despotism'.[61] Joel Barlow went further and stated that all the 'tyrannies of the world' are 'aristocratical tyrannies'.[62] The *abbé* Sieyès's *Essay on privileges*, translated into English in 1792, was promoted as an important radical text because its influence in France had contributed in particular to 'the abolition of Titles and Nobility'.[63] An anonymous pamphleteer confirmed that to 'banish Kings and Courts', as the French had done, was 'to extirpate the most destroying Pestilence that ever desolated the Universe'. In France, he continued, 'the vagrant Train' of the 'routed court' consisted of 'Priests, Pimps, Parasites, Strumpets, Princes'. Courts would always turn 'all the rich men into a 'pampered' and 'profligate Aristocracy'.[64] In England too, 'Servile courtiers and pensioners . . . form a numerous body . . . an Aristocracy'.[65] Indeed, John Oswald declared, 'A Peer is a sort of political monster, who is born a law-giver, sucks from his nurse's breast the wisdom of legislation, and comes in Parliament to represent himself.'[66] Ultimately, 'the House of Peers' was responsible for 'Every oppression we labour under'.[67] Such vitriolic rhetoric had not previously been used during the eighteenth century against the English nobility as a class.

Moreover radicals either explicitly or, more often, implicitly identified the English government as an aristocratic oligarchy. The term 'oligarchy' was not commonly used by radicals of 1791–2; only two uses of the term were found in the radical pamphlets of that period. Butler stated, 'I am inclined to think our government nearly equal to an oligarchy'.[68] And Oswald agreed that 'The whole representation of this country has fallen into the hands of a few great families' possessing 'great masses of property', 'a certain circle of the Aristocracy'. So few had the right to vote in elections that at best the 'House of Commons can represent *only* an Aristocracy'. Indeed, the 'English government, IS OLIGARCHY . . . TYRANNY, CORRUPTION'.[69] In addition an anonymous pamphleteer argued that the 'Aristocracy by various unwarrant-

---

[61] Anon., *The political crisis: or, a dissertation on the rights of man*, 1791, in Claeys, *Political writings*, iii. 114.

[62] Barlow, *Advice to the privileged orders*, part 1, iii. 262.

[63] *Abbé* Emmanuel Sieyès, *An essay on privileges, and particularly on hereditary nobility*, trans. 1792, p. iii.

[64] Anon., *An address to the Jacobine and other patriotic societies of the French: urging the establishment of a republican form of government: by a native of England and a citizen of the world*, 1792, 1–2, 15–16.

[65] Anon., *Political crisis*, 114.

[66] John Oswald, *A review of the constitution of Great Britain: being the substance of a speech delivered in a numerous assembly on the following questions: "Is the petition of Mr. Horne Tooke a libel on the House of Commons, or a just statement of public grievances arising from an unfair representation of the people?"*, London 1791, 3rd edn Paris, in Claeys, *Political writings*, iii. 417.

[67] Butler, *Brief reflections*, 366.

[68] Ibid. 369.

[69] Oswald, *Review of the constitution*, 419, 425, 446.

able arts, especially by creating fraudulent and fictitious votes', had acquired 'the absolute power of nomination'.[70] Even the reformer John Cartwright, who had tempered his earlier radicalism for fear of revolution spreading to England, identified Parliament as a 'cobweb of *aristocratic connexion*'.[71] He warned that if the constitution should 'perish through the pride and tyranny of an *aristocracy*, obstinately determined to resist the people's just claim for a fair representation in their own House of Parliament, it is for that aristocracy to consider, what place they would have in a new system'. In these times when 'men may live and thrive without Lords' and are happy 'where there are none' and 'even good laws can be made, and justice well administered, without either hereditary legislators or hereditary judges', the aristocracy would be wise to consider reform.[72]

It is noticeable among the great range of pamphlets produced in 1791–2 that it was now 'aristocracy', rather than the crown or government, that was accused by radicals of being the source of corruption. It was 'titled persons' who procured 'the rich places and wealthy livings' for their relations and dependants, to ensure that their designs, '*sinister in quality, or inimical to the public welfare*' would be supported.[73] Charles Piggot's *The Jockey Club* was a direct criticism of easily identifiable members of the aristocracy. His explanation for so bold a move was that he hoped to take 'dust out of the eyes of the multitude' by 'exhibiting to public view, the corruption and filthy debauchery of those, who are thus wickedly attempting to establish an eternal and destructive authority over them'.[74] Aristocracy were 'the large beasts of the field, who solace themselves under the shadow of the British oak, chewing the cud of national bribery, and impoverishing the state by taking large pensions as emoluments for simple services'.[75] Moreover the leaders of the Anglican Church formed part of this 'aristocracy'. As one anonymous pamphleteer put it, 'The whole National Church is under the control of a few pampered bishops, who live at the rate of ten thousand a year' and form 'an aristocratic branch of the national legislature!'[76] Parallels were drawn with the *ancien régime* French Church, in which the 'mitred clergy . . . the drones

---

[70] Anon., *Confederacy of kings*, 194.
[71] John Cartwright, *A letter to the duke of Newcastle: together with some remarks touching the French Revolution, a reform of parliament in Great Britain and the royal proclamation of 21 May 1792*, 1792, 86. For biographies see J. W. Osborne, *John Cartwright*, Cambridge 1972, and F. D. Cartwright, *Life and correspondence of Major Cartwright*, London 1826.
[72] Cartwright, *Letter to the duke of Newcastle*, 97–9.
[73] Benjamin Damm, *An address to the public, on true representation and the unity of man*, Sheffield 1792, 13.
[74] [Charles Pigott], *The Jockey Club: or, a sketch of the manners of the age*, 1792, i. 3–4. This contained damning condemnation of many members of the aristocracy from Marie Antoinette, the duke of York, the duke of Bedford and other dukes and earls, to many lesser peers, for the numerous vices associated with aristocracy.
[75] Butler, *Brief reflections*, 350.
[76] Anon., *Political crisis*, 141.

of the church' had 'nothing to do for their four or five thousand a year, but to wear a great wig or lawn sleeves occasionally'.[77]

Many of the attacks on aristocracy took up issues raised in the *Rights of man*, in particular criticisms of the hereditary rights and privileges of the English aristocracy. Emotive attacks upon the game laws, primogeniture, hereditary succession and titles are prominent in radical writings. It was these privileges that had defined Paine's polarised society of aristocracy and people, so representative of *ancien régime* Europe. Parallels were drawn in radical writings between the privileges in England and those of the French *noblesse*. In France the aristocracy had owned 'Hunting Forests, from which their Sport has driven the Spirit of Agriculture, . . . this enormous Waste had reduced near 20 millions of . . . Citizens so as scarcely to earn a Meal by their Labour'.[78] In England too the 'beasts of the field, and the fowls of the air', which 'man has a natural right to take' were reserved by law 'for the sport and luxury of the Great'.[79] Radicals complained that whilst a Lord might trample down fences and crops in pursuit of game, a labourer could be imprisoned for shooting a partridge.

Primogeniture was condemned as another feudal law that usurped the rights of man. It was the source of subordination for it 'habituates the people to believe in an unnatural inequality', which 'prepares them for servility and oppression'.[80] Indeed primogeniture was the very basis of aristocratic power and one anonymous pamphleteer warned that there would remain 'a formidable aristocracy to act in opposition' to reformers, so long as primogeniture endured.[81] A radical broadside asked a labourer if he would have one son 'proudly exalted above the rest of the family, and that we should first be obliged . . . to contribute towards his pomp and splendour, and then to fall down and worship this God raised by extortion, on the ruins of the family?'.[82]

Such laws were, radicals argued, representative of a larger problem, that in England the law was only available to the few. Justice was out of the reach of the people.[83] One broadside declared that it was 'an insolent falsehood' to claim that 'the Laws are the same for the poor as the rich', for 'various laws like the Game Laws . . . are expressly made against the POOR'.[84] It was claimed that the aristocracy used their legislative power entirely in 'their own interest' and passed laws 'intended to *augment* and keep up the *landed interest*'.

---

[77] Sieyès, *Essay on privileges*, 16–17. Interestingly, this comment appears in a footnote, and the footnotes were apparently added by the 'foreign nobleman, now in England', who translated the work into English 'with notes'.
[78] Anon., *Address to the Jacobine*, 3–4.
[79] Anon., *Political crisis*, 122.
[80] Barlow, *Advice to the privileged orders*, part 1, iii. 270–7.
[81] Anon., *Political crisis*, 138.
[82] Anon., *A few words but no lies from Roger Bull to his brother Thomas*, 1792, in Claeys, *Political writings*, iii. 406.
[83] Barlow, *Advice to the privileged orders*, part 1, iii. 310.
[84] Anon., *War*, 1792, in *Political broadsides*, fo. 26.

Consequently 'the great mass of the people and the . . . multitude of *Tradesmen*, *Artizans*, and *Labourers*' were drawn into the 'vassalage and intolerable oppression' of a feudal *ancien régime*.[85]

In their condemnation of hereditary rights many radicals invoked the 'Norman yoke' theory and argued that such rights of the aristocracy had no legitimacy but were rooted only in conquest. The 'original ancestors of the present generation of nobility were robbers', Paine's 'banditti of ruffians'.[86] They had obtained their lands and power by 'plunder and murder'.[87] The aristocracy put great store by a 'train of ancestry', of 'being descended from men, who existed in the thirteenth or fourteenth century', the 'good feudal times'. As the *abbé* Sieyès had said, it was in such genealogical trees that the idea that 'birth' denotes 'rank' was fostered.[88] But, an anonymous pamphleteer argued, the history of the acquisition of 'hereditary property', which was 'first acquired by the sword', justified 'abolishing hereditary right'.[89] As Thomas Cooper declared, 'an hereditary Monarchy, and hereditary Nobility, hereditary Legislators, and hereditary Judges', which make 'the happiness and welfare of the many, subservient to the pride and emolument of the few', cannot be justified on grounds of utility.[90] Ultimately 'TYRANNY IS THE SURE OFFSPRING OF HEREDITARY OFFICE'.[91]

Moreover radicals argued that, as a result of its roots in conquest, the aristocracy thrived on war and consequently promoted it. Barlow complained that the nobility of Europe 'are always fed upon human gore. They originated in war, they live by war', and without it they would starve.[92] This, according to Oswald, had created a warmongering aristocracy, 'a rapacious Aristocracy', who 'plunge the nation into war' for no legitimate reason and then expected the 'poor man' to go and fight for 'a piece of silver'.[93] Consequently, as Paine said, 'War is the Faro table of governments, and nations the dupes of the games.'[94]

Radicals challenged the aristocratic culture and language, which had promoted concepts of honour and glory and associated them with aristocracy. As an anonymous pamphleteer put it, the aristocracy would 'shoot or stab their brethren' for 'wounding (what they call) their *honour*'. 'Knaves are called and calling each other "honourable" and "right honourable" – when nothing is necessary to the making of a modern young gentleman but money

---

85 Damm, *Address to the public*, 11, 10.
86 Anon., *Political crisis*, 138; *Rights of man*, 168.
87 Barlow, *Advice to the privileged orders*, part 1, iii. 264, 269.
88 Sieyès, *Essay on privileges*, 31–2.
89 Anon., *Political crisis*, 137–8.
90 Thomas Cooper, *A reply to Mr Burke's invective against Mr Cooper and Mr Watt*, 1792, 17.
91 Anon., *Address to the Jacobine*, 44.
92 Barlow, *Advice to the privileged orders*, part 1, ii. 291.
93 Oswald, *Review of the constitution*, 415.
94 Paine, *Rights of man*, 169.

and effrontery.'⁹⁵ Barlow proclaimed that the principle of honour should be associated with morality but 'It is capable of total perversion, of losing sight of its own original nature, and still retaining its name; of pursuing the destruction of moral sentiments, instead of being their ornament; of debasing, instead of supporting the dignity of man.'⁹⁶

He lamented that 'Honour' had been 'utilised by governments for their own convenience' to symbolise killing in battle. It was a device used by kings to make war fashionable, hence the acclamation of warriors as heroes. The 'trade of war' has been 'ennobled' and presented as 'descended to us from our Gothic ancestors'. Consequently *ancien régime* governments must maintain that 'all occupations which tend to *life*, and not to *death*, are dishonourable and infamous'.⁹⁷ But, radicals argued, such days were gone and only the 'gay phantom of glory' remained.⁹⁸ Indeed the true 'Spirit of Philosophy and Heroism' had pervaded France since 1789 and given it 'the grandest Opportunity ever enjoyed by mankind'.⁹⁹

Titles were another honorary privilege universally and boisterously condemned by radicals and there is much on titles in radical writings. You do not make a 'GREAT MAN', scoffed Oswald, 'by awarding a red or blue ribbon, or affixing to his breast some glittering toy'.¹⁰⁰ Cartwright noted that whilst titles may have 'an intrinsic pecuniary value in the market of matrimony, and in the Register-office for servants at St. James's', they did not denote any genuine superiority or merit.¹⁰¹ Indeed a satirist argued that a nobleman without a title and his pride was 'no more than a common man'.¹⁰² Titles, Benjamin Damm declared, created inappropriate class divisions, suited to an *ancien régime*, whereby one man is 'distinguished by the ostentatious title of *Duke, Earl, Lord, Count*' with the 'epithet of *Noble*', whilst another who is 'perfectly useful to society, with his utmost industry and oeconomy', is still 'branded with the odious and degrading term of *vulgar, common, peasant*'.¹⁰³ Moreover radicals argued that titles did not denote 'real glory' or 'laudable ambition'.¹⁰⁴ They created only artificial distinctions of birth and blood. As a satirist put it:

---

⁹⁵ Anon., *A rod for the Burkites: consisting of remonstrative answers to the objections and invectives, of the interested, bigoted, and misguided inhabitants of Stockport by the 'Friends of Universal Peace, and the Rights of Man'*, by one of the 'swinish multitude', 2nd edn c. 1792, 10, 13.
⁹⁶ Barlow, *Advice to the privileged orders*, part 1, iii. 288.
⁹⁷ Ibid. iii. 290–1.
⁹⁸ Oswald, *Review of the constitution*, 415.
⁹⁹ Anon., *Address to the Jacobine*, 1.
¹⁰⁰ Oswald, *Review of the constitution*, 418.
¹⁰¹ Cartwright, *Letter to the duke of Newcasle*, 98.
¹⁰² Launcelot Light, *A sketch of the rights of boys and girls*, part 1, 1792, 47.
¹⁰³ Damm, *Address to the public*, 7.
¹⁰⁴ Anon., *Political crisis*, 140.

When mortal monarchs please to give,
Unto a fawning creature here,
The appellation of a Peer,
This vocal badge, this empty sound,
Makes veins with better blood abound?[105]

Consequently, the radicals identified titles as a means of false distinction, a form of show and display. As Damm stated, a *'high titled man*, as he can shew no native, or personal superiority, over his equal brother the labourer or mechanic, must have recourse to *art and parade* alone', for that is 'all that is to distinguish him'.[106] Such pageantry and parade was designed to 'entrap the admiration of the ignorant'. And 'NO nation ever seemed more stupidly rooted in admiration' of such 'glare and parade' than the English.[107] Such display, radicals claimed, was used as a diversion from the excessive expenditure of public money on aristocracy. A broadside declared, 'through the medium of sycophantic newspapers' the government gave the public 'a pleasing detail of Diamond Epaulets, superb Carriages, coloured Ribbands, brilliant stars, glorious petticoats, and diamond necklaces!'[108]

Radicals also suggested that aristocratic codes of behaviour accentuated such inappropriate elevation. As the *abbé* Sieyès said, the aristocracy wished to be distinguished *from*, rather than *by*, their fellow citizens.[109] A nobleman regulated his behaviour towards others, not according to their 'virtues or their talents', for these are 'beneath his notice', but by 'their comparative situations'.[110] Aristocratic manners were such that 'a look, a stretching out the arm, or walking across a room are published as acts of uncommon *condescension*'.[111] To Oswald it was 'a barbarous refinement of tyranny' that the rest of society should be obliged to salute such men as 'his Grace, his Highness, his Excellency', when they may in reality be 'the lowest lacquey' or the 'veriest dunce'. Such practice had caused a 'defilement of the public manners', a 'disorder of manners'.[112]

Moreover some radicals noted that titles were increasingly utilised by the aristocracy as a means of shoring up their supremacy against challenges from a people spurred on by the example of the French Revolution. As one satirist observed, at a time when the people of Europe 'combine in regarding the more elevated orders of society with a jealous and suspicious attention', it becomes increasingly necessary for the aristocracy to exhibit 'the true and genuine dignity of titles and honours, derived from a long line of illustrious

---

105 J. Sharpe, *A rhapsody to E***** B**** Esq.*, Sheffield 1792, 10.
106 Damm, *Address to the public*, 8.
107 [Pigott], *Jockey Club*, i. 2, 13.
108 Anon., *Rod for the Burkites*, 12.
109 Sieyès, *Essay on privileges*, 23, 26.
110 Light, *Sketch of the rights*, 48–9.
111 Anon., *Rod for the Burkites*, 11.
112 Oswald, *Review of the constitution*, 418; Sieyès, *Essay on privileges*, 20.

ancestry' and to 'treat with proper scorn and contumely the observations of the baser Vulgar'. In the face of the increasing 'equalizing spirit', the aristocracy might be wise to 'direct a contrary mode of conduct', but they treat such ideas with 'ridicule and contempt'.[113] Certainly, the challenge to aristocracy expressed in radical pamphlets was explicit and vicious.

Merit versus birth

The most universal and enduring issue raised in radical writings, which brought the issue of leadership to the forefront of the debate, was the value of merit over birth and wealth. As Charles Pigott put it, 'Popular esteem should be attached only to purity of principles, or an union of virtue and talents' and 'poor indeed is the claim to public affection, that consists in rank alone'.[114] 'Talents and Abilities . . . Knowledge, Experience and Integrity' were needed for good government but, in hereditary government, 'are left entirely to the production of chance'.[115] The message was clear and widely voiced: 'MERIT is not confined to a PEERAGE'.[116] As a manufacturer speaking at a public meeting in Sheffield declared, 'Hearken then, to a plain man (good sense is not confined to rank)'.[117] In fact, Oswald claimed, it was rarely to be found there; after all, 'what occasion has a Lord for ability', if he is 'born a Legislator'. At present in England 'the places of great honour and trust' were filled 'by sycophants and idiots'.[118]

The traditional defence of aristocratic 'independence' was also held up for scrutiny by radicals and found wanting. As one anonymous pamphleteer declared, 'men of birth and education are not *naturally* better calculated to regulate the great machine of government than those less independent'. Indeed, 'we often find as great geniuses spring from the dunghill, as ever boasted the pompous title of Lord or Duke' and in such cases 'merit, and not wealth or high birth triumphs over prejudice'.[119] The issue of merit versus birth appeared in writings on social status throughout the eighteenth century and before, but clearly the stress on merit was rising to a crescendo during the 1790s.[120]

For radicals, wealth and birth damagingly excluded men of merit from obtaining positions of power. As Oswald noted, a rich man may enter the

[113] Light, *Sketch of the rights*, 49–50.
[114] [Pigott], *Jockey Club*, i. 1, 4.
[115] Cooper, *Reply to Mr. Burke's invective*, 20.
[116] Anon., *Political crisis*, 112.
[117] Anon., *A speech by a manufacturer at a public meeting in Sheffield on 11 June 1792*, 1792, 23.
[118] Oswald, *Review of the constitution*, 425, 431.
[119] Anon., *Political crisis*, 145–6.
[120] See, for example, Corfield, 'The rivals', 12–18, and also her *Power and the professions*, 1–17.

House of Commons with 'a pittance of intellect', little greater than 'his mule', while those 'whom the love of mental wealth sublimes above the sordid stench of ore, are excluded'.[121] There were 'numerous characters' with 'minds that would do honour to the higher ranks' but who were at present 'bowed with poverty and oppression'.[122] By restricting government to the aristocracy, 'wealth' had become 'the criterion of worth'. This 'debauches the people and impoisons the public mind with a false opinion of the excellence of riches'.[123] Cartwright asked 'Who has the greatest stake in the country; he who has most *wealth*, or he who has most *happiness* in it?' The man of virtue and education was 'superior to the mere man of wealth'.[124]

Moreover, the suggestion, and indeed often the accusation was not merely that birth and wealth did not naturally or necessarily denote merit but that they actually precluded it. In a direct challenge to Burke's assumption that the aristocracy was well educated and qualified for leadership, radicals claimed the opposite. The *abbé* Sieyès had observed that as 'honour is assigned' to the aristocracy 'as their inheritance', they see no need to pursue it, but leave it to other less privileged men to strive to 'obtain it by merit'.[125] Cooper argued that the aristocracy were 'almost inevitably brought up to an habitual indulgence in Luxury and Vice'. Consequently, the 'Idleness and Ignorance of the Titled orders' rendered them 'unfit for positions in government'. It was kings and nobles who furnished 'the compleatest Specimens of mental Depravity'.[126] Mary Wollstonecraft in her *A vindication of the rights of woman* (1792) maintained that 'Riches and honours prevent a man from enlarging his understanding, and enervate all his powers by reversing the order of nature which has ever made true pleasure the reward of labour.'[127] One anonymous pamphleteer stated that pride acted as an 'admirable substitute for learning', which a young nobleman may not have pursued 'so much as many of his inferiors in rank'.[128] And another, that the 'education and habits of our Noblemen' render them 'incompetent of judging in cases of intricacy, which depend on the nice distinctions of law'.[129] Thus the aristocracy was condemned as unqualified for the positions it held.

A number of radicals further identified the aristocracy as positively idle. It was well established that the French aristocracy had lived 'in idleness at the expence of the public'.[130] Radicals followed Paine and entrenched the unfa-

---

121 Oswald, *Review of the constitution*, 425.
122 Anon., *The case of Thomas Spence . . . who was committed to prison for selling Paine's Rights of man*, 1792, 11.
123 Oswald, *Review of the constitution*, 420.
124 Cartwright, *Letter to the duke of Newcastle*, 109–10.
125 Sieyès, *Essay on privileges*, 56–7.
126 Cooper, *Reply to Mr Burke's invective*, 20–1, 25.
127 Wollstonecraft, *Vindication of the rights of woman*, 134.
128 Light, *Sketch of the rights*, 47.
129 Anon., *Political crisis*, 38, 65.
130 Sieyès, *Essay of privileges*, 62.

vourable connections he had made between the English aristocracy and the *ancien régime* French aristocracy. Barlow expanded this theme: there is one 'genuine feudal claim', which affects all the aristocracy and 'extends to every drop of feudal blood' and that is '*idleness*'.[131] Cooper concurred: 'hereditary Titles, Privileges, and Orders . . . are from their natural tendency . . . the Hot-beds of Luxury, Idleness, and Immorality'.[132] And Oswald defined an aristocracy of 'the rich, the luxurious, and the idle'.[133] One pamphlet asserted that, 'The present prosperity in trade' is due to 'the ingenuity and labour of the bulk of the people' rather than to the aristocracy.[134] Here radical calls for supremacy based on merit rather than birth coincided with long-standing Dissenter views about virtue and merit, industry and idleness. As the Dissenter Anna Barbauld commented in 1792, the virtuous people are not 'the dissolute, idle intemperate' and 'profligate . . . who prey upon the honest industry of others' but those 'who are sober, industrious and thoughtful'.[135] The 'general corruption of morals, and depravity of manners' amongst the people 'is in great measure owing to' the 'extravagant examples of luxury and dissipation' provided by the aristocracy.[136] Wollstonecraft too declared that 'Happy it is when people have the cares of life to struggle with; for these struggles prevent their becoming a prey to enervating vices, merely from idleness!' which afflict those 'from birth . . . placed in a torrid zone, with the meridian sun of pleasure' upon them.[137]

Thus in the early 1790s radicals were largely united in the belief that the positions of power and influence should be awarded to those of merit and virtue. Clearly, however, where within society such virtuous men were to be found and how they were to be elevated to positions of power was not agreed, or even always considered, at this stage. A number of radicals argued that it was only in 'equal', 'popular' government that 'greater statesmen' would be found.[138] France and America were frequently held up as examples of such equal government. Joel Barlow declared that the National Assembly was a truly 'great body of men'.[139] And an anonymous pamphleteer argued that in America, where 'there are no nobility; every one depends on his virtue for pre-eminence'.[140] But, as illustrated below, not all radicals were consistent in their condemnation of aristocracy and proposals for reform. One point

---

[131] Barlow, *Advice to the privileged orders*, part 1, iii. 277.
[132] Cooper, *Reply to Mr Burke's invective*, 21–2.
[133] Oswald, *Review of the constitution*, 415.
[134] Anon., *Rod for the Burkites*, 8.
[135] Anna-Laetitia Barbauld, *Civic sermons to the people*, 1792, 17–19.
[136] Damm, *Address to the public*, 9.
[137] Wollstonecraft, *Vindication of the rights of woman*, 124.
[138] Anon., *Political crisis*, 125.
[139] Joel Barlow, *A letter to the National Convention of France*, 1792, in *The political writings of Joel Barlow*, New York 1796, 160.
[140] Anon., *Political crisis*, 139–40.

radical representations were united in making most strongly at this stage, however, was that little merit or virtue were to be found amongst the aristocracy.

Inequality of rights

Not surprisingly much of the radical literature focused on inequality. Here 'a plain ploughman', 'a peasant' or 'a mechanic' has the 'ambitious wish to enjoy the Rights of Man' which are his natural rights.[141] All men were born equal and consequently it was 'proper to enquire why some men are set over and govern other men'.[142] Radicals proclaimed that 'A principle of equality reigns in every breast', and it was equality of political rights they primarily wanted. And here radicals followed Paine and challenged the established traditional assumption held by conservatives and Whigs alike that political rights must be linked to property ownership. Radicals argued that every individual, whether or not they own property, should have an equal vote. Oswald was not alone in arguing that in any event all men had property; 'Is there any man without property? Is not the daily labour of the peasant or the mechanic, as much his property, and as precious to him, as the wide possessions or funded wealth of the landholder, or man of money?'. He went on to argue that the House of Commons 'are chosen by a number of electors, not exceeding, at a very extravagant calculation, an hundredth part of the people of Great Britain. At best, therefore, the House of Commons can represent *only* an Aristocracy'.[143] Thus radicals challenged the established political status of land that had, for so long, shorn up aristocratic hegemony.

Furthermore the disparity between rich and poor was a major concern to radicals and many followed Paine and raised the issue of inequality of property. Some radicals even went so far as to call for a redistribution of land. Thomas Cooper expressed support for the radical agrarian law proposed by William Ogilvie in his *Essay on the right of property in land* (1781).[144] Thomas Spence published his lecture given in 1775, the *Real rights of man* (1790), which advocated a redistribution of property.[145] Spence wanted to decentralise government and advocated that all the land be owned on behalf of the citizens by parochial corporations and administered by parish councils. He

---

141 Anon., *Few words*, 405.
142 Barbauld, *Civic sermons*, 9.
143 Oswald, *Review of the constitution*, 415–19.
144 Claeys has noted that both Thomas Cooper and John Oswald had praised Ogilvie's schemes but neither of them made a similar proposal in their own works during this period: *Thomas Paine*, 133.
145 This tract was a later publication of a lecture Spence had given in 1775 and then published as a cheap broadside entitled *The rights of man*. Spence's ideas did not receive much attention until he re-published them in 1790: Goodwin, *Friends of liberty*, 479.

particularly condemned hereditary land ownership.[146] He pointed out that land was not like the produce of manufacturing industry, for 'whilst manufacturers . . . have the right in what they produce . . . man should have equal rights in land as they do in air or light'.[147] Whilst Paine did not make a direct challenge to private property *per se*, and declared it 'impolitic to set bounds to property acquired by industry', he forcibly attacked hereditary landed estates. Paine contended that in 'hereditary estates, the law has created an evil' and consequently primogeniture should be abolished. Vast hereditary estates should be prohibitively taxed to force their division. An anonymous pamphleteer concurred, arguing that 'hereditary estates' should be 'made partable' so that 'in a very little time estates would get so distributed as to place the inhabitants of an opulent kingdom more on a level with each other'.[148] Barlow, echoing Wollstonecraft,[149] also acknowledged that many agreed that 'industry and cultivation' are 'best promoted on small estates'. He further suggested that individuals should be entitled only to 'the surplassage' of their property after society has deducted 'what is necessary to the real wants of society', for society should be 'the first proprietor'.[150]

However most radicals did not promote an abolition of the laws of property. Indeed a few radical pamphleteers actually defended property laws. As one anonymous writer put it, to 'render property insecure would destroy all motives to exertion, and tear up public happiness to the roots'; radicals were not 'LEVELLERS'.[151] The 'true essential rights to which every man is alike duly entitled' are 'the preservation of life, liberty and property'.[152] Whilst more should be done to relieve want, private property was consistent both with 'good order among men' and 'necessary to the existence of society'.[153] The 'Footman' is equal to the Esquire' but only under the law and regarding his natural rights.[154] Yet Damm reflected the feeling expressed by many radicals: abhorrence at the inequalities in society but stopping short of a desire for the abolition of property laws: 'Why is so vast a difference made amongst men . . . both in titles and the appropriation of goods, and fruits of the earth which, (exclusive of private property justly obtained) was originally intended for the general use and benefit of all?'[155]

Moreover radicals did focus on the causes of such inequality, and corrup-

---

[146] See Thomas Spence, *The real rights of man*, 1775, in H. T. Dickinson (ed.), *The political works of Thomas Spence*, Newcastle-upon-Tyne 1982.
[147] Spence, *Real rights*, 2.
[148] Anon., *Political crisis*, 139.
[149] See p. 48 above.
[150] Barlow, *Advice to the privileged orders*, part 1, iii. 270, 305.
[151] Anon., *The perverse definitions imposed on the word equality*, c. 1792, in Claeys, *Political writings*, iii. 403.
[152] Ibid.
[153] Barlow, *Advice to the privileged orders*, part 1, iii. 305.
[154] Anon., *Few words*, 406.
[155] Damm, *Address to the public*, 4.

tion in government was identified as a major source of inequality. The aristocracy were accused of obtaining their wealth from government revenue. Like the French aristocracy, the English was completely idle and unproductive and must live off the industry of the poor, both directly on the land and in industry, and indirectly through corruption. As Paine put it, in old governments 'we still find the greedy hand of government thrusting itself into every corner and crevice of industry, and grasping the spoil of the multitude'.[156] And, as already established, to radicals 'old governments' denoted 'aristocracy'. One of the major objections to the 'Establishments' of government 'is the expense of them', which the poor must bear.[157] Damm declared that any 'person of integrity and ingenuity' must view

> with abhorrence, and utter detestation, that superfluous number of places, and pensions paid out of industrious labour, and the hard earnings of the poor, for the meer purpose of agrandizement and luxury, that is, to support a set of idle and useless beings, favourites of a court, in splendour, riot and all manner of wanton extravagance, whilst the obvious fund that supplies this channel, is the sweat & blood of the great multitude, the bulk or mass of the nation.[158]

It was such inappropriate spending of the 'public money', which was to blame for the 'very low incomes of multitudes'. And as 'equipages, diversions, and pride and luxury in general, increase among our rich men and rulers; so hunger and nakedness, poverty and wretchedness keep an equal pace among the poor, and lower orders'.[159]

Taxation was another source of corruption and inequality identified by radicals. In part two of the *Rights of man*, Paine proposed a system for the redistribution of wealth by means of taxation and a form of welfare. He focused his ideas for such taxation against a definition of 'luxury', which reflected annual income. Indeed 'an overgrown estate . . . is a luxury at all times', and Paine advocated a tax of 100% on the largest estates worth £23,000 or more.[160] Here he reflected the French criticism of the tax privileges of their aristocracy of the *ancien régime*. Radicals also took up the issue of taxation in England favouring the aristocracy. Taxes 'fall heavy on those who are compelled by necessity to labour hard to support a miserable existence', Butler lamented, and consequently they are 'already reduced almost to a state of slavery'.[161] One broadside proclaimed that all taxes 'ultimately fall on the *laborious* part of the nation'. Taxation 'takes the poor man's shilling out of the rich man's hands. Thus the "*swinish multitude*" are hood-

---

156 Paine, *Rights of man*, 160.
157 Cooper, *Reply to Mr Burke's invective*, 19.
158 Damm, *Address to the public*, 12.
159 Thomas Bentley, *The rights of the poor*, 1791, in Claeys, *Political writings*, iii. 173.
160 Paine, *Rights of man*, 251; Claeys, *Thomas Paine*, 254.
161 Butler, *Brief reflections*, 379.

winked, whilst they are deprived of the fruits of their labour'.¹⁶² Oswald confirmed that the tax, 'which lessens the luxuries of the son of wealth, and thins a little the crowd of his lacqueys, shall rob the poor man of his morsel of bread, and turn his wife and children naked into the street', for 'the whole robbery of government' falls on 'the poorer class of citizens'.¹⁶³ A number of radicals also identified 'industrious tradesmen and manufacturers of England' as bearing the brunt of taxation.¹⁶⁴ Thus all were united here as the people, who worked and paid taxes, opposed to an aristocracy who did neither but merely 'roll in luxury'. Paine confirmed that 'There are two distinct classes of men in the nation those who pay taxes and those who receive and live upon the taxes.'¹⁶⁵

It was within the context of corruption ensuring that the aristocracy deprived the people of their share of the country's wealth that Paine and others introduced the issue of economic equality into the debate. As McNally has said, part 2 of *Rights of man*, 'made the critique of poverty and inequality a central part of the radical defence of the French Revolution'.¹⁶⁶ As importantly for the unfolding arguments about England, part 2 also pushed economic inequality into the centre of the debate about domestic politics. Paine suggested that as a result of 'the aristocratical system' of primogeniture, 'The peer and the beggar are often of the same family. One extreme produces the other: to make one rich many must be made poor.' This, Paine argued, was the 'natural consequence of aristocracy', both within the family and society at large.¹⁶⁷ An economic as well as a political 'aristocracy', which incorporated the 'rich' and Paine's 'landed interest', was set against the people. As Thomas Cooper commented, there was 'too much Inequality of Rank – too much Inequality of Riches – too much inequality of Labour'.¹⁶⁸

Much was made in radical pamphlets, particularly from 1792, of economic inequality. Here the poor and labouring interest were set against the rich, an 'aristocracy' of wealth. Distinctions were no longer made between good and bad possessors of wealth. Instead radicals represented the 'people' in opposition to all the rich and powerful.¹⁶⁹ One pamphleteer declared: 'You have heard, no doubt . . . a great deal of . . . the government interest, the landed interest, the moneyed interest, the mercantile interest, the church interest, and I know not how many interests, but all of them wealthy interests; but never a word of the *labouring* interest, as if labourers had no interest at all.'¹⁷⁰

---

162 Anon., *Rod for the Burkites*, 6.
163 Oswald, *Review of the constitution*, 415.
164 Butler, *Brief reflections*, 374, 379.
165 Thomas Paine, *Letter addressed to the addressers on the late proclamation*, 1792, in M. Foot and I. Kramnick (eds), *The Thomas Paine reader*, London 1987, 376–8.
166 McNally, 'Political economy to the fore', 430.
167 Paine, *Rights of man*, 257.
168 Cooper, *Reply to Mr Burke's invective*, 75.
169 Wahrman, *Imagining the middle classes*, 75.
170 Anon., *Few words*, 405.

The 'pride and pleasure and covetousness' of the rich 'naturally' caused a rise of rents and taxes, and the cost of the necessaries of life which fall 'first and most heavily upon the poor'.[171] In England, 'the whole weight of aristocracy falls heavy on the poor' and again it was an 'aristocracy of wealth'.[172]

Thus radicals represented England as an economic as well as a political *ancien régime*, with a polarised society of 'aristocracy and people', incorporating the division of 'rich and poor'. This model directly contradicted the incumbent Whig representation of England as a modern, commercial country with a polite and commercial people. Unfortunately for radicalism, as time would tell, many Englishmen and women were still very much attached to the Whig position.

Interpretations

Having identified the radical representations of aristocracy it is now appropriate to consider what such radical depictions of 1790–2 meant for the French Revolution debate. Ultimately they suggest that the majority of radicals and reformers believed that the practices and privileges, which were the foundation and support of aristocratic hegemony, were untenable. Barlow voiced the view of many when he said that such hereditary rights were a 'discouragement to agriculture, an embarrassment to commerce, – they humiliate one part of the community, swell the pride of the other, and are a real pecuniary disadvantage to both'.[173] In effect the abrogation of privileges and hereditary rights would bring the abolition of aristocracy and equality of rank, which some like Paine stipulated and others did not. One problem that arises when trying to understand the extent and scope of such radical representations is that the anti-aristocratic rhetoric did not always reflect the actual reforms proposed in the pamphlets.

Early 1790s radicalism certainly did not produce an entirely homogeneous discourse; nor were radicals consistent in their proposals. As J. A. Epstein has pointed out, 'there was no unitary radical response to the French Revolution, not least because the revolution itself was in constant motion; the 1790s was a decade of great ideological diversity'.[174] Certainly this research into representations of aristocracy in radical pamphlets reveals a diversity of political ideas and does not provide a clear picture of precise divisions between radicals and reformers. Nor is it possible always to identify an individual's

---

171 Thomas Bentley, *A few queries to the Methodists in general and especially to the teachers amongst the people*, 1792, in Political broadsides, fo. 5.
172 Oswald, *Review of the constitution*, 429.
173 Barlow, *Advice to the privileged orders*, part 1, iii. 270–7.
174 J. A. Epstein, *Radical expression: political language, ritual and symbol in England, 1790–1850*, Oxford 1994, 6; Philp, 'Fragmented ideology', 56.

political allegiances with total clarity. In this new political terrain options and opinions were in flux.

In her study of radicalism Jenny Graham has identified a strong republicanism and a revolutionary radicalism in the early years of the French Revolution.[175] She described the early radical leaders as having the 'republican spirit' and referred to 'the republican Joel Barlow'.[176] Certainly Joel Barlow stated that the 'republican principle' is 'proper and safe for the government of any people'.[177] And a number of the more radical writers, such as Thomas Cooper and John Oswald, wanted to abolish the English constitution and to replace it with a republic or democracy. Oswald argued that reform of the English government would not be sufficient and that 'Our only hopes of renovation are suspended on a NATIONAL ASSEMBLY.' He went on to predict, in somewhat vaguer terms, that the French Revolution 'sooner or later will be imitated by every nation in Europe'.[178] An anonymous pamphleteer took a more common approach, however, and advocated a 'FREE and EQUAL REPUBLIC' in France but not specifically in England.[179] Another described the republics in Switzerland, Holland, France and America as outstripping 'every other nation in the world, in the improvements in government, in credit, in riches, in power and in the arts and sciences' and as a 'glorious example to other nations!'. Yet for England the author promoted only the reform of the existing government'.[180]

As has been well documented, during this period a number of radical popular societies were formed and were growing rapidly, in provincial towns as well as London.[181] Certainly these societies quickly gained a reputation for attracting radicals and promoting revolution and republicanism.[182] Popular radical societies pledged their support to the French Revolution and sent addresses of congratulation to the French National Convention in 1792. Many such addresses contained criticisms of government in England. The London Corresponding Society's address to the National Convention, declared that the real enemy in Europe was the 'all-consuming Aristocracy – Wisely have you acted in expelling it from France'.[183] Radical societies also

---

[175] Graham, *The nation, the law and the king*, 16–27.
[176] Ibid. 73, 83.
[177] Barlow, *Advice of the privileged orders, part 1*, iii. 236.
[178] Oswald, *Review of the constitution*, 437.
[179] Anon., *Address to the Jacobine*, 49.
[180] Anon., *Political crisis*, 148, 134.
[181] The London Corresponding Society (LCS) was formed in January 1792 and the Sheffield Society for Constitutional Information had grown to a membership of approximately 2,000 by summer of the same year: Stevenson, 'Popular radicalism', 70.
[182] Graham has claimed that the popular societies such as the LCS and, particularly the Society for Constitutional Information and its leader, the Revd John Horne Tooke, were republican: *The nation, the law and the king*, 85–6, 90–1.
[183] LCS, *The address to the French National Convention, 27 September 1792*, in Mary Thale (ed.), *Selections from the papers of the London Corresponding Society, 1792–99*, Cambridge 1983, 21.

promoted and distributed copies of the *Rights of man* free, or at reduced rates, to ensure it reached a wide audience among the people.

It is clear that many radicals and their societies did have 'the republican spirit' in that they celebrated events in France, promoted liberty and the rights of man and looked forward to a 'new condition of the world', which would reflect government in France and/or America.[184] Yet often this 'spirit', generally reflected in forceful rhetoric, did not extend to concrete proposals for a republic in England.[185] Certainly in the early years of the French Revolution a general enthusiasm for revolution was widely expressed by English pamphleteers. But as John Dinwiddy has pointed out, such enthusiasm was for the most part 'rather disembodied and vicarious' and few actually advocated a revolution in England.[186] Clearly this lack of concrete proposals was partly due to the style of writing adopted by many radicals. The norm was to write in terms of an attack against what was already in place, often in heated and dramatic terms. Concise delineation of a solution, as provided in *Rights of man, part 2*, was rarely found in radical pamphlets of 1791-2.

Moreover there was much in radical writings that is familiar from the 1780s and before. In particular in 1790-2 many radicals promoted the reforms proposed in the duke of Richmond's 1783 plan, for universal male suffrage, increased representation and annual parliaments, although a far more numerous and vociferous radicalism promoted such ideas in the 1790s than had done so in the 1780s. Analysis of the radical societies' public documents suggests that, despite their vehement support for the revolution in France and for Paine, in the main their aims were for reform rather than revolution in England. Calls to curb violence and for peaceful reform of the existing government are common in such documents. Indeed during 1791-2 even anti-aristocratic pronouncements were rare in the public documents of the radical societies.[187]

Furthermore during the early 1790s many radicals who condemned aristocracy and promoted merit over birth also expressed a desire to retain the constitution. Benjamin Damm produced a vitriolic tirade against aristocracy but, in the same pamphlet, claimed that reform of representation and election, which reflected the will of the people, was what was required to avoid despotism and arbitrary power.[188] Pigott, having written a lengthy and direct condemnation of the aristocracy, called only for the speedy and liberal reform of the constitution as 'it would be unwise to annihilate it altogether'.[189] One

---

184 Priestley, *Letters to the Rt. Hon. Edmund Burke*, 384.
185 Of course not all radicals held the same views as to what form of republic they would favour.
186 John Dinwiddy, 'Conceptions of revolution in the English radicalism of the 1790s', in Hellmuth, *Transformation of political culture*, 539.
187 Although anti-aristocratic rhetoric is present primarily in their later private correspondence published subsequently.
188 Damm, *Address to the public*, 3.

anonymous pamphleteer declared that in a 'State really free, a privileged cast of men cannot possibly exist'.[190] He went on, 'the SOVEREIGN WILL of Nations must finally triumph over the exertions of an Aristocracy, and Despotism be sacrificed on the altar of Liberty', but later in the same pamphlet stated:

> I am far from wishing a revolution, and would spill my blood to prevent it. I only wish to see some reform; and perhaps a reformation in the expenditure of money and the established church, and in the modes of election, so as to produce a more equal representation of the people, which would render the present government as lasting as the pillars of time.[191]

This ambivalence is common in radical pamphlets of the period and suggests that in many cases the criticisms of aristocracy were more radical than the reforms actually proposed.

Ultimately it is not clear how radical writers envisaged the abolition of aristocracy if a mixed form of government, in which aristocracy formed an essential part, was retained. Oswald argued that 'No sooner was the French nation fairly represented, than the order of the *noblesse* was abolished' and, correspondingly, when in England the people obtained 'an equal representation, our Barons must bid adieu to their political existence'.[192] But clearly 'an equal representation' would not on its own, introduced within the English constitution, result in the abolition of the House of Lords. It is true that the introduction of manhood suffrage would sever the ties between property and political rights that reinforced aristocracy supremacy. Manhood suffrage also might, as many radicals clearly hoped, have paved the way for other more drastic reform, but such further reform was rarely proposed.[193]

Interestingly Major Cartwright did propose a system of representation by election for the House of Lords, albeit with a 'suitable qualification in property and character' to prevent a 'degradation of the peerage'.[194] Yet Cartwright's was the only such proposal uncovered in the pamphlets viewed here. Indeed Oswald dismissed the idea of an elective nobility on the grounds that 'the voice of the people cannot give permanency to the character of men'.[195] Although much admiration for the American system was expressed, radicals did not directly promote an elected senate as instituted in America. The majority of radical writings of 1791–2 merely promoted the concept of merit over birth without actually providing concrete proposals as to how such a change should be achieved.

---

[189] [Pigott], *Jockey Club*, i. 5.
[190] Anon., *Political crisis*, 137–8.
[191] Ibid. 114, 134.
[192] Oswald, *Review of the constitution*, 419.
[193] Dinwiddy, 'Conceptions of revolution', 542.
[194] Cartwright, *Letter to the duke of Newcastle*, 118–19.
[195] Oswald, *Review of the constitution*, 418.

Similarly, whilst radicals published an anti-aristocratic tirade against inequality of property, they did not formulate concomitant proposals to remedy it. As illustrated above a number of radicals wanted to abolish hereditary estates and a few promoted the redistribution of land or subscribed to an agrarian law. But clearly many radicals were wary of interfering with the laws of property. Actual economic reform proposals were also few and far between in radical pamphlets. The historian Gwyn Williams has stated that English radicalism failed to integrate ' "economic" grievances into a political attitude, as *sans-culottes* did'.[196] This lack of alternative economic thinking amongst radicals reflects the nature of the swiftly moving pamphlet debates in which, at this stage, radicals focused predominantly on the attack rather than upon detailed solutions.

It is possible that the government action to quell radicalism initiated in May 1792 in response to the publication of *Rights of man, part 2*, may have influenced radicals, and particularly the societies, to tone down what they expressed in print. Dickinson claimed that the radical Thomas Cooper, 'fearing a charge of treason', stated that he had no intention of overturning the English constitution and only wanted political equality.[197] But fear of reprisals surely cannot account for the frequent conjunction of radical anti-aristocratic rhetoric with only modest proposals for reform in pamphlets published during this period, many of which were certainly written, if not published, before May 1792. It is also possible that, despite the rhetoric, many radicals wanted only to put an end to corruption in government.

It has been the general consensus amongst historians in this field that the radicalism of the 1790s differed from the reform of the 1780s in the ideology it promoted and/or its efforts to involve the people.[198] Yet, as Philp has noted, another difference can be identified in the French Revolution debate of the 1790s: a marked shift from ideology to rhetoric and propaganda. The high-flown rhetoric made it more difficult for historians to determine what radicals actually meant.[199] Events in France encouraged the shift from ideology to rhetoric and propaganda in England.[200] And the radical focus on aristocracy, so much the subject of rhetoric and abuse in France, also influenced it. The anti-aristocratic rhetoric invoked in England was the most consistently radical material to be found in the pamphlets. Moreover the focus on 'aristocracy', which carried with it negative connotations and accompanying models of society, obscured rather than clarified radical proposals for reform in England. For one thing, as Penelope Corfield has pointed out, there was not a power vacuum to fill in England in the 1790s as there had been in revolutionary France in 1789. Consequently things moved

---

[196] Williams, *Artisans and sans-culottes*, 101.
[197] Dickinson, *Liberty and property*, 247.
[198] Ibid. 240–58; Stevenson, 'Popular radicalism', 70.
[199] Philp, 'Fragmented ideology', 72, 65.
[200] Ibid. 65.

more slowly.[201] Thus, as this book illustrates, the radical rhetoric adopted from France was curiously out of alignment with both the political situation in England and with much of the specific reform demanded by radicals. And none more so than the rhetoric aimed at the English aristocracy.

The challenge to aristocracy

It is clear that in the early 1790s radical writings reflected a strong and almost universal condemnation of aristocracy. It is a contention of this book that it was anti-aristocratic rhetoric coupled with the revolutionary rhetoric espoused so forcefully by Paine and his followers that gave the movement of 1790–2 its strongly radical identity. This was an identity that did not fully reflect the majority of radical reform proposals. Moreover the term 'aristocracy' became increasingly a term of abuse, taken from France, used to define for the first time a class of aristocracy, which incorporated the nobility but increasingly the rich who were naturally opposed to the poor. The Painite model of England as an *ancien régime* society of 'aristocracy and people' was adopted and promoted by radicals. Those radicals and reformers who supported a mixed government in England, and those who did not, attacked aristocracy at the very least as the source of corruption. The radical challenge to the established system that tethered political power to land-ownership further intensified that attack. Thus the representations of aristocracy in England had both changed and increased in response to the French Revolution. During the years 1791–2 Paine and his fellow radicals developed an anti-aristocratic rhetoric, which in its force and public expression was new.

In promoting the Painite model of society radicals also invoked an inclusive language of natural rights intended to appeal to all 'the people'.[202] The language and concepts which had formulated aristocratic codes and ideals and shorn up aristocratic hegemony, were constantly challenged. Aristocratic language, the language of an *ancien régime* and the language of Burke, was held up for scrutiny and found wanting. As Oswald declared, the plight of the poor is 'no tale of artificial sorrow, no eloquent fiction'. Here there are no 'gew-gaws . . . to dazzle the understandings, no dagger to glitter through the shining superficies of courtly pamphlets'. It is a 'plain story of humble grief'.[203] This inclusive language of the people and the accompanying radical model of society as 'aristocracy and people' posed a new and powerful challenge to the loyalists. They then had to find a way to respond in order to attract the mass of the people, previously excluded from the political world, to the loyalist cause.

---

[201] Corfield, *Power and the professions*, 6.
[202] Wahrman, *Imagining the middle class*, 77; Smith, *Politics of language*, 35–67.
[203] Oswald, *Review of the constitution*, 417.

3

Loyalist Responses to Paine, 1791–1792

> In England, commerce, fostered by freedom, daily extends her empire, opening new sources of industry, and thereby facilitating the acquisition of splendid fortunes.[1]

Many historians have identified the loyalist response to radical attack as a conservative defence of the church and state establishment and the social order.[2] Dozier has described loyalism emerging as the mass support shown by Englishmen to king and constitution at the time of the Royal Proclamation on sedition in May 1792. One way in which this loyalty was shown was by attendance at public meetings held around the country and the signing of prepared addresses of loyalty to the king. Dozier stated that 'in this manner, and over this issue, the English loyalists made their first appearance . . . a new group of Englishmen had appeared on the political stage'. The addresses loyalists signed were, however, lost. Consequently, 'how many loyalists there were, their stations in life, and their political attachments are impossible to trace'.[3] But these loyalists clearly displayed their support for the monarchy, the government and the Church in the face of the radical attack. Dozier described a form of 'organised loyalism', that is, the movement which took steps physical, legal and propagandist to quash radicalism.[4]

In addition some historians detect the source of 1790s loyalism in the sermons and writings of Anglican clergy. Jonathan Clark has identified Anglican high churchmen as leaders in conservative loyalism. It was they, he argues, who 'were the most effective spokesmen: they possessed the most intellectually powerful doctrine of the State'.[5] Certainly the Anglican Church was mobilised behind the loyalist movement and a mass of Anglican tracts, largely supporting a traditional, conservative loyalism, were published.[6] Two high churchmen, William Jones and George Horne, were

---

1 [[John Gifford], A plain address to the common sense of the people of England, 1792, 49.
2 See, for example, Schofield, 'Conservative political thought', 601–22; Hole, *Pulpits, politics and public order*, 18–37; and Dickinson, 'Popular conservatism', 103.
3 Dozier, *King, contitution and country*, 20–5. Dickinson defines loyalism on similar terms: 'Popular conservatism', 113–17.
4 Claeys, *Thomas Paine*, 139–46.
5 Clark, *English society*, 247–9.
6 See, for example, Hole, *Pulpits, politics and public order*; Richard A. Soloway, 'Reform or ruin: English moral thought during the first French Republic', *Review of Politics* xxv (1963), 110–28; and Nancy U. Murray, 'The influence of the French Revolution on the Church of England and its rivals, 1789–1802', unpubl. DPhil. diss. Oxford 1975. It should be noted

among the first to condemn the revolution in France and defend the Church and State in England. In 1789 they both gave sermons condemning the French revolutionaries for disregarding the 'doctrine of the divine authority of government' and usurping God's power by taking power for the people. The people, they asserted, owed a duty of absolute obedience to government at all times and never had a right, whatever the circumstances, to rebel against their government.[7] Such ideas were adopted by many loyalist Anglican churchmen in their sermons and tracts. In particular the *Rights of man* triggered a substantial response in the form of Anglican political sermons, many of which emphasised the obligation of obedience and justified subordination and the social order. Homilies against disobedience and rebellion from 1547 and 1570 formed the basis for many Anglican pamphlets published during the pamphlet war.[8] Many stressed that the established Church was an essential part of the State.[9] Charles Hawtrey in 1792 confirmed that the people could not be the source of power, as radicals claimed, since all power derived from God. William Sewell declared in 1791 that: 'Whatever be the public Language of the French Democrats, their concealed Doctrine is truly this . . . they are exercising the deep Policy of their great Master, *Lucifer*; they are loosening the Bands of civil Society, and undermining the Influence of natural Religion.'[10]

Furthermore Anglican clergymen had always justified the social order upon the prospect of just rewards in the next life and continued to do so in support of the loyalist cause. William Paley argued in 1792 that religion eased the problem of inequality of rank, for 'religion smoothes all inequalities, because it unfolds a prospect which makes all earthly distinctions nothing'.[11] Some Anglican writers clearly put the Church, rather than the constitution, at the centre of the state. Clark has stated that during war with France from 1793 'circumstances had led churchmen to defend aristocracy and monarchy as outworks of the Church itself'.[12] And Gunn has identified within Anglican loyalism an influential and strong 'un-Whiggish' and indeed 'High

---

that whilst the Anglican Church gave the strongest support to the loyalist cause, other denominations also pledged their support. Scottish presbyteries, Methodists and even the official leaders of the older, more conservative dissenting churches around the country declared their loyalty: Dickinson, 'Popular conservatism', 112.

[7] See Hole, 'English sermons and tracts', 19–21
[8] Ibid. 32–3.
[9] Charles Hawtrey, *Various opinions of the philosophical reformers considered; particularly Pain's Rights of man*, 1792, in Claeys, *Political writings*, vi. 89–93. See also Revd David Scurlock, *Thoughts on the influence of religion on civil government*, 1792; John Erskine, *The fatal consequences, and the general sources of anarchy*, Edinburgh 1793; and Thomas Somerville, *Effects of the French Revolution*, Edinburgh 1793.
[10] [William Sewell], *A rejoinder to Mr Paine's pamphlet, entitled, Rights of man*, 1791, in Claeys, *Political writings*, v. 135.
[11] William Paley, *Reasons for contentment*, 1792, 20–1, as quoted in Clark, *English society*, 262.
[12] Clark, *English society*, 263.

Tory' element that invoked ideas with roots in the writings of the likes of Charles Leslie and Sir Robert Filmer. As well as preaching the doctrine of passive obedience and non-resistance, such loyalists inflated the royal prerogative, placing the monarchy in a position of supremacy over the Lords and Commons.[13] Thus many Anglican clergy were publishing pamphlets with a traditional conservative agenda that acted as a bulwark to conservative loyalism.[14]

Yet it was not just Anglican churchmen who were promoting this conservative loyalism. A number of loyalist laymen adopted the conservative political ideas of Anglican churchmen. Some of them were also committed Anglicans. Clark has claimed that Edmund Burke's achievement in his later works (including *Reflections*) was 'to give eloquent but unoriginal expression to a theoretical position largely devised by Anglican churchmen'.[15] John Reeves found himself on trial for sedition in 1796 for publishing a pamphlet in which he argued that the king could legitimately rule alone without parliament.[16] Hannah More was a particularly outspoken conservative, evangelical Anglican who promoted obedience and quiet acquiescence among the labouring poor in her pamphlets aimed at working people.[17] More became involved in both the luxury debates and in the French Revolution debate. Clearly Anglican ideas were absorbed into a wider conservative loyalism that defended the established Church and State alliance, the hereditary monarchy and aristocracy, the social order and private property. It is this conservative reactionary force that most historians have identified as the loyalism of the 1790s. This loyalism, they argue, developed over time into a more cogent conservative ideology and emerged in the next century as a new Tory Party.[18]

But this conservative loyalism is not the only loyalism to be found in the political writings of the 1790s. Nor was the Anglican Church the only Church to pledge its support to the loyalist cause. Other denominations, including the Scottish presbyteries, the Methodists and even the official leaders of the older, more conservative dissenting Churches around the country, also declared their loyalty.[19] The loyalism that is the focus of this book is that expressed in the mass of loyalist pamphlets published between 1791 and 1796, which incorporated representations of aristocracy. These pamphlets provide a broad view of loyalism and those who may loosely be

---

[13] Gunn, *Beyond liberty*, 174–184. See also Clark, *English society*, 247–64.
[14] It should be noted, however, that the majority of these religious works do not mention aristocracy and consequently the majority are excluded from this book, although a few which are relevant may be found amongst the footnotes.
[15] Clark, *English society*, 249.
[16] Gunn, *Beyond liberty*, 178.
[17] For a discussion of More's pamphlets see chapter 5 below.
[18] Dickinson, 'Popular conservatism', 103.
[19] Ibid. 112.

defined as loyalists, both individually and ideologically.[20] Taken as a whole they may be described as invoking an 'intellectual loyalism', which inevitably coincided with both 'organised loyalism' and the traditional 'Anglican loyalism'.

Certainly pamphlets were used as a means of disseminating the propaganda of organised loyalism, particularly during the years 1793–6.[21] Taken together they not only reveal strong elements of a traditional defence of the establishment but also a majority support for the constitution. That is not to say that the loyalist defence, as delineated in the pamphlets, amounted to a unified and coherent argument or that loyalism was one unitary movement. In particular one area of clear conflict within loyalism can be identified: between conservative Anglican loyalists, who promoted the Church above the constitution and the king above the Lords and Commons, and the more moderate Whiggish loyalists. The latter followed a Whig Lockeian tradition and focused on the state, defending a primarily secular, mixed and, crucially, balanced constitution. For them property-ownership was at the root of all political rights. As Jonathan Clark so succinctly put it, some historians have argued that the 'Glorious Revolution substituted the divine right of property owners for the divine right of kings, so that eighteenth-century England was, in a secular idiom, preoccupied with an oligarchic defence of property.'[22] For eighteenth-century England one can here substitute 'Whigs'. John Reeve's prosecution for seditious libel well illustrates this conflict within loyalism. Indeed the pamphlets suggest that, rather than one dominant conservative Anglican loyalism surviving until 1832, as Clark has suggested, loyalism was from the start a multifaceted movement, a number of 'loyalisms'.

In fact the loyalist pamphlets published in 1791–2 reveal a variety of often incoherent and incompatible views, which do not lend themselves to precise categorisation. A number of early loyalist pamphleteers expressed support for the French Revolution insofar as it represented the overthrow of French absolutism.[23] Many also concurred with limited reform of parliament, although generally not reform of the constitution itself, provided that such reform was carried out peacefully.[24] A couple even concurred with the

---

[20] In view of the loss of the loyalist addresses referred to by Dozier, the pamphlets also provide a valuable source of information about those who put pen to paper in defence of the *status quo*.
[21] For a full discussion of the propaganda aimed largely at the mass of the people see chapter 5 below.
[22] Clark, *English society*, 347–8
[23] For examples see [John Saint John], *A letter from a magistrate to Mr William Rose*, 1791, in Claeys, *Political writings*, v. 177, and Boothby, *Observations on the appeal*, 214, 254.
[24] For example see anon., *Considerations on Mr. Paine's pamphlet on the rights of man*, Edinburgh 1791, in Claeys, *Political writings*, v. 96; [Graham Jephson], *Letters to Thomas Payne: in answer to his late publication on the rights of man*, 1792, ibid. v. 368; Alexander Peter, *Strictures on the character and principles of Thomas Paine*, Portsmouth 1792, ibid. vi. 141; [D. Rivers],

abolition of the game laws.[25] Sir Brooke Boothby, for example, identified himself as neither a Painite nor a Burkite, but a Whig and expressed largely moderate views in his 1792 pamphlet[26] (which reflects a shift from his earlier more reformist response to Burke).[27] This book shows that John Bowles, identified by the majority of historians as a conservative, Anglican loyalist and placeholder who wrote many pamphlets for Pitt's administration,[28] also promoted in his pamphlets ideas more commonly associated with more moderate loyalists. Thus the loyalist movement, at its most theoretical and least propagandist as represented by the responses to Paine in 1791–2, displayed a broad spectrum of loyalists, incorporating not just conservatives but also those who may be classed as moderate loyalists and/or conservative Whigs. This diversity in loyalism is not surprising for, at this time of turmoil in France and early response in England, political allegiances were in flux and political ideas were evolving.

Taken together early loyalist pamphlets incorporated a number of interweaving themes and issues. There was also some overlap between what may be identified as political, social and religious tracts. Most important, however, they reveal new loyalist strategies of combining the old with the new. The loyalists defended the *status quo* and, particularly here the aristocracy, on traditional grounds, but also on new economic grounds. A two-fold loyalist model of society began to emerge in loyalist pamphlets during 1791–2. First the traditional, conservative loyalist version and second a new loyalist commercial model evolved.[29]

Cursory remarks on Paine's Rights of man, 1792, ibid. vi. 134; anon., *A whipper for levelling Tommy*, 1793, ibid. vi. 403–4; and anon., *An humble address to the most high, most mighty, and most puissant the sovereign people*, 1793, 29.

[25] See [Green], *Slight observations*, 221; Hunt, *Rights of Englishmen*, 72.
[26] Boothby, *Observations on the appeal*, 178–9.
[27] Boothby's earlier pamphlet, *A letter to the Rt. Hon. Edmund Burke*, is discussed in chapter 1 above.
[28] For example Gunn, *Beyond liberty*, 176. Emma Vincent states that he was paid £100 by the Treasury for his efforts: 'John Bowles and the French revolutionary wars, 1792–1802', *History* lxxviii (1993), 394–420.
[29] In order to gain a full sense of the unfolding of the French Revolution debate, this chapter focuses predominantly upon the loyalist responses to Paine published between 1791–2. As direct responses to Paine, these pamphlets reflect the interactive nature of the debate and form an important sector of pamphlets in their own right. Moreover, although *Rights of man, part 1* was first published in 1791, *part 2* was not published until February 1792. Consequently, in order to review fully the responses to Paine, it was deemed appropriate to include here those published in 1793. This does result in a slight time over-lap with chapter 5, which commences in 1793. Chapter 5 does not, however, focus on responses to Paine, but upon loyalism generally. Moreover, although many loyalist pamphlets, which were not direct responses to Paine, were published during the period 1791–2, only a few of these have been included here. One reason for this is the sheer volume of pamphlets, which necessitated a process of selection. Another reason is that the loyalist pamphlets of 1791–2 include many which were aimed at the 'people' and such pamphlets are discussed in chapter 5.

A new model of society

The radical attack left early loyalists with something of a problem in terms of their defence of the *status quo* in England. Politically they must defend and preserve intact the English constitution and its established mixed government, with its concomitant social order. Yet Paine and his radical followers, and indeed even Burke to some degree, had represented England as an *ancien régime* with the obvious links to France before the revolution such a definition would reflect. Radicals had also promoted England on the Painite, French model of society, consisting of an aristocracy and people. In order to attract the much-needed support of the people it was clearly necessary for loyalism to move away from such radical representations of England.

Furthermore, crucial to this problem was the aristocracy, necessary to government and the control and order of society, yet increasingly a central focus of condemnation by radicals. One loyalist identified 'the order of Nobility and the honors and privileges of the House of Lords' as the 'principal object of the spleen and malice of the levellers,[30] from the fifth monarchy-men[31] down to the reformers of the present day'.[32] Paine had warned that the days of aristocratic hegemony in England were numbered. The swift demise of the French order of aristocracy served only to endorse this claim. Loyalist representations of aristocracy were considered crucial to its survival and also to the very survival of the constitution itself. Consequently some loyalists clearly recognised that they could not reproduce a Burkean defence of an ancient and established aristocracy, because Paine had represented that aristocracy as the despotic oligarchy of an *ancien régime*. Worse, Paine had compared the English aristocracy to its French counterpart.

It appears that, in order to resolve these problems, some loyalists began to develop and to promote a different model of English society and concomitant representations of aristocracy. Many loyalists rejected both Burke and Paine as out of date. Paine was as old-fashioned as Burke, for his 'levelling principles' were 'not of a very modern date' and a number of loyalists categorised him with Wat Tyler, Jack Straw and the seventeenth-century levellers.[33] Not only did some early loyalists reject Burke's representations of an *ancien régime* England, but they also rejected his corresponding aristocratic language.[34] Nor were links with chivalric ideals and the 'medieval' generally made by loyal-

---

[30] For the levellers in the 1640s see G. E. Aylmer (ed.), *The Levellers in the English Revolution*, London 1975.
[31] The reference to the 'fifth monarchy-men' indicated an interesting awareness of the mid seventeenth-century millenarian radicals, for whom see B. Capp, *The fifth monarchy men: a study in seventeenth-century English millenarianism*, London 1972.
[32] Anon., *Defence of the constitution*, 11.
[33] [Rivers], *Cursory remarks*, 131–2.
[34] [Thomas Hearn], *A short view of the rise and progress of freedom in modern Europe . . . in answer to the calumnies of Thomas Paine*, 1792, in Claeys, *Political writings*, vi. 322, 341–2; Boothby, *Observations on the appeal*, 261.

ists.³⁵ This rejection of Burke's depiction of an *ancien régime* England and his language already suggests a modernising element within loyalism. Loyalists also began to invoke a more complex social model. Hence the discussion that follows challenges the view commonly held by historians, that society was represented by loyalists as simply polarised between patrician peers and rebellious plebs.³⁶

Loyalist representations in the 1790s suggest that they did not, all or entirely, defend the aristocracy in conservative terms or within the *ancien régime* paradigm of aristocracy and people. Instead a number of loyalists invoked the well-established Whig identification of England as an imperial, commercial and prosperous state, and developed a new model of England on that basis.³⁷ Loyalists represented this commercial model as spawning a multi-layered, gradated society with an open elite. In reality for loyalists this model was firmly rooted in the existing frameworks of the established constitution and government, so dramatically defended by Burke. At this stage loyalism mixed the old with the new. The development and success of this new loyalist commercial model has not been fully explored by historians. Claeys and Dickinson did note that loyalists promoted a commercial and opulent England, but neither of them then explored how this model developed new dimensions or how it affected representations of aristocracy.³⁸ Indeed Dickinson also argued that the 'conservative theorists' were in favour of an aristocracy based on birth and fortune dominating politics.³⁹ The new loyalist commercial model and its accompanying representations of aristocracy are central to this study. The loyalist respondents to Paine, the subject of this chapter, were in the vanguard of the process.

The English constitution

The mixed constitution, always promoted by Whigs as the source of England's greatness, was of crucial importance to the loyalists' argument. Most loyalists did not in their pamphlets follow the more conservative Anglican churchmen and promote royal supremacy. Quite the contrary, the majority was at pains to stress the importance of the balance within the mixed constitution. The English constitution was also important now as a means to differentiate England from France. Unlike republics that were at a

---

35 For example anon., *Remarks on Mr Paine's pamphlet*, 1791, in Claeys, *Political writings*, v. 50.
36 See Wahrman, *Imagining the middle class*, 32. 86.
37 See Pocock on Whig social theory in Burke (ed. Pocock), *Reflections*, pp. xvii–xx.
38 Claeys, 'French Revolution', 59–80. See also his *Thomas Paine*, 153–6, and Dickinson, *Liberty and property*, 273.
39 Dickinson, *Liberty and property*, 316. See also Schofield, 'Conservative political thought', 620.

primitive stage of civilisation, England, it was claimed, had reached the pinnacle, or pretty near it. The majority of loyalists represented England as a leading, commercial empire. Alexander Peter declared that, 'The vast extension of commerce possessed by this favourite island, furnishes resources which would astonish the wisest of our progenitors.'[40] The 'nation' had 'carried the arts and sciences, mechanical as well as liberal to a very high pitch of perfection'.[41] Cusack Smith confirmed that, 'The progress from savage life to citizenship is through a long course of gradual civilization', it is now completed and 'we behold perfect civilization'.[42]

This prosperity and modernity was, the loyalists proposed, largely due to the English constitution. Frederick Hervey observed that it was by 'preserving the forms and principles of our constitution' and the security it provided that 'makes the riches and luxuries of the earth flow through the hands' of English merchants' and rendered England a rival to 'the greatest empires'.[43] One anonymous pamphleteer described the English constitution as 'an historical painting of prodigious beauty and magnitude, executed by the most eminent masters, in which the progress of civilization from the date of the Magna Charta to that of the Bill of Rights may be seen at one view'.[44] The constitution had produced 'this vast and wonderful assemblage of laws, manners and customs on which the whole fabric of society has been constructed and happily been brought to perfection'.[45] Indeed, Boothby declared, 'Commerce and arts and industry and riches and population are invariable signs of good government.'[46] For John Bowles government was 'the only source of all protection and all security, and alone enables us to enjoy the gifts of fortune and the fruits of industry . . . it protects the labours of the husbandman, and defends the harvest and the vineyard from rapine and degradation'.[47]

Moreover it was the freedom, the liberty allowed to the English people under the constitution that engendered such universal prosperity. John Jones asserted: 'We enjoy all the advantages of an extensive and well regulated liberty, and founded upon that liberty, a national prosperity that has no example in the world.'[48] England, loyalists confirmed, was prosperous and her

---

[40] Peter, *Strictures on the character*, 140.
[41] Anon., *A rod in brine: or, a tickler for Tom Paine, in answer to his first pamphlet, entitled the Rights of man*, Canterbury 1792, in Claeys, *Political writings*, vi. 25.
[42] [William Cusack Smith], *Rights of citizens: being an examination of Mr Paine's principles, touching government*, Dublin 1791, in Claeys, *Political writings*, v. 286.
[43] [Hervey], *Answer to the second part*, 384.
[44] Anon., *Rod in brine*, 159.
[45] Anon., *Letter to Mr Paine*, vi. 159.
[46] Boothby, *Observations on the appeal*, 270.
[47] [John Bowles], *A protest against T. Paine's 'Rights of man'*, 5th edn 1792, in Claeys, *Political writings*, vi. 49.
[48] [John Jones], *The reason of man: with strictures on Rights of man, and others of Mr Paine's works*, Canterbury 1792, in Claeys, *Political writings*, v. 406.

prosperity was due to 'the goodness of our constitution'. It was not just the elite who benefited from such prosperity but all those who worked for their living including the labourer, the mechanic and the merchant.[49] Indeed John Gifford argued that in no other European country 'is the *soldier* so well paid, or possessed of so many privileges . . . are the *poor* so amply provided for . . . are the people, less burthened with taxes!'.[50]

Consequently England did not need a change of government. Many loyalists applied the proverb 'the proof of the pudding is in the eating' and George Mason asked 'if we really enjoy the comforts of civilization under our present political establishment, shall we idly look for them in the reveries of maniacs?'.[51] The message was clear: prosperity was shared by all, or almost all, in England. As Claeys has noted, vindicating the country's 'opulence became the focus of loyalist exertions'.[52] One loyalist declared: 'We have a government to defend and a prosperity to maintain – unequalled and unexampled in the annals of history.'[53] In England, a broadside proclaimed, 'Each enjoy'd his faith, his hearth, his work, his art, his wealth, his farm.'[54]

Not surprisingly many loyalists emphasised the essential political role of the aristocracy in the English constitution. In England the rank of aristocracy was emphatically not, as Paine had represented it, 'a frivolous exterior distinction'.[55] Nor was it, as radicals claimed, an aristocratic oligarchy. Aristocracy was an essential part, but only part, of government and England undoubtedly had the best form of government in the world. This mixed government required 'not only a gradation of rank, but also an intermediate legislative order' between monarch and commons, which was 'rendered thereby the natural guardians of both, and an insuperable barrier against the encroachments of either'.[56] Government with 'an overgrown power of aristocracy' was not only unacceptable but also it was now unthinkable in England.[57] And here again loyalists were promoting the essentially Whig concept of the balanced constitution.

Most interestingly, however, many loyalists argued that history showed that it was republics which sank into 'Aristocratic, or into Despotic Governments'.[58] It was, Boothby declared, republics, such as America, which must

---

49 Anon., *Letters to Thomas Paine: in answer to his late publication on the rights of man*, 1791, 81.
50 [Gifford], *Plain address*, 49.
51 [George Mason], *A British freeholder's address to his countrymen, on Thomas Paine's Rights of man*, 1791, in Claeys, *Political writings*, v. 10.
52 Claeys, 'French Revolution', 75.
53 [Jones], *Reason of man*, 410.
54 Anon., *Tom the bodice maker*, c. 1792, in *Political broadsides*, fo. 42.
55 [Bowles], *Protest*, 56.
56 Ibid.
57 Anon., *The interests of man in opposition to the rights of man*, Edinburgh 1793, 41.
58 James Brown, *The importance of preserving unviolated the system of government in every state . . . to which is added an appendix containing some strictures on the writings of Mr. Paine*, 1793, 58.

inevitably 'become an aristocracy like that of Holland' and to 'compare the constitutional nobility of England with these little tyrants' was wicked.[59] Loyalists argued that republics could only function in primitive states, for once commerce and industry were introduced, luxury would soon follow and, without the restraining effect of a mixed government, an aristocracy would inevitably develop.[60] The loyalists' point, then, was that an 'aristocracy' would arise only in states that did not have a mixed government, for mixed governments ensured that aristocracy both maintained the balance and was kept within check.

Although to loyalists history confirmed the existence and legitimacy of the constitution that Paine had denied, most did not dwell unduly on the past. Loyalists did not generally share Burke's reverence for a feudal past.[61] In fact many of them discarded the outward symbols of the old, whilst retaining the tenets upon which they were based. Feudalism was no longer necessary to the aristocracy, an anonymous pamphleteer declared, for although 'VAS-SALAGE has long since CEASED in England ... the NOBILITY still continue in respect and esteem.'[62] Nevertheless patronage and paternalism were still of importance. For, this pamphleteer continued, whilst masters claim 'a kind of property ... in their servants and apprentices', the 'obedience, and submission of these is fully repaid by the instruction, protection, and support afforded them'.[63] Moreover, as Boothby put it, the fact that 'the feudal nobility' had enjoyed 'territorial jurisdiction ... privileges and immunities', which were inconceivable in civil society, did not mean that 'in great rich commercial extensive empires, *the optimates, the better sort*, are to be excluded from a fair determined share in the government, such as their weight and interest and consequence entitles them to expect and demand, and which their influence ... will always enable them to acquire'.[64]

Defence of the aristocracy

Faced with the radical attack, loyalists clearly saw the need to defend the English aristocracy on both traditional and new terms during 1791–2. The picture, presented by radicals, of an idle, parasitic elite similar to the French aristocracy was swept away by loyalist propaganda. French aristocrats were compared unfavourably with their English counterparts. The English were promoted as leaders of an open elite, with an important constitutional role

---

[59] Boothby, *Observations on the appeal*, 283, 237.
[60] Anon., *Interests of man*, 48.
[61] William Lewelyn, *An appeal to men against Paine's Rights of man*, 1793, 39; anon., *Interests of man*, 40.
[62] Anon., *Rod in brine*, 15.
[63] Ibid.
[64] Boothby, *Observations on the appeal*, 234–5.

and with no legal privileges. As Green said, whilst 'the French Noblesse were ignorant, proud and tyrannical . . . we order the matter better in England', indeed, 'our *aristocracies* have . . . the best chance of being the best men in the nation'.[65] Hearn declared that *ancien régime* France was 'marked with profusion and licentiousness' in which the nobility were allowed to 'plunder the lower order' and thus the state sunk towards disaster. He went on to stress that, in England, 'A duke or lord has very little influence more than other private gentleman of equal fortune'.[66] Unlike the French aristocracy, the English 'are vested with no privilege superior to the other orders of citizens'.[67] Indeed, English peers were subject to the law: 'Persons of the highest rank are equally amenable to justice, for their transgressions, with the lowest among us . . . some of our Peers, even in the memory of many, have DIED for rape or murder, BY THE HALTER, and others suffered by the HATCHET for treason and rebellion'.[68]

Nor was the English aristocracy, as Paine suggested, effeminate and feeble. It was instead manly and purposeful. Indeed its members were renowned for their willingness to 'box with a porter, ride races with a professed jockey, and perform a thousand feats of vigour and activity, to the full as well as the most athletic ragamuffin'.[69] The message was clear. England did not have an aristocracy like the French and, thus, it did not need a revolution like the French Revolution.[70]

The hereditary nature of aristocracy was also defended on grounds both old and new. A hereditary aristocracy was essential to the constitution and defended by loyalists on traditional grounds of independence. As Green argued, it was to the '*hereditary*' nature of the House of Lords that 'peers owe their independence, which if they had not they might be influenced by the monarch or the people'.[71] An anonymous pamphleteer confirmed that the 'House of Peers is indeed hereditary; complete independence both of the king and representatives of the people, being deemed necessary for the more effectual exercise of their power of controul'.[72] The 'hereditary nobility', he continued, is 'the great bulwark against all infringements of our rights'.[73] And

---

65 [Green], *Slight observations*, 227.
66 [Hearn], *Short view*, 328, 366.
67 Anon., *Considerations on Mr. Paine's pamphlet*, 85–7.
68 Anon., *Rod in brine*, 15.
69 [Green], *Slight observations*, 229.
70 It should not be forgotten that many French aristocrats, who were the victims of the Revolution, sought asylum in Britain and had connections with the English aristocracy. It is not surprising, therefore, that not all loyalists represented the French unfavourably. Indeed, one pamphleteer suggested that the French aristocracy were 'brave, full of sentiments of honour, benevolent, and polite, especially to strangers': anon., *Defence of the rights of man; being a discussion of the conclusions drawn from those rights by Mr Paine*, 1791, in Claeys, *Political writings*, v. 293.
71 [Green], *Slight observations*, 227–8.
72 Anon., *Considerations on Mr Paine's pamphlet*, 86–7.
73 [Hervey, Frederick], *A new friend on an old subject*, 1791, in Claeys, *Political Writings*, v. 71.

Saint John, clearly disassociating himself from the traditional high Tory position, declared that 'Hereditary Right is the law of the land, and the peace and security of the people depends on it . . . *indefeasible and divine Hereditary* Right is, quite another thing, and cannot be too strongly resisted.'[74]

Hereditary aristocracy was also defended by loyalists on the broader, more egalitarian issue of general laws of inheritance. All individuals, it was argued, had the right to bequeath their property to whom they pleased in civilised societies and the same rules applied to the rank of aristocracy.[75] Saint John stated that any nation had the right to maintain 'an hereditary House of Lords if it so pleases', on the grounds that 'men in all countries have still too much regard for their property and too much affection for their children, not to be desirous of transmitting it to them'.[76] And Hervey warned that the 'destruction of hereditary honors . . . would lead to the subversion of every species of inheritance. Wealth is not more strictly property than rank, and it is only hereditary upon the same principles'.[77] Such representations suggested that the aristocracy was not a separate class defined by special privileges but part of a homogeneous society where rights were defined by laws shared by all.

Some loyalists also argued that primogeniture was practised out of economic expediency in a commercial England, rather than to bolster aristocratic hegemony. Primogeniture ensured that large estates remained viable economic units and should not, therefore, be abolished as radicals claimed. At the same time loyalists asserted that primogeniture also benefited younger siblings by forcing them into commerce and industry where many made fortunes as great as, or greater than, their elder brothers. Indeed in England 'the younger branches of the family are rarely left destitute', for 'the quantum of personal estates in all countries where commerce and trade make a part of the national occupation, exceeds in an infinite degree the value of the *landed* property'.[78] Such younger sons should not be pitied for 'they commonly arrive, by honourable and worthy means, at the end of their pursuits and enjoy with credit what they have obtained by perseverance'.[79] Here again the old and new were comfortably united in loyalists' representations.

Corruption in government was identified by a number of loyalists as an inevitable side effect of England's progressive and advanced civilisation. An anonymous pamphleteer declared that 'corruption and venality . . . pervades all ranks of men, in an advanced state of society'.[80] Although radicals had

---

[74] [Saint John], *Letter from a magistrate*, 230.
[75] Charles Harrington Elliot, *The republican refuted: in a series of biographical, critical and political strictures on Thomas Paine's Rights of man*, 1791, in Claeys, *Political writings*, v. 351.
[76] [Saint John], *Letter from a magistrate*, 187.
[77] [Hervey], *New friend*, 74.
[78] [Saint John], *Letter from a magistrate*, 225–6.
[79] [Jephson], *Letters to Thomas Payne*, 373.
[80] Anon., *Interests of man*, 69.

firmly identified aristocracy as the major proponents and beneficiaries of corruption, it was generally agreed by loyalists that 'no such corruption is to be now imputed either to our ministers or the members of the legislative bodies', as in 'former periods'.[81] One loyalist went so far as to declare that 'the robes of the nobility of England have never yet blushed at the imputation of corruption'.[82] However, a more common view was expressed by Frederick Hervey: 'though amongst our nobility there have been very profligate and worthless individuals, yet, as a branch of the legislature, they have ever merited our affection and respect'.[83] To many loyalists it was the House of Commons, rather than the upper house, which was the source of corruption.[84] Moreover influence, the very source of corruption according to radicals, was still deemed by loyalists a necessary system in government. As John Saint John commented, 'I am no advocate for a slavish and mercenary House of Commons, but I am ready to profess myself a friend to influence.' For, he argued, influence 'is and ought to be the principal instrument in the carrying on a free government' and he distinguished between 'clandestine bribery and the public acceptance of beneficial employments'.[85]

Thus, as the debate developed in 1791–2, the loyalists' representations extracted the aristocracy from the *ancien régime* environment in which, for different reasons, both Burke and Paine had placed it. Instead loyalists located it in a modern, prosperous world, governed under the admirable English constitution, where the old was compatibly bound up with the new.

Aristocratic leadership

The issue of leadership so crucial to the loyalist argument, although often raised, has not been fully explored by historians within the context of this debate. On the question of leadership many loyalists recognised that it was no longer appropriate to seek justification for the pre-eminence of the aristocracy in a Burkean gothic past. Despite the fact that loyalist pamphleteers had defended the role of the hereditary aristocracy in government, when it came to the question of its suitability for political leadership, many loyalists shifted the emphasis away from issues of birth and blood.[86] An anonymous pamphle-

---

81 Anon., *Considerations on Mr Paine's pamphlet*, 101.
82 Anon., *Remarks on Mr Paine's pamphlet*, 54.
83 [Hervey], *New friend*, 74.
84 See, for example, anon., *A few minutes advice to the people of Great Britain on republics*, 1792, 11; anon., *Constitutional letters, in answer to Mr Paine's Rights of man*, 1792, in Claeys, *Political writings*, vi. 143.
85 [Saint John], *Letter from a magistrate*, 196–7.
86 Concern was expressed from time to time, however, that the nobility would be weakened by infiltration from below: anon., *Defence of the constitution*, 13. Here a fear is expressed that 'contamination of the blood' as a result of 'improper marriages and alliances', would effect the nobility for generations.

teer claimed that 'the distinction of birth' in the English government 'is extremely feeble' and 'much inferior to what is paid to riches'.[87]

Indeed loyalists snapped up the radical issue of qualification for leadership. The loyalists were clear: those who constituted the political elite were also the best qualified.[88] Boothby declared that 'no public assembly has preserved a higher character for wisdom and integrity than the House of Peers'.[89] The leadership was compared with that of republics, which were invariably led by 'artful and ambitious men' with no credentials and with 'spirits more ardent, more vain, more daring, and more cunning than the rest'.[90] 'In republics the best and ablest citizens do not obtain the highest offices but are ignored or banished by the unreliable multitude.'[91] One pamphleteer suggested that republics such as America would inevitably eventually 'fall victim of ambition' and so: 'be happy to submit to an Hereditary Magistrate restrained by law, rather than to an equal, elevated perhaps by the chance of the moment, who in his exalted situation must ever retain the passions and prejudices of a private citizen'.[92] The suggestion here was that the aristocracy had developed a disinterested, public *persona*, an ability to keep its private interest out of public office.

Loyalists defended aristocratic leadership in England on two main grounds which, they suggested, were inextricably linked. First, the traditional role of the aristocracy as property-owners with a stake in society was invoked. Land had long been identified by both Whigs and Tories as the vital stabilising force in British politics and society. And the aristocracy, as the hereditary owners of great estates, were still seen as the bulwark against other more unstable and insecure forms of property. Within the debate Burke had led the way with his promotion in *Reflections* of the political status of land. For him it provided both a defence of aristocracy and a safeguard against unstable commercial politics of the kind in play in France. Indeed it was largely the radicals' apparent desire to follow France and dismantle the long-established link between property-ownership and political rights that had provoked the decline in support in parliament for the reforming Foxite Whigs.[93] Second, loyalists represented the aristocracy as promoters of industry, commerce and general prosperity in accordance with the new commercial model of society.

Hervey argued that there were 'two sets of men in society who have a great and natural influence over its inferior classes. These are the landholder and

---

[87] Anon., *Considerations on Mr. Paine's pamphlet*, 99.
[88] See on this Dickinson, *Liberty and property*, 316.
[89] Boothby, *Observations on the appeal*, 232.
[90] Anon., *Few minutes*, 15.
[91] Anon., *Interests of man*, 22.
[92] Anon., *A letter to a friend in the country: wherein Mr Paine's letter to Mr Dundas is particularly considered*, 1792, 15–16.
[93] The influence of the Foxite Whigs in Parliament declined during the early 1790s as opposition to radicalism, and by implication, any reform of government, grew: Turner, *British politics*, 61–70

the merchant'.⁹⁴ Yet he took a conservative stance on this issue and voiced concern that 'the merchant, the monied man, the stockholder . . . may all have temporary interests widely different from the rest of the nation'. Land was still the greatest source of prosperity and security and, Hervey continued, the House of Lords 'is, perhaps, the only set of individuals in the kingdom, who must always forward the interests of the country, by pursuing their own'. For the 'interests of the landlord' are 'always in unison with the interests of the country'.⁹⁵ Green confirmed that the House of Lords should be entrusted with legislative powers because 'of the immense *interest* they have in the community – because the stake they hold in the fund of national property, is equal in value to a fifth of the whole stock of the kingdom'.⁹⁶ Similarly an anonymous pamphleteer stated that of course 'the people of property in every country must be the governors'.⁹⁷

Correspondingly the loyalists largely defended England politically on the established propertied and property-less model. However, unlike Paine's model of aristocracy and people, this model inevitably reflected a gradated society which incorporated a broad spectrum of the populace who as 'forty-shilling freeholders' qualified for the franchise. Political rights were firmly linked to property ownership for the majority of loyalists. Political assemblies should be composed of those who own property for '*property alone is capable of representation*'.⁹⁸ Elliot, invoking a common loyalist view, stated that those without property were more susceptible to corruption and bribery and were therefore '*not as eligible* to a place of trust as the man who has a property at stake'.⁹⁹ Most loyalists agreed that only those with an 'interest' in society as a 'fixed householder, or a proprietor of land', should have the franchise.¹⁰⁰ The moderate Isaac Hunt argued that England should 'afford an opportunity to the middle class and all who acquire property by their industry, to become voters'.¹⁰¹ Clearly then the belief in the essential link between property and political rights was one that united loyalists, both conservative and moderate. Radical demands for universal political rights unconnected to property ownership, some specifically for male suffrage, served only to entrench such loyalist beliefs. The pamphlets reveal that this debate about the political meanings of land bolstered loyalist support for the owners of great estates, the aristocracy. But it also linked the aristocracy more

---

94 [Hervey], Answer to the second part, 397.
95 Ibid. 390.
96 [Green], Slight observations, 229.
97 Anon, Candid inquiry, 19, 136–7.
98 Ibid. 133. See also Tobias Molloy, An appeal from man in a state of civil society to man in a state of nature, . . . and strictures on Mr. Paine's Rights of man, Dublin 1792, 255.
99 Elliot, Republican refuted, 359.
100 Anon., Defence of the constitution, 14. Indeed, he claimed that the rest of society was 'destined to servility, as vagabonds, and unfit to be ranked among citizens'.
101 Hunt, Rights of Englishmen, 70.

closely with other landowning sectors of society, particularly the gentry, on the propertied and property-less model.

Some loyalists also identified landed property as the very source of commerce and industry. As one anonymous pamphleteer commented, 'the great object of society is the preservation of property', for 'the strongest inducements to the acquisition of wealth, and the cultivation of talents are held out by annexing the right of power to property alone'.[102] Indeed 'All power emanates from *landed* property, it is the parent of all property ... The landed proprietor, however, if he is wise, will encourage trade, arts, manufactures, commerce' and 'give a *permanent residence* to these'.[103] Another anonymous pamphleteer proposed that the 'House of Lords is the most respectable and the most honourable' and 'To prove that it enlivens ambition, and stimulates industry is to prove that fire warms, or the sun shines.'[104] The 'existence of such a rank in the State', Bowles observed, 'is conducive to the promotion of a spirit of virtuous enterprise and honourable emulation'.[105] Thus again loyalists suggested that the old was the source of the new. The pre-eminence of landed property was justified because it was the life spring to commerce and industry and the source of the wealth and talents necessary to leadership.

Furthermore, in direct contradiction to radical claims, many loyalists argued that the aristocracy had earned its supremacy through a mixed bag of talents and qualifications, with the emphasis on education. It is the emphasis on aristocratic supremacy being directly connected to merit, but also to commerce, that places the developing loyalist argument in a different paradigm from the traditional defence of supremacy through hereditary rights and land ownership. Loyalists suggested that those who 'possess a splendid independence' had earned it 'by their industry, bravery or their talents'.[106] Indeed 'The possession of wealth, of abilities, or reputation' were the 'means or motives of all public virtue' and the 'strongest springs of private industry and exertion'.[107] Peers, one pamphleteer confirmed, had 'ample means of education, a necessary qualification to render them compleat'. He continued, whilst 'it be urged that SOME of them be WEAK in intellect and not capable of improvement', it may be concluded that 'MANY, from the extraordinary advantages afforded them, will surpass other men'.[108] One Tobias Molloy went so far as to suggest that 'Positions of public trust and confidence' ought to be filled by those of '*superior abilities, splendid talents, or exemplary virtues*' and in the first civil societies it is likely that those who possessed such virtues

---

[102] Anon., *Humble address*, 17–8.
[103] Ibid. 15–16.
[104] Anon., *Defence of the constitution*, 12.
[105] [Bowles], *Protest*, 56.
[106] Anon., *Letter to Mr Paine*, 169.
[107] Anon., *Interests of man*, 21.
[108] Anon., *Rod in brine*, 14.

'resulting from age and long experience' would be singled out 'by the multitude. Hence the true origin of a natural aristocracy'.[109]

Hearn confirmed that it was the aristocracy who, above all others, tended to have the greatest qualifications. The aristocracy 'not only should be, but confessedly are from constitution, temper of mind, and habits of education, . . . more competent to the duties of government' than commoners. And other private citizens may become just as competent 'when the advantages of education are equal'.[110] An anonymous pamphleteer concurred that the 'people in general' recognised their own 'incapacity' for politics and government. Hence 'they naturally look up to the great proprietors of land, and to men of education and leisure, to take these provinces for themselves'.[111] Only those who had large estates and/or, great wealth, it was argued, would also have sufficient leisure to devote to 'those studies which will best qualify' them for government.[112] On a practical basis Richard Hey declared that 'Taylors, Masons, and Labouring Farmers' are as 'ill qualified' for making laws as 'Ministers of State are for making clothes, building houses and ploughing fields'.[113] Thus the existing social order was justified on the basis of qualifications.

The loyalists generally agreed with Paine that wisdom was not hereditary but they took the view that 'neither is idiotism'. A good and appropriate education was more often to be found amongst hereditary peers than among the 'lower persons' who were generally 'by education, less qualified for . . . office'.[114] Green confirmed 'we read in the books of the ancients, of hereditary virtue, an hereditary sense of honour' but this is now perceived as a 'false philosophy'.[115] And Saint John declared that 'all disputants admit that Peers are not born with peculiar talents for legislation, or great knowledge of an abstruse science', but their great property and circumstances 'renders it wise to invest them with a share in the legislature'.[116] Many agreed with Elliot that 'the advantages of education are generally in favour' of the nobility and 'Among two hundred and fifty men bred with all the didactic advantages of a refined nation, of whom twenty-six in particular are some of the most learned men in *Europe*, a wise and virtuous council may well be looked for.'[117]

However, the appropriate education and qualifications for leadership at the highest level were not, according to some loyalists, available to all. Although wisdom was not hereditary, it was 'education and habits trans-

---

109 Molloy, *Appeal from man*, 143.
110 [Hearn], *Short view*, 341.
111 Anon., *Defence of the constitution*, 22.
112 Anon., *Candid inquiry*, 136–7.
113 Richard Hey, *Happiness and rights: a dissertation upon several subjects relative to the rights of man and his happiness*, 1792, 32.
114 Elliot, *Republican refuted*, 350–1. See also anon., *Rod in brine*, 14.
115 [Green], *Slight observations*, 227.
116 [Saint John], *Letter from a magistrate*, 193.
117 Elliot, *Republican refuted*, 32.

mitted from generation to generation, and still more the culture and application to particular walks of life', which 'contribute most essentially to qualify men' for leadership.[118] Indeed Hunt declared that 'In point of wisdom' the aristocracy had the advantage for their 'more refined education, superior rank, and many other circumstances qualify them' better than others 'to legislate with knowledge, judgment, and prudence'.[119] Many believed that it was only those 'with the opportunity of leisure', who could develop 'the wisdom of a learned man'.[120] Lewelyn confirmed that wisdom was not so much due to 'natural parts and faculties, as a doctrine, a system acquired and learned scientifically and practically by suitable advantages ... A person thus properly bred in the seat of government, and educated for the purpose, will be wiser and abler to govern than one educated elsewhere with twice his natural parts'.[121] Thus loyalists suggested that only a very specific culture and education, which was primarily available to the aristocracy, prepared men suitably for the highest positions in government. Lewelyn concluded that it was a combination of 'advantages, and diligence', which 'makes men fit for the different offices of life'.[122]

As well as defending the supremacy of a hereditary aristocracy and its superior education and culture, the loyalists also represented the English aristocracy as an open elite and rejected suggestions that England had a specific class of leadership. The fact that the crown could, and did, make new peerages in England was highlighted by loyalists. Many loyalists promoted the aristocracy as primarily an open elite, playing down the existence of a hereditary element. In fact the pamphlet literature has revealed that those who championed an open elite during 1791–2 were not, with a few exceptions, the pamphleteers who specifically promoted a hereditary aristocracy.[123] This reinforces the argument for defining loyalism not as one united movement but as a number of divergent but connecting groups.

The moderate Whig Sir Brooke Boothby asserted that 'The house of peers is not a *separate class of citizens*, but a legislative judicial senate ... instituted for the *public utility*; to which all ranks are equally admissible.'[124] England had an open elite that included anyone who through industry and talents had risen to a position of power. An anonymous pamphleteer confirmed that 'The highest and the proudest situations in the state are within the reach of talents and industry.' By 'the creation of new titles ... the chief magistrate is enabled to reward the performers of eminent services to the state by advancing them

---

[118] Anon., *Rights upon rights with observations upon observations*, 1791, 107.
[119] Hunt, *Rights of Englishmen*, 45.
[120] [Saint John], *Letter from a magistrate*, 188.
[121] Lewelyn, *Appeal to men*, 83.
[122] Ibid.
[123] But, as mentioned above, it is not always possible to ascertain from the pamphlets the precise political inclinations of those who may generally be classified as loyalists.
[124] Boothby, *Observations on the appeal*, 235.

to its first honours, and that order of merit cannot be very offensive in any country which is always within the attainment of talents and exertion'.[125] And another stated that 'the *great* in talents, industry, and consequently in wealth will always be *great* in powers'.[126] Under their 'glorious constitution' Englishmen benefited from 'political equality', and under the law 'no monopoly of rank or power is authorized; the road to wealth and honours is open to every man; the means of elevation are infinite: industry, application, genius, either separate or combined, can raise men from the lowest to the highest stations in life'.[127]

'As the road to the peerage is open to all it may be attained, and is attained, by all ranks.'[128] Indeed Isaac Hunt was one loyalist who, in the same pamphlet, noted the superior education and advantages of the aristocracy and promoted an open elite. In other countries, Hunt argued, 'all lucrative appointments, all the posts of honour and profit are confined only to men of birth and fortune' but 'No merit is here excluded from its proper recompence . . . no parentage or condition, however humble are here neglected.' In fact 'every person, however low his station or his origin . . . may aspire and arrive at the first honours and emoluments of his calling or profession'. 'The nobility', Hunt concluded, are the 'pillars, which are reared from among the people'.[129] For the more moderate loyalists, then, England had an open elite, which provided opportunities to a far greater sector of society than the reality of new peerage creations suggested.[130]

The rationale for titles and glamour

It was the awarding of titles in England, some loyalists claimed, that had created this open elite. The nobility consisted 'chiefly of men taken from the commons as the merited reward bestowed by the country for services themselves or their fathers have performed by sea or by land, in law or in trade'. Titles were therefore 'rewards which the lowest may hope for and enjoy, as the lowest have obtained them by ability and diligence'.[131] In England, a pamphleteer declared, the king 'is enabled to reward the performers of eminent services to the state, by advancing them to its first honours, and that order of merit . . . is always within the attainment of talents and exertion'. He later added, however, that 'by ascertained and well constituted gradation of

---

125 Anon., *Remarks on Mr Paine's pamphlet*, 40, 52.
126 Anon., *Letters to a friend*, 4.
127 Gifford, *Plain address*, 48. It should be noted that Gunn identifies 'Gifford' (a pseudonym of James Richard Green) as one of the later group of 'High Tories' who edited the *Anti-Jacobin Review and Magazine: Beyond liberty*, 176.
128 Anon., *Considerations on Mr. Paine's pamphlet*, 96.
129 Hunt, *Rights of Englishmen*, 59, 79.
130 Cannon, *Aristocratic century*, 21–3.
131 Anon., *Few minutes advice*, 10.

rank, the limits of ambition are pointed out'.[132] English titles were differentiated from those of the French nobility, which were entirely honours for birth and blood. The 'old feudal names of Duke and Baron' may still be utilised but only because they had 'ancient custom and popular opinion in their favour' and were as good as any other.[133] Ultimately, another added, 'The institution of honours has for its object, to provoke and remunerate exertion'; it gives 'encouragement to virtue, dignity to worth, adds the idea of great to good, and makes that splendid which was useful'.[134]

Titles were also represented as valuable because they provided something to aspire to and excited in others 'a laudable ambition'.[135] Titles ensured that 'the proud monuments of a long and illustrious nobility' provided a 'record of what is great, and the stimulant to what is good'.[136] One pamphleteer declared that 'some among us, men of understanding too . . . do not look upon titles as altogether so *puny and senseless*' and 'Not a few indeed . . . would gladly lay hold of a title, was it within his reach.'[137] A number of loyalists made the point that titles denoted an important role in government and the law. Like that of 'a Justice of the Peace, or a Constable', all 'titles imply the office of a Judge in the Supreme Court of Judicature, as well as a Member . . . in Parliament'.[138] Boothby observed that 'When we speak of a peer of the realm, or a lord of parliament, we . . . associate with it the idea of office and character just as much as when we speak of a judge or a general.'[139] Thus a number of what appear to have been more moderate loyalists suggested that titles in England represented anything but merely hereditary position.

Similarly show and display, that other glitter and dazzle of aristocracy, were represented as necessary assertions of legitimate pre-eminence in government and, like titles, a mark of office. John Bowles argued that the people could see that 'the pomp and splendour annexed to the rank of English Nobility, are but appendages to a high situation, and to important public duties both of the legislative and judicial kind'.[140] Show and display fulfilled a civic function. They ensured that the people looked up to those in government and the judiciary with 'some degree of reverence and awe' and were not 'dazzled' by any interlopers.[141] They were also necessary as a replacement for prerogatives and privileges no longer held by those in power. Boothby stated that the king was clothed in 'all the attributes and distinctions of personal dignity that can

---

[132] Anon., *Remarks on Mr Paine's pamphlet*, 52.
[133] Boothby, *Observations on the appeal*, 236.
[134] Anon., *Remarks on Mr Paine's pamphlet*, 49–51.
[135] Hunt, *Rights of Englishmen*, 77.
[136] Anon., *Remarks on Mr Paine's pamphlet*, 49–51.
[137] Anon., *Rod in brine*, 12.
[138] [Jephson], *Letters to Thomas Payne*, 366, 372.
[139] Boothby, *Observations on the appeal*, 235.
[140] [Bowles], *Protest*, 56. Wahrman describes Bowles as 'a place-holding magistrate and one of the most prominent anti-Painite pamphleteers': *Imagining the middle class*, 84.
[141] Anon., *Interests of man*, 51–2.

create respect and veneration; to supply the want of coercive powers by the influence of opinion' and 'these marks of reverence and submission have been carefully preserved . . . as necessary substitutes for the real prerogative which they took away'.[142]

Moreover, and more important, some loyalists stressed that a legitimate civil list paid for the genuine services of judges, admirals, diplomats and other public servants and 'these appointments are in general far from exorbitant'.[143] Paine's accusations that public money was being squandered and siphoned into the pockets of the aristocracy were dismissed by loyalists. It was not the case that 'the greater part of the revenue of this country is spent on idle profusion'.[144] Loyalists suggested that fair payment was made for legitimate employment. In reality it was predominantly the aristocracy and their families and connections who took up such offices and were awarded with titles. But loyalists represented that such office-holders were being rewarded for their qualifications and industry rather than for their pre-eminence in society through birth.

Thus by accepting the issue of qualifications and promoting the aristocracy primarily as a meritocracy, some loyalists defended the aristocracy on radical terms. They adopted the radical criteria, in whole or in part, for an acceptable elite and applied it to the present aristocracy. Many loyalists represented the meritocracy so desired by radicals as the reality in England. In fact, in common with Burke, the loyalists were defending the establishment, but in such a way as to denote a change in the criteria for leadership. And it was their representations that counted in the French Revolution debate. Thus, and this is a crucial point, loyalist representations taken as a whole masked continuity with the suggestion of change.

Defining 'true' equality

Two social issues were particularly relevant to the loyalist defence, inequality and the multi-strata structure of society controlled by means of subordination. Both these issues were inextricably linked with the political issues and in particular the loyalist defence of the constitution. Much of the loyalists' writing was concerned with inequality and there is a great deal of material on this issue. Radical calls for equality of rights were dismissed by loyalists, who accused radicals of wanting equality of property. Part 2 of Rights of man was identified as an example of this aim. According to Gifford, Paine was advocating that 'every man ought to resign all he possesses, and put all his property into one common stock-purse'.[145]

---

142 Boothby, Observations on the appeal, 232–3.
143 Anon., Interests of man, 49–50.
144 Ibid. 49.
145 Gifford, Plain address, 32.

The accusation that Paine sought to undermine the existing system of private property was fully utilised by loyalists. They warned that it was not just the aristocracy that would suffer if England followed the example of France. The radical proposal 'goes to affect directly or indirectly, the liberty and property of every individual in these kingdoms'.[146] If England sank into a revolution, Saint John warned, 'property of every kind would then be at the mercy of lawless ruffians and assassins who would in their turn plunder and be plundered'. Paine's arguments, he continued, 'all extend to the equalizing of property', the destruction of 'all inheritance, and all power of bequeathing property, and an Agrarian law, or equal distribution of land would be next proposed by him'. Indeed, Saint John concluded, the equalising of property 'puts an end to all industry; cuts off the fruits of labour, robs the fair trader and farmer of all profits of his toil; places the idle and worthless in the seat of the meritorious; and unhinges all society'.[147] Loyalist accusations of levelling were also commonplace and, 'wherever the levelling doctrines of THOMAS PAINE are received, religion and morality will be turned out of doors... and the order of nature reverted'.[148] 'Equality' became a term of abuse for loyalists, as 'aristocracy' had become a term of abuse for radicals. Transposing the radical issue of equality of rights into one of equality of property had the effect of suggesting to the people that they should be defending their property rather than fighting for their rights. Significantly this transposition also challenged the Painite model of aristocracy versus people and, again, moved the debate into the context of the propertied versus the property-less, model of society.

Historians have generally suggested that loyalists defended inequality on traditional grounds. Schofield asserted that loyalists 'all agreed in 'their defence of inequalities of wealth, rank and power'.[149] It is true that some loyalists did argue that inequality was natural, created by God, necessary to society and prosperity, and mutually beneficial to rich and poor. Anglican clergymen had traditionally preached that inequality was the will of God and that the poor must wait until the next life to reap their rewards and many continued to do so in the loyalist defence.[150] This stance was also invoked by some loyalist laymen.[151] It was deemed natural and necessary that 'some must till the ground, sow the grain, and reap the corn, that all may have the means of supporting life'.[152] Cusack Smith argued that 'inequality of property' was beyond the control of man, for 'in natural inequality we behold the unsteady swell and fluctuation of a sea'.[153] Yet other loyalists also defended inequality

---

[146] Anon., *Interests of man*, 56.
[147] [Saint John], *Letter from a magistrate*, 206.
[148] Peter, *Strictures on the character*, 42.
[149] Schofield, 'Conservative political thought', 605.
[150] See, for example, Paley, *Reasons for contentment*.
[151] See [Hervey], *New friend*, 72–3.
[152] Anon., *Letters to a friend*, 3.
[153] [Cusack Smith], *Rights of citizens*, 283, 281.

as an inevitable result of commercial progress, prosperity and civilisation. Whilst republicanism might bring greater equality, it would inevitably result in a return to primitivism.[154] Jones asserted that 'republican government, which can only exist in its simple state by the principle of equality, can never be congenial to science or friendly to commerce', it is close 'to a state of nature' and, thus, the French had 'uncivilized themselves'.[155] It was generally propounded by loyalists that an 'inevitable inequality of condition . . . necessarily results from . . . advancing prosperity and opulence'.[156] Indeed the modern, commercial society promoted by many loyalists was the cause of inequality. This rendered a 'fixed and permanent government' ever more essential to ensure that 'honest industry' need not 'fear the attack of the profligate and the abandoned'.[157]

Moreover although it was argued that men were naturally unequal, again, in the main, this was not said to occur because some were superior in blood or birth, but because some had greater talents and virtues than others.[158] One anonymous pamphleteer declared that 'the mental faculties of men are very variable'. Therefore, as 'Some men are endowed with a far greater portion of understanding than others . . . these will always take the lead, and be looked up to with respect and veneration' by the others.[159] A broadside declared that wealth and possessions were 'obtainable by any of you or your children as their talents and merits shall deserve'.[160] Indeed the '*rights of the mechanic and artist* are proper and just returns for their ingenuity'.[161] But the important point to keep in mind here – one not generally noted by historians – is that this elaborate rhetoric about equality served primarily to defend the aristocracy. For the most part inequality was defended on the same grounds as was aristocratic political leadership. This rhetoric about equality also reinforced the loyalist argument that England had an open elite.

By linking success with merit loyalists had plenty of ammunition with which to fight radical calls for greater equality. There was no reason why, loyalists argued, those who had earned their wealth, or whose ancestors had earned their wealth through their own industry, should be called upon 'to share it with those who have nothing; that is, with those whose stupidity disqualifies them, or whose idleness prevents their providing for themselves'.[162] Saint John asked of Paine: 'Are men born, and must they continue equal in respect of their property? The world is not yet so mad as to endure the assertion of such an absurdity – Property is in its nature changeable, and

---

154 See Claeys, 'French Revolution', 77.
155 [Jones], *Reason of man*, 401.
156 Anon., *Considerations on Mr Paine's pamphlet*, 95.
157 Anon., *Interests of man*, 10–11.
158 Claeys, 'French Revolution', 71–2.
159 Anon., *Letters to a friend*, 3.
160 Anon., *Few minutes advice*, 11.
161 Anon., *Defence of the constitution*, 23.
162 Anon., *Constitutional letters*, 169.

must vary according to industry or idleness of individuals.'[163] Loyalists argued that if the levellers had their way 'the indolent and the industrious, the lazy and the laborious; the extravagant and the frugal; the bad and the good, would, then be placed on one common level'.[164] It was only the 'needy, the desperate, and the licentious' who favoured levelling.[165] Moreover loyalists claimed that the system of inequality affected the aristocracy in the same ways as everyone else. Aristocrats too could lose as well as gain on the seesaw of good fortune. Great landed proprietors who, 'through ignorance and bad passions, oppress their laborious inferiors', find that their 'folly brings with it its own punishment, in the depopulation and waste of barrenness of their property'.[166] Those who preferred to 'go idle, and be drunk' became the burden that is the poor.[167]

A number of loyalists, in terms not dissimilar to those used by radicals, promoted industry as the source of happiness. Richard Hey argued that for 'the generality of persons whose daily labour is their livelihood ... Their Labour is their Riches, and, in some sense their Happiness'.[168] John Bowles concurred that it was 'contentment and cheerful industry' which were 'so beneficial to the individual and the community'.[169] Without 'industry it is impossible for mankind ... to enjoy the comforts of existence' and so idleness or sickness must 'render men without these comforts'.[170] Ultimately Hervey exclaimed that 'Commerce is the true corrective of mankind, and by pursuing it, we shall gradually exterminate the wretched remains of ignorance and error.'[171] Thus promoting England as an industrial and commercial country enabled loyalists to invoke the virtues of personal industry. If prosperity was to be maintained and increased the majority must labour and only industry could be, and indeed was, rewarded.

Economic and social value of aristocracy

The loyalist commercial model was also further used in defence of the aristocracy. Loyalists argued that the aristocracy and indeed the wealthy were necessary. They provided the rest of society with work and a market for manufactured goods. Loyalists stressed that it was also predominantly the wealthy who provided relief for the poor by charity. 'The rich', Dalrymple

---

163 [Saint John], *Letter from a magistrate*, 179.
164 Gifford, *Plain address*, 32.
165 Anon., *Interests of man*, 55.
166 Anon., *Defence of the constitution*, 22.
167 Brown, *Importance of preserving*, 67.
168 Hey, *Happiness and rights*, 8.
169 [Bowles], *Protest*, 44.
170 Alexander Dalrymple, *The poor man's friend: an address to the industrious and manufacturing part of Great Britain*, Edinburgh 1793, 17.
171 [Hervey], *Answer to the second part*, 390.

asserted, 'not only pay our taxes, but they are the market for our commodities. If we were all brought to the same level . . . tradesmen of all kinds, would neither find a merchant for their articles, nor price for their labour.'[172] An anonymous pamphleteer suggested that the rents of wealthy landowners

> are mostly divided amongst people of the working class, employed in husbandry, or as tradesmen, mechanicks, or people from the same class, whom he maintains as domesticks, or who are unable to work and reduced to poverty, so that this great proprietor has, in effect, nothing more than the power of distributing these rents.[173]

Another confirmed that property 'costs much to the possessor, and his expence to support the possession administers the means of subsistence, and diffuses wealth and happiness to numbers of his fellow citizens'.[174] Hearn even went so far as to claim that

> [the] luxury of the few becomes a source of prosperity to the whole – it is a spring which communicates new motion to the engine of public labour, and calls forth all the resources of industry and invention – it animates the efforts of the manufacturer, and is the greatest stimulus which excites the ingenuity of the artist, the speculation of the trader, and the enterprize of the merchant. Luxury, in a word, may be considered as the *primum mobile* of national exertion, and the vital principle of public prosperity.[175]

So even luxury benefited all and promoted industry in the loyalists' prosperous, commercial England.

In a further vindication of English prosperity, loyalists suggested that the poor were now better off than in feudal times and than their brethren were in most other European countries. Even the 'children of deepest poverty' were 'few . . . in comparison with other countries' and were protected with 'vigilance and tenderness' under the constitution.[176] In 'England every one EATS BREAD, and enjoys the fruits of his labor, and industry, in security and quiet'.[177] 'Look around you . . . Is there any industrious man who has not the means of earning a full competency for himself and his family?'[178] Brown noted that 'even in the trading and manufacturing towns, it is pleasing to observe how plentifully and comfortably the generality of industrious tradesmen live and keep their families'.[179] And another pamphleteer asked what other 'nation can boast such benevolent and multiplied endowments,

---

172 Dalrymple, *Poor man's friend*, 18.
173 Anon., *Defence of the rights*, 299.
174 Anon., *Candid inquiry*, 84.
175 [Hearn], *Short view*, 367.
176 Anon., *Letters to Thomas Paine*, 81.
177 Anon., *Rod in brine*, 27.
178 Dalrymple, *Poor man's friend*, 8.
179 Brown, *Importance of preserving*, 67.

hospitals and charities? In what country but England were poor laws ever heard of?'[180] Alexander Peter even went so far as to suggest that the wants of the poor were not real but were prompted by the aspiration and emulation which were provoked by luxury. For, 'when the price of labour doth not rise in proportion to those new created demands, murmurings and complaints are as frequently the consequence, as if dire necessity drew them from a heart harrowed by distress'.[181] Inequality of rank, raised so boldly by Paine, was also defended by loyalists within the framework of their defence of subordination. Two arguments were invoked here, the traditional and the commercial, and this again suggests that were at least two 'loyalisms' within loyalism.

Some conservative loyalists followed the sermons of conservative Anglican clergymen, such as William Jones and George Horne, and argued that men were naturally evil, having been born with Original Sin. Hence subordination was a necessary bulwark against man's natural passions. A number of loyalists implied that the social order reflected gradations of evil, from the savage who lived in primitive society to the nobility in a civilised society such as England. 'The equality of savage man is that chaos of the species; – a regulated and subordinate inequality is the fair creation', produced by nature.[182] Indeed subordination could be justified by, and traced back to, the Bible. The Apostle Peter said that 'in our *civil* establishments, GOD never meant there should be an *equality* of *degrees*, or of *officers*, or of *rank*'.[183] An anonymous pamphleteer explained that 'the sons of Noah . . . were the natural rulers and judges of their own prosperity'. When 'their different branches separated, and settled in different countries, single families became in time great nations . . . The father of each of those separate families was its natural judge and ruler' and such patriarchs then left their dominions to their eldest sons.[184] Thus the more conservative loyalists argued that subordination was a naturally occurring system and that hereditary rulers and primogeniture were a natural part of the system.

Subordination was, however, also represented by the less traditional branch of loyalism as the inevitable result of English civilisation and prosperity. Many agreed that in 'rich and populous countries . . . The powers of government must necessarily be confined to a proportionally small part of the community'.[185] The social order was also linked to merit, as one anonymous pamphleteer declared: 'eminence and inferiority of worth, will always produce degrees of estimation, which will constitute ranks'.[186] And another

---

[180] Anon., *Few minutes advice*, 11.
[181] Peter, *Strictures on the character*, 140–1.
[182] [Cusack Smith], *Rights of citizens*, 282.
[183] Anon., *Letters to a friend on the Test Laws . . . also strictures on Mr Paine's Rights of man*, 1791, 183.
[184] Anon., *Defence of the rights*, 294.
[185] Anon., *Considerations on Mr Paine's pamphlet*, 95. See also anon., *Letters to a friend*, 2–3.
[186] Anon., *Remarks on Mr Paine's pamphlet*, 48.

concurred: 'Superior sagacity and superior strength take place of stupidity and weakness, and give rise to a distinction of ranks, and orders.'[187] Thus a few loyalists represented inequality of rank as the natural result of a meritocracy.

It was also a loyalist contention that subordination normally sprang from, but also supported, the multi-layered society to be found in England. Hunt claimed that 'A body of nobility . . . is peculiarly necessary to our mixed . . . constitution'; it 'creates and preserves that gradual scale of dignity, which proceeds from the peasant to the prince, rising like a pyramid from a broad foundation, and diminishing to a point as it rises'.[188] Indeed, John Jones elaborated, 'there is a chain of connection through the whole of our community' which incorporates 'the GENTLEMAN, the MERCHANT, the FARMER, the TRADESMAN, the MECHANIC, and the LABOURER'.[189] This chain was one of commercial connections, for each link was economically reliant on the others. Jones continued, 'if the Gentleman loses his property, neither the manufacturer or the tradesman, can find a consumption for their articles; and of course the means of an honest livelihood for the mechanic and the labourer are done away'.[190] One loyalist used an industrial simile to define this economic subordination: 'The whole system of creation is connected together like one vast machine by the *difference* of its component parts; inequality, gradation, dependence, influence, and subjection, hold together the moral world.'[191] The implication was, of course, that the aristocrats, at the head of the chain, were not just the political but also the economic leaders of this industrial and commercial England.

A two-fold defence of the establishment

Thus it is clear that the loyalist pamphlets of 1791–2 reveal not just one conservative loyalism, but a number of 'loyalisms'. What the majority had in common was, as Dozier said, their defence of the English constitution.[192] In their support for the constitution loyalists invoked traditional defences but also began to develop a new commercial model of society, based on Whig social theory. Nor, contrary to Wahrman's suggestion, did all loyalists represent English society as polarised on the Painite model. Such polarisation can be identified in the traditional, conservative defence of the establishment and also in loyalist propaganda specifically aimed at the working people. But a number of loyalists represented England on the new model as a modern, commercial and prosperous country with, significantly, a gradated society and

---

187 Anon., *Defence of the constitution*, 21.
188 Hunt, *Rights of Englishmen*, 78–9.
189 [Jones], *Reason of man*, 410.
190 Ibid.
191 Anon., *Rights upon rights*, 106.
192 Dozier, *King, constitution and country*, 20–5.

an open elite. These loyalists described a society structured and focused in ways which would clearly have been more acceptable to the English people than the models of either Paine or Burke.

The emergence of this two-fold loyalism suggests that loyalists were not a unitary group but that there were at least two, if not more, groups within loyalism. During the years 1791–2, both conservative and non-traditional 'loyalisms' can be identified. Various religious groups, often with their own agenda, also pledged their support to loyalism, in what may be identified as another branch of the debate. As will become apparent loyalism further diversified during the years 1793–6.[193]

Between 1793 and 1796 the radicals continued to attack the aristocracy in much the same terms as they had begun. They continued to attempt to rally the people in a reflection of the revolution in France but without, for the most part, by 1796, promoting its violent conclusion. With the revolution turning the corner into terror and the government mobilising to repress radical writings, radicals appear to have been fighting against the odds. That was particularly so in that they were now also polemicising against a newly vocal and 'modernising' loyalism that was fighting back formidably in defence of an open aristocracy.

---

[193] See chapter 5 below.

4

Radical Debates and Diversification, 1793–1796

> If there really exist persons, who are endeavouring to destroy the true constitution of our country, point them out and punish them. But it is the prevalent presumption of thinking men, that we have no such persons among us.[1]

During the year 1793 a number of events occurred which inevitably affected the French Revolution debate. These events included, in France, the execution of Louis XVI in January, the outbreak of war between England and France on 1 February 1793, and the increase of violence and the development of 'the Terror', instituted by the Jacobins in September. In England, Pitt's government stepped up attempts to suppress radicalism.[2] As a result radicalism, taken as a whole, became considerably more reactive than pro-active during the period 1793–6. Whilst anti-aristocratic rhetoric in radical pamphlets became, if anything, more vitriolic, connections with France and the French aristocracy were less commonly made. The focus of radicalism was fragmenting to some degree. It was no longer a question of condemning England and its aristocracy as an *ancien régime*, on a model similar to that of pre-revolutionary France, as Paine had done. The strong radical anti-aristocratic rhetoric continued, and possibly even increased, but it was no longer generally accompanied by revolutionary rhetoric. It became common radical practice both to condemn aristocracy and to promote the English constitution, even in one pamphlet. This ensured that aristocracy, at least in terms of the presence of rhetoric against it, remained central to the radical argument, but in an increasingly abstract role.

And the French Revolution debate certainly raged on. Gregory Claeys has argued that the controversy was most heated between 1791 and 1793[3] and Mark Philp has claimed that the intellectual argument had been overtaken by the activities of radical and loyalist societies by the end of 1792. These societies 'carried the debate over into a practical struggle for and against

---

1 William Hughes, *Justice to a judge: an answer to the judges's appeal to justice*, 2nd edn 1793, in Claeys, *Political writings*, iv. 9.
2 For details of the sedition legislation see introduction n. 12 above.
3 'Introduction', in Claeys, *Political writings*, i, p. xliii.

parliamentary reform'.[4] Whilst the popular societies did become dominant in the struggle on the ground, the pamphlet debate still continued to make a significant contribution to the ongoing intellectual debate. The flow of radical and loyalist pamphlets continued into 1795 and even 1796, albeit at a reduced rate.[5] It is significant that one of the last innovative acts of pamphlet radicalism during 1790–6, was the publication of the Norwich *Cabinet*. This periodical was published during 1794–5 and contained political and literary pieces which took a broad intellectual view of reform.[6] Moreover it should not be forgotten that the popular societies were themselves also participants in the intellectual debate and contributed pamphlets, broadsides and publications of their addresses and resolutions. And whilst sedition proceedings silenced some writers the war with France provoked others to put pen to paper.

The pamphlets published during the years 1793–6 clearly suggest that the French Revolution debate was a true, constantly developing debate about current political issues and between rival and interacting sides. The political flux within parliament also indicates that during this period people were constantly rethinking their positions. Most notably, in July 1794, the Portland Whigs abandoned Fox and the opposition benches to join Pitt's wartime government.[7] This left Fox's reform Whigs further weakened and unable to affect any reforms from within parliament. Radicalism and loyalism were, thus, not merely two separate traditions running parallel. In particular the adverse effect of war on the living standards of the poor in England meant that radicals and loyalists came into direct conflict over the loyalist promotion of an opulent nation in which prosperity was shared by all.[8]

Representations of aristocracy in the radical writings of this period present the historian with a particular problem. Whilst the pamphlets contain much damning anti-aristocratic rhetoric, radicalism did not pick up the radical impetus provoked by Paine and take it to its logical conclusion. The political reforms proposed by radicals during 1793–6 did not contemplate revolution or, for the most part, include measures to alter or to abolish the role of the aristocracy. This dichotomy raises the question: what did the anti-aristocratic rhetoric mean? Its dominance within radical representations is of considerable importance and forms the major focus of this chapter.

A secondary focus of this chapter is the apparent diversification of radicalism as a result of events during the period. The representations of proposals for reform were heterogeneous and owed as much to the reform

---

4 Philp, *French Revolution*, 1.
5 For a survey of the publication figures see Goodrich, 'Peers or parasites?', 217–19.
6 Goodwin, *Friends of liberty*, 375–7. For the background of the Norwich and other writers, who contributed to *The Cabinet* see Penelope J. Corfield and Chris Evans (eds), *Youth and revolution in the 1790s: letters of William Pattisson, Thomas Amyot and Henry Crabb Robinson*, Stroud 1996, 32–3, 111, 120–1, 187–95.
7 O'Gorman, *Whig party*, 192–208; Goodwin, *Friends of liberty*, 365–6.
8 For the interactivity of the debate see conclusion.

movement of the 1780s as to the radicalism of the French Revolution. Despite the dominant anti-aristocratic rhetoric, an increased condemnation of government and in particular of William Pitt and his ministers, especially regarding war with France and enforcement of the sedition legislation, is also to be found in radical pamphlets. On the issue of inequality, the third theme of this chapter, again condemnation of aristocracy remained at the forefront of radical debate. But a shift away from aristocracy can also be detected as a few radicals began to focus on the capitalist economic system as a cause of inequality and as other elites too came in for criticism.

Anti-aristocratic rhetoric

During the period 1793–6 radicals produced some of the most damning representations of aristocracy to date. Their pamphlets contain a sustained, vehement and vitriolic attack upon aristocracy in which the Painite model of England as 'aristocracy and people' was dominant. The term 'aristocracy' continued to be used by radicals both in classical terms and to describe a social class or caste. Radicals continued to challenge the aristocracy on the same grounds as were expressed in the years 1791–2. James Parkinson's *Knaves acre association* (1793) was not alone in raising issues of aristocratic corruption in government, the inequality of taxation, of property, and under the law.[9] The game laws, titles and all the privileges of a hereditary aristocracy still featured in radical pamphlets.[10]

Above all Henry Redhead Yorke ranted for pages against the aristocracy.[11] Inequality, both political and economic, was the central focus of his writing. He declared that where there were unequal divisions in society there would also be unjust unequal divisions in government. 'Thus the millions of the People, or their Representatives, can compose but a very subordinate branch of the Legislature, when it is in the power of the Aristocracy . . . to negative or control their operations.' He went on:

> It is true, they may style themselves the Nation, but the experience of their conduct, will always give the lie to the assertion; It will prove them to be an embodied phalanx, unrestrained by remorse, and uncontrolled by popular opinion: it will prove that they never form any calculations on the mischiefs

---

9 [James Parkinson], *Knaves acre association*, 1793, in Claeys, *Political writings*, iv. 13–20; Joseph Gerrald, *A convention the only means of saving us from ruin*, 1794, ibid. iv. 192.
10 For the game laws see Hughes, *Justice to a judge*, 4; William Frend, *Peace and union recommended to the associated bodies of republicans and anti-republicans*, 1793, in Claeys, *Political writings*, iv. 112. On titles see anon., *Extermination: or, an appeal to the people of England, on the present war, with France*, 1793, ibid. iv. 143; and Yorke, *Thoughts on civil government*, ibid. iv. 267.
11 See, for example, Yorke, *Thoughts on civil government*, 257–71.

which their evil administration may bring upon a country, but that they decree rewards, honours and glory to themselves, when they merit infamy and disgrace.[12]

Moreover Yorke complained that aristocrats considered themselves exempt from the rules of morality and that 'they demand an exemption, which is nothing less than a privilege of doing wrong with impunity. They call in Religion to their aid, they misconstrue and torture its precepts, to sanction their injustice'. When challenged the aristocracy wrap 'themselves under the mystic robe of an immaculate privilege'. Ultimately, Yorke declared, 'aristocracy . . . appropriates exclusively to itself, that quantity of happiness which is the natural inheritance of all'.[13]

William Vaughan was also clear in his condemnation of aristocracy and promotion of equality of political rights. He vehemently promoted the people as the true source of merit:

> If you wanted an able Lawyer, an elegant Historian, or an acute Philosopher, would you seek him among Kings, Princes, Dukes and Lords? fruitless in general, in that case, would be your labours. It is the People who have been the authors of almost every thing either illuminating in science, or useful in art. Who discovered the circulation of the blood? – *The People*. – Who the art of Printing? – *The People*. Who the power of the Magnet? *The People*. Who the use of Logarithims? – *The People*. Who the continent of America? – *The People*. Ask, in short, Who have been the Authors of all the remarkable discoveries which have been made? and the answer, with a very few exceptions, will still be – *the People*. Without frequent draughts from the People to infuse fresh vigour into the puny bodies of Nobles, and genius and taste into their weak minds, what a pitiful race would they quickly become![14]

He scoffed that it was from the corporation of aristocracy 'where Birth supplies the place of Abilities, Virtues, Knowledge, and Experience; where Fortune alone doles out pre-eminence, the Executive Officers of the Nation are selected'.[15] The Unitarian George Dyer declared that, it was 'the pride of rank, that supercilious insolence, that leads those who are born noble, and others, who are mere upstarts, to treat the poor man with contempt'.[16] In England, Joseph Gerrald argued, unlike in America the poor were 'broken down to support the expensive trappings of royalty, or to pamper the luxury of an insolent nobility'.[17] There was little doubt that the aristocracy was the enemy of 'a poor and oppressed people'.[18] William Godwin also attacked aris-

---

[12] Ibid. 257.
[13] Ibid. 256–7.
[14] [Vaughan], *The catechism of man*, 216.
[15] Ibid. 260.
[16] G. Dyer, *The complaints of the poor people of England*, 1793, 14.
[17] Gerrald, *A convention*, 190.
[18] [James Parkinson], *An address to the Hon. Edmund Burke from the swinish multitude*, 1793, in Claeys, *Political writings*, iv. 129.

tocracy in his *Enquiry concerning political justice* (1793), identifying 'privilege and aristocracy' as directly opposed to 'equality' and universal justice.[19] He declared that in England 'the feudal spirit still survives that reduced the great mass of mankind to the rank of slaves and cattle for the service of the few'.[20] While Godwin's general philosophy was abstract and theoretical, his specific denunciations of aristocratic feudalism chimed with the radical mood in 1793–6.

Corruption was still the focus of radical attack and aristocracy was still the target. Indeed, according to one anonymous pamphleteer, 'Intrigue and Corruption' were 'the only *trades*' of an intrinsically idle 'Aristocracy'. Whilst the people 'are to be loaded with fresh taxes, the Kings and Ministers may . . . sleep in security, and Aristocracy continues to gorge itself on the industry of the nation and at the public expense. The truth is YE ARE SLAVES'.[21] Yorke declared that 'the People, it is said, are made for the Government, not the Government for the People'. As a result, public money was not used for the public good but was

> squandered among those idle, monstrous, and useless harpies, who hover about Palaces, and waste that Property which they have never contributed to gather; to reward the well-earned services of nobility *in its cradle*, to support ennobled vice, to encourage influence, patronage, and servility; and, finally, to corrupt the People with the produce of their own labours.[22]

One anonymous satirist asked 'surely, the Money . . . squeezed from the People in Taxes . . . is not squandered on Drones?'.

> Are not the great Placemen, and truly noble Pensioners, who fill the high offices of the state useful thereto? Is it not for the dignity of the Nation to have such Places filled by the first Nobility, Lords, Earls, and Dukes? What could be done without a Master of the Horse, and Keeper of the Stag hounds, . . . Lords of the Treasury, of the Admiralty, and of the Bedchamber; Groom of the Stole or Stool . . . &c. &c? Is not such a fine string of them an Ornament to the Nation? Do they not strengthen the hands of Government?[23]

William Vaughan stated that in England, the 'pitiful race' of nobility had become '*The unblushing companions of Grooms and Sharpers, and the detestable Patrons of Boxers and of Strumpets.*'[24]

Furthermore, aristocracy was identified as the very source of corruption.

---

[19] William Godwin, *Enquiry concerning political justice*, 1793, 3rd edn 1798, ed. Isaac Kramnick, London 1985, 296–7.
[20] Ibid. 726. For debates on this concept as crystallised in the seventeenth and eighteenth centuries see Susan Reynolds, *Fiefs and vassals: the medieval evidence reinterpreted*, London 1994.
[21] Anon., *Extermination: or an appeal*, 140.
[22] Yorke, *Thoughts on civil government*, 234.
[23] Anon., *An enquiry into the present alarming state of the nation*, 1793, 5.
[24] [Vaughan], *Catechism of man*, 216 (italics in original).

There was not 'a single placeman or pensioner' who was not 'the creature of Aristocracy'.[25] The members of the Reeve's Association[26] were inevitably accused of being 'Placemen and Pensioners'.[27] Gerrald scoffed: 'The red book (properly so called, indeed, for the outside blushes for the contents of the in) since the commencement of the war, has been swelled by additional bands of pensioners and placemen.'[28] And an anonymous pamphleteer commented sarcastically, that 'most of the property of the Association is to be found in the Red Book ... in the list of Placemen and Pensioners, it is very necessary, that *such kind of property* should be preserved'. He added in the same vein:

> I cannot but applaud the Association for giving so early a proof of their *patriotism* in the choice of their chairman, a man, who, on account of his possessing immense property, being totally free from aristocratical influence, and not holding any place under the present Government (though a very virtuous one) is the more to be depended on by the public at large.[29]

Clearly the hardships experienced in England as a result of war heightened such radical anger.[30] The British Convention in Edinburgh[31] stressed '*we* do not servilely feed on the patronage of the great' or 'on the spoils of an injured country'.[32] Even a petition of the Friends of the People to the House of Commons called for an end to 'PRIVATE PARLIAMENTARY PATRONAGE' as it resulted in 'the interference of Peers in elections'.[33] The message was clear, the country was still an *ancien régime*. As Gerrald put it, 'divided into an oppressed peasantry and an overgrown aristocracy' England was dominated by an aristocracy of nobles and bishops, of 'chicanery in ermine' and 'hypocrisy in

---

[25] [Parkinson], *Knaves acre association*, 14.
[26] The loyalist Association for the Preservation of Liberty and Property against Republicans and Levellers was founded by John Reeves on 20 November 1792: Black, *The association*, 237.
[27] Anon., *More reasons for a reform in parliament*, 1793, in Claeys, *Political writings*, iv. 53.
[28] Gerrald, *A convention*, 186.
[29] Anon, *More reasons for a reform*, 53.
[30] See, for example, Roger Wells, 'English society and revolutionary politics in the 1790s: the case for insurrection', in Philp, *French Revolution*, 191–5, and John Rule, *The vital century: England's developing economy, 1714–1815*, London 1992, 253–5.
[31] The British Convention was an assembly of Scottish and English radicals which consisted of 180 delegates who met in Edinburgh in November and December 1793. Their aim was to form a democratic union between England and Scotland for radical reform, proposed by Joseph Gerrald. This convention was to consist of 375 delegates elected by the people. Due to government repression, the Convention did not survive beyond December 1793. Its leaders, including Joseph Gerrald, were arrested and tried for sedition: Goodwin, *Friends of liberty*, 296–306.
[32] British Convention, *The address of the British Convention, assembled at Edinburgh*, 1793, in Claeys, *Political writings*, iv. 92.
[33] Anon., *Petition of the friends of the people to the Honourable the Commons of Great Britain, in parliament assembled*, 1793, in Claeys, *Political writings*, iv. 156–8.

lawn'.[34] In England, Yorke declared, 'there still exist some bloody fragments of Gothic barbarity'.[35]

It is notable that during these years aristocracy was by no means the only target of criticism. Government in general, and Pitt and his ministry in particular, came under considerable attack for instituting sedition proceedings against radicals and for entering into war with France.[36] Nevertheless the majority of radical writers suggested that government was an aristocratic oligarchy or at least a conspiracy led by the aristocracy. As Vaughan protested, England had the 'Aristocratic form' of government which 'vests the power . . . in a few called Grandees, Peers, Nobles, Barons, Lords spiritual or temporal'.[37] Godwin also particularly disliked 'the aristocratical system' and claimed that both aristocracy and monarchy were despotisms 'founded in falsehood'. All 'adherents of the old systems of government' and the tenets they fostered were, Godwin argued, 'a partisan of aristocracy'.[38]

A number of radicals identified government as a conspiracy of corruption led by the main beneficiaries, the aristocracy. Such a government, complained Yorke, '*is a downright tyranny*', it is 'a GOVERNMENT OF CONSPIRACY'.[39] Governments carried out 'plots' against the people, 'plots against liberty, or plots against peace'.[40] The great, according to John Baxter, were colluding with 'our corrupt Legislators' in 'the infamous System of Monopoly' and it was only by introducing 'universal suffrage' that 'the Monopoly of Power may be divided'.[41] John Oswald also identified the government as consisting of 'aristocratic corporations' and 'aristocratic conspiracies'.[42] And an anony-

---

[34] Gerrald, *A convention*, 190.
[35] Henry Redhead Yorke, *Reason urged against precedent: in a letter to the people of Derby*, 1793, in Claeys, *Political writings*, iv. 70.
[36] For criticisms of government regarding sedition proceedings see, for example, Yorke, *Reason urged against precedent*, 79, and *These are the times that try men's souls!*, 1793, 64; Thelwall, *Natural and constitutional rights*, 17; anon., *Reflexions of a true Briton, continued*, in Eaton, *Politics for the people*, pt i, 154; LCS, *Circular letter to other reform societies*, c. 1 March 1794, in Thale, *LCS selections*, 119; LCS, *Account of general meeting*, 29, ibid. 25; and LCS, *Proceedings of a general meeting*, 26 Oct. 1795, ibid. 326. For pamphlets condemning government and ministers regarding the war see LCS, *Address to the nation*, July 1793, ibid. 75–6; Thelwall, *The tribune*, i. 1795–6, in Claeys, *Politics of English Jacobinism*, 85–7; Gerrald, *A convention*, 193; anon., *Advertisement to the electors of Westminster, 14 June 1796*, in T. Hardy (ed.), *Moral and political magazine of the London Corresponding Society*, London 1796, 16; anon., *Some account of a very seditious book lately found upon Wimbledon Common*, 1794, 53; Daniel Stuart, *Peace and reform, against war and corruption*, 2nd edn 1794, in Claeys, *Political writings*, iv. 318–19; Yorke, *Thoughts on civil government*, 230; and anon., *Considerations on the French war*, 1794, 5–6, 66.
[37] [Vaughan], *Catechism of man*, 216, 227.
[38] Godwin, *Enquiry concerning political justice*, 167, 296–7.
[39] Yorke, *Thoughts on civil government*, 235.
[40] Anon., *Some account of a very seditious book*, 21.
[41] John Baxter, *Resistance to oppression: the constitutional rights of Britons asserted*, 1795, in Claeys, *Political writings*, iv. 440–2.
[42] John Oswald, *The government of the people*, Paris 1793, in Claeys, *Political writings*, iv. 101–2.

mous pamphleteer identified a conspiracy between 'Extravagant Courts, selfish Ministers and corrupt Majorities' as at the root of the 'war with France'.[43] Aristocracy, then, was still at the root of the corrupt government in England. Consequently the Painite model of society of 'aristocracy and people' in an *ancien régime* remained dominant in radical writings. As Yorke said 'In the haughty and imperious language of Aristocracy, the Government and the People are two distinct terms.'.[44]

Aristocracy was also represented, in similar terms, as responsible for the war with France. Indeed the outbreak of war clearly contributed to the groundswell of anti-aristocratic rhetoric during this period. As in the period 1791–2, war was condemned as initiated by a war-mongering aristocracy. As Yorke said, the '*fields of battle*' were 'the nurseries of the Nobility'.[45] Radicals argued that ambitious leaders of European monarchies were waging an inappropriate war against a fledgling free France, which was still trying to find its constitutional feet. Cartwright argued that the war was not instigated by France but waged against her 'by the European allies'. England should have 'supported the infant state' of France, not gone to war against her.[46] Thomas Spence complained of 'the inveterate war commenced by the aristocracy of the world against France'.[47] This was, according to one anonymous pamphleteer, 'A WAR AGAINST FREEDOM, a War in which the King, the Nobility and the Priesthood can alone be interested, and from which the People can derive no possible advantage whatever'.[48] England was allied with European despotic monarchies, true *ancien régimes*, in this war, which reinforced radical representations of England on the same model. As in 1791–2 radicals condemned the traditional aristocratic language of war and the issue of honour was again raised.[49]

The pamphlets and broadsides aimed directly at the people were also particularly vicious in their condemnation of aristocracy and inevitably reflected a polarised society of 'aristocracy versus people' on the Painite model. There was much material on Burke's reference to the '*swinish multitude*'.[50] James Parkinson sardonically described Burke as 'thou flower of chivalry and spirit of civility' and as to his term 'swinish multitude':

---

[43] Anon., *The evidence summed up: or, a statement of the apparent causes and objects of the war*, 1794, 1.
[44] Yorke, *Thoughts on civil government*, 235.
[45] Ibid. 265.
[46] John Cartwright, *The commonwealth in danger*, 1795, 4–5. See also Stuart, *Peace and reform*, 305.
[47] Thomas Spence, *The end of oppression*, 2nd edn 1795, in Dickinson, *Political works*, 34.
[48] Anon., *Extermination: or, an appeal*, 140; Yorke, *Reason urged against precedent*, 268.
[49] See, for example, Yorke, *Reason urged against precedent*, 75; Gerrald, *A convention*, 169; Frend, *Peace and union*, 127; anon., *The pernicious effects of the art of printing upon society, exposed*, c. 1793, 4; Yorke, *Thoughts on civil government*, 262; and John Thelwall, *Miscellaneous subjects, 7 June 1796*, 1796, in Hardy, *Moral and political magazine*, 16–17.
[50] For Burke's reference to the 'swinish multitude' see p. 43 above.

Alas, Good Sir! We much fear the contrary of what you suppose will take place; and that men, instead of supposing that the honest, industrious, and suffering part of this nation are meant by the *swinish multitude*, will conclude that the compliment was really intended for the sordid herd, which help to fill up a court.[51]

Parkinson continued that whilst the people are 'driven to the irksome employment of grubbing for our livelihood in stony and barren grounds', the 'noble and highborn Swine' are 'wallowing in all the luxuries which a Stye can yield'. The system of hereditary ascendancy and primogeniture resembled 'the choosing *a pig in a poke*'.[52] Another anonymous satire described 'the Golden Age' of feudalism wherein 'the different orders of society were kept perfectly distinct and separate – there were kings, barons, priests, yeomanry, villains or slaves'. It was 'The villains, or lowest class', Burke's '*Swinish Multitude*' who 'tilled the earth, and performed all manual labour' but who were paid only with 'subsistence'.[53] Spence, in a pamphlet that took the form of a dialogue between a poor woman and the aristocracy, described 'the haughty Aristocracy, sneering and tossing up their noses' while the woman of the people raged:

> Hear me! ye oppressors! ye who live sumptuously every day! ye for whom alone all human and brute creatures toil, sighing, but in vain, for the crumbs which fall from your overcharged tables; ye, for whom alone the heavens drop fatness, ... ye, who are not satisfied with usurping all that nature can yield; ye, who ... would deprive every heart of joy but your own, I say hearken to me! Your horrid tyranny, your infanticide is at an end! Your grinding the faces of the poor, and your drinking the blood of infants, is at an end! The groans of the prisons, the groans of the camp, and the groans of the cottage, excited by your infernal policy, are at an end! And behold the whole earth breaks forth into singing at the new creation, at the breaking of the iron rod of aristocratic sway, and at the rising of the everlasting sun of righteousness![54]

Such brilliant and expressive phraseology and language could surely not fail to attract the attention of the people. But it was the radical printer and bookseller, Daniel Isaac Eaton's *Politics for the people, or a salmagundy for swine*, a series of publications in 1794, which contained some of the most savage tracts and broadsides published during this period.[55] A typical tract told the tale of 'A Certain Court candidate, the Polite Courtier', who tried to bribe 'honest

---

51 [Parkinson], *Address to the Hon. Edmund Burke*, 129.
52 Ibid. 130–2.
53 Anon., *Pernicious effects*, 6.
54 Thomas Spence, *The rights of infants*, 1796, in Dickinson, *Political works*, 50.
55 These publications are in two parts with part i consisting of 16 editions of *Politics for the people* and part ii consisting of 12 editions. Each edition contains such radical material as tracts, short pieces, publications of popular societies, letters, poems and trial details. This version was found in the British Library, bound as one volume merely entitled 'Tracts'.

Crispin' the cobbler to vote for him. Honest Crispin says to the courtier ' "kiss my a-se or no vote for me" ' and 'The polite Courtier, offended at such indelicacy, offered any sum, &c' but honest Crispin does not want it and repeats his demand. As 'the fate of the election depended on his single voice, the polite Courtier complied'. But 'the honest cobler voted for *t'other side*, as his conscience directed; declaring that a scoundrel that could be mean enough to "*kiss my a-se*" was unworthy of a seat in Parliament'.[56] Another 'Anecdote' relayed the tale of a beggar:

> A few days ago, as a Beggar in a Rag Fair was picking something off his clothes, he was thus angrily accosted by one of Mr. Reeve's associates: – 'You dirty rascal what are you about?' – 'Nothin, Sir, but guillotining a few Aristocrats.' – 'Aristocrats! You seditious scoundrel! How dare you call such vermin Aristocrats?' – 'I can't find a better name for them an' please your honour, for they always prey upon the poor'.[57]

A common theme in such pamphlets for the people was corruption. The wealth of the aristocracy was obtained from public funds and was consequently derived from the labours of the poor. One tract lamented that the people must 'Burn' in 'miserable garrets' to provide for 'honourable members of the illustrious House of Peers'. Another tract claimed that 'if we examine the origin of Nobility and Royal Grandeur ... we shall find the first fathers of these noisy pedigrees to be cruel Butchers of Men, Oppressors, Tyrants, perfidious Truce-Breakers, Robbers, and Parricides' and 'all the successive continuation of it ... even to these modern times' are 'the greatest Oppressors, Hypocrites, Atheists and Outlaws in the world'. Indeed, 'Kings, Princes, Courtiers and Pharisaical Priests' had merely 'put on the mask of wisdom and virtue' and they 'have great reason to take care, that their mask be not pull'd off'.[58]

One particularly vitriolic tale from John Thelwall's *The peripatetic*, which was included in Eaton's *Politics for the people*, claimed that the English aristocracy was composed of 'those illustrious characters who derived their *hereditary wisdom*, and *hereditary virtues* from the intrigues of *Gallic Courtezans*, and the amours of *Theatrical Prostitutes*'. Another piece entitled 'The Genealogy of a modern Aristocrate' described

> THE Devil begat Sin, Sin begat Error, Error begat Pride, Pride begat Ignorance ... Superstition begat Priestcraft, Priestcraft begat lineal Succession ... Non Resistance begat Oppression, Oppression begat Corruption, Corruption begat Want of Public Virtue, Want of Public Virtue begat Ministerial Influence, Ministerial Influence begat Time-Serving Sycophants, [and] Time-Serving

---

[56] Eaton, *Politics for the people*, pt i, 3.
[57] Ibid. pt ii, 16.
[58] Ibid. pt i, 6, 26, 46, 99.

Sycophants begat Modern Aristocracy on the Body of the Whore of Babylon when she was deemed past Child-bearing.[59]

Such rhetoric suggests that during the period 1793–6 'aristocracy' became increasingly a term of abuse and a subject of ridicule to English radicals. The term was adopted by those writing tracts for the people as well as those directly engaged in the literary debates. Universally these authors depicted England as having a corrupt and oppressive aristocracy. The rhetoric ensured that representations of aristocracy remained central in the French Revolution debate until at least 1796. Most significantly, however, as this continuing plethora of anti-aristocratic rhetoric illustrates, the representations of aristocracy were the most consistently and universally radical to be found in the pamphlets.

Revolution or reform?

Despite the virulence of the anti-aristocratic rhetoric the gap between that rhetoric and the reforms actually proposed was, if anything, even wider between 1793 and 1796 than in 1791–2. No such radical and influential text as *Rights of man* was published during this period. In England the anti-aristocratic rhetoric did not, amongst the majority of radicals, reflect a desire for revolution. Gwyn Williams has argued that radicalism was in England 'not in any meaningful sense revolutionary' but mostly defensive. This was because 'never at any stage did the English movement concern itself with power except as its victim'.[60] Certainly after 1792 the radical movement was increasingly pushed on to the defensive by Pitt's counter-attack.

This is nowhere more apparent than in radical representations of aristocracy. Radicals ranted and raved at aristocracy but very rarely did they actually directly attack the legitimacy of the House of Lords as a sector of government. It is clear that in reality the issue of leadership was raised primarily to promote reform of representation in the House of Commons and to argue for an extension of the franchise, neither of which would affect the existence of the House of Lords.

As in 1791–2 a few radicals did advocate the abolition of aristocracy. Thomas Spence, the radical lecturer on agrarian equality, suggested that the people should go to war to confiscate the land of the aristocracy. It would be a 'war' between the 'soldiers of liberty' and the 'wealthy enemy', 'the aristocracy'.[61] He confirmed that 'such a combination of spoilers' as the European aristocracies should be rooted up and the world set free from all 'exactions,

---

[59] Ibid. pt i, 120; pt ii, 6.
[60] Williams, *Artisans and sans-culottes*, 101.
[61] Spence, *End of oppression*, 37.

imposts, and abuses at once and for ever'.⁶² Furthermore William Godwin proclaimed that the 'dissolution of aristocracy is equally the interest of the oppressor and the oppressed'.⁶³ Henry Yorke also advocated abolition of aristocracy.⁶⁴ One pamphleteer calling himself Citizen Randol, conceded that a mixed government might be workable but claimed 'I do not see any hereditary branch of a legislature as congenial to a people's welfare.'⁶⁵ And Dyer noted that America had successful government, 'yet the Americans have no nobles. The system of aristocracy, they think, tends to weakness'.⁶⁶ Many radicals suggested, on the same grounds as in 1791–2, that the aristocracy were not the best qualified for leadership.⁶⁷ Yet the majority of radical writers provided no direct proposals for its abolition or replacement.

Moreover during this period even those calling for the abolition of aristocracy did not form a united group making uniform proposals. Far from it: the aims and intentions of the more radical element were, to say the least, disparate. Godwin advocated abolition of government, as it was known, altogether and his proposals for an entirely new anarchic society were somewhat outside those of the radical movement in general.⁶⁸ Godwin's *Enquiry*, a highly literate work, focused on the creation of an idealised and experimental society, with the emphasis on moral integrity and intellectual development. Meanwhile, Spence continued to propose a radical agrarian equality in the form of a collective ownership of land. He claimed that Paine did not go far enough in his land reforms, as proposed in the *Rights of man* and in *Agrarian justice*.⁶⁹ Although Spence, and Godwin each developed a small band of followers, neither had anything like the impact of Paine.⁷⁰ Within the more mainstream radicalism John Oswald continued to make radical proposals. Living in Paris, and an active member of the Jacobin Club, he promoted a form of direct democracy.⁷¹ Yorke advocated that 'the People govern themselves' and the 'jimcrack nonsense . . . the *balance of power*' be abolished.⁷² Joseph Gerrald advocated creating a convention like that of 'our Saxon ancestors' in their 'folk-mote', where '*the majority of wills*' dominated government. But he also

---

⁶² Ibid. 35.
⁶³ Godwin, *Enquiry concerning political justice*, 475.
⁶⁴ Yorke, *Thoughts on civil government*, 257.
⁶⁵ [Citizen Randol, of Ostend], *A political catechism of man*, 1795, 30.
⁶⁶ Dyer, *Complaints of the poor people*, 8.
⁶⁷ See, for example, John Lovett, *The citizen of the world*, 1793, 13.
⁶⁸ Philp has argued that Godwin was not 'just another enthusiastic radical taking up his pen to add his weight to the radical side of the debate', but was involved in 'a very different kind of activity': *Godwin's political justice*, Ithaca, NY 1986, 59. Godwin's *Enquiry concerning political justice* does not feature as a major contributor to this study because, as a very long and philosophical book aimed at a literate elite, it remained distant and distinct from the polemical pamphlet debates: Philp, *Godwin's political justice*, 73–9.
⁶⁹ Spence, *The rights of infants*, 52.
⁷⁰ Claeys, *Thomas Paine*, 133–4.
⁷¹ Oswald, *Government of the people*, 96; Dinwiddy, 'Conceptions of revolution', 539–40.
⁷² Yorke, *Thoughts on civil government*, 257.

declared that 'To the want of an adequate representation in parliament may be traced all our sufferings, under whatever aspect they are presented.' He therefore wanted 'not a breach, but a renovation of our constitution'.[73]

It is true that there was still some revolutionary rhetoric to be found in the pamphlets. Yorke celebrated that 'Despotism is in agony . . . Hear ye not, the *tocsin* of Freedom ringing throughout the world, and calling the dead to life . . . the clanking of chains, and their millions of living Beings preparing to take a terrible vengeance on their Oppressors'.[74] Randol lauded Paine and his followers for waving 'the celestial banners of the rights of man, over the tottering bastiles of Europe; to break the shackles of despotism from the ankles of millions, and destroy those yokes of oppression, vainly reserved by the impious ministers of misguided monarchs'.[75] Paine continued to support his own vision of republicanism and declared in 1795: 'I have always considered the present Constitution of the French Republic the *best organized system* the human mind has yet produced.'[76] Nevertheless for the most part revolutionary rhetoric did not reflect a desire to introduce a republic into England. Even the radical John Thelwall, whilst lauding the 'brave republic of France – whose republicanism ought to be no crime in our eyes', in 1795 advocated for England only 'annual parliaments, and universal suffrage; by which, and which alone, plenty and happiness can ever be extended to the majority of the people in this country'.[77]

Clearly events in France had diluted enthusiasm for Painite republicanism amongst many radicals. As William Frend[78] said, 'The assassinations, murders, massacres, burning of houses, plundering of property, open violations of justice, which have marked the progress of the French Revolution, must stagger the boldest republican in his wishes to overthrow any constitution.'[79] An anonymous pamphleteer in 1795 declared an 'ardent wish' that 'our glorious and much loved constitution' may not 'fall to pieces and make room for a much-dreaded republic'.[80] And Major Cartwright, the veteran reformer, argued that 'to restore the constitution at home' was the only way to 'contend with republican *France*'.[81] John Baxter even suggested resorting to 'Addresses, Petitions, or Remonstrances . . . either to the King or Parliament'

---

[73] Gerrald, A convention, 202, 193.
[74] Yorke, Thoughts on civil government, 229.
[75] [Randol], Political catechism, 8.
[76] Thomas Paine, Letter to the legislature and executive directory of the French Republic, attached to his Agrarian justice, 1796, in Foot and Kramnick, Thomas Paine reader, 472.
[77] John Thelwall, Peaceful discussion, and not tumultuary violence, the means of redressing national grievance, 1795, in Claeys, Political writings, iv. 401.
[78] Claeys has identified William Frend as a 'Unitarian reformer' but included him in his collection of radical pamphlets: Frend, Peace and union, 105.
[79] Ibid.
[80] Anon., A political freethinker's thoughts on the present circumstances, 1795, in Claeys, Political writings, iv. 434.
[81] Cartwright, Commonwealth in danger, 44.

as the means to provoke reform.⁸² Moreover a number of radicals promulgated the traditional English belief that England enjoyed greater political liberty than pre-revolutionary France. In apparently direct contradiction to the general condemnation of aristocracy, Frend declared that, whilst the origin of both governments was 'the feudal system', England had long-since abolished the evils of such a system which the French did not accomplish until the revolution.⁸³ And Daniel Stuart remarked that the English were 'much more happy and wealthy' because 'we have much less of the old system remaining' and 'more Liberty than is enjoyed under any other Monarchy'.⁸⁴

Even Thelwall stated that England did not require the 'violent resolutions' invoked by the French for 'we, in England' are 'happier' than the French for 'Political discussion has long been common among Englishmen'.⁸⁵ In his response to Burke's *Letter to a noble lord*, Thelwall went further and, in a somewhat out-of-character defence of aristocracy, suggested that it would be necessary to abolish the English aristocracy only if it became as reprehensible as the French. Thelwall condemned Burke's suggestion that the English aristocracy was similar to the French. He rebuked:

> if the titled great of Britain were what those of France had been, then should I exclaim in bitterness of my soul, that their crimes and their oppressions ought no longer to be endured – no longer protected by the laws and institutions of the land; but that they, also, in their turn, ought to be driven into ignominious banishment.⁸⁶

But, he confirmed, 'Never-never (let us hope) will the vices, the profligacy, the insolent oppression, and immeasurable rapacity of the French aristocracy, ravage and depopulate this country.'⁸⁷ Clearly many radicals were keen to show that whilst revolution had been necessary in France, it was not necessary in England.

Moreover, despite the fact that the popular societies became the major force of radicalism during this period, their focus too remained firmly on non-violent reform of the constitution. It is interesting to note that, whilst radical pamphlets aimed at the people contained some of the most vitriolic anti-aristocratic rhetoric, writings published by the popular societies did not generally focus on aristocracy. As in 1791-2, the popular societies included little anti-aristocratic rhetoric in their public documents,⁸⁸ although such rhetoric can be found in the private correspondence subsequently

---

⁸² Baxter, *Resistance to oppression*, 439.
⁸³ See, for example, Frend, *Peace and union*, 106.
⁸⁴ Stuart, *Peace and reform*, 303.
⁸⁵ Thelwall, *Peaceful discussion*, 396-7.
⁸⁶ Idem, *Sober reflections on the seditious and inflammatory letter of the Rt. Hon. Edmund Burke to a noble lord*, 1796, in Claeys, *Politics of English Jacobinism*, 380.
⁸⁷ Ibid.
⁸⁸ In fact, only three such references to aristocracy were discovered in this research: LCS, *Address to the nation*, 29 June 1795, in Thale, *LCS selections*, 270; Birmingham SCI, *Resolu-*

published.⁸⁹ Dickinson has argued that one of the reasons for the societies' failure to attack the aristocracy overtly, was that, like the Yorkshire Association a decade earlier, they feared alienating those from whom they hoped to gain support.⁹⁰ This may have been the case but fear of prosecution under sedition legislation is a more likely explanation.⁹¹ Many prominent radicals and leaders of the societies, including John Horne Tooke, Thomas Hardy, Daniel Adams, Henry Yorke and John Thelwall, were arrested and tried in 1794 and, in the same year, Joseph Gerrald was tried in Scotland and transported.⁹²

The LCS was accused of being involved in the 'Pop-Gun Plot' of 4 September 1794 and of intending to acquire arms from the 'arming societies'.⁹³ Yet in common with other radical societies it consistently reiterated its desire only for the reform of government and education of the people.⁹⁴ In April 1794 the LCS stated that although members 'will despise the frivolity of Aristocratic POLITESSE', they will 'not offend against the mild and necessary decrees of urbanity and civilized Society'.⁹⁵ The pan-Britain Convention at Edinburgh also confirmed that they wished only for 'THE RESTORATION OF ANNUAL PARLIAMENTS AND UNIVERSAL SUFFRAGE. WE GO NO FURTHER.'⁹⁶ As John Stevenson has confirmed, analysis of the radical societies' pronouncements 'reveals no more than outraged constitutionalism'.⁹⁷

Indeed, although Paine had condemned such methods, societies still promoted petitions to the king or government as a legitimate form of redress.⁹⁸ Joseph Gerrald, a member of the SCI and the LCS, in a pamphlet

---

tions, 4 March 1793, in Political broadsides, fo. 36; LCS, Resolutions and address at a general meeting, 14 April 1794, in Thale, LCS selections, 134.
⁸⁹ See, for example, LCS, The correspondence of the London Corresponding Society, London 1795, and Thompson, Making of the English working class, 131–3.
⁹⁰ See Dickinson, British radicalism, 14.
⁹¹ For studies of the trials see Clive Elmsley, 'An aspect of Pitt's "Terror": prosecutions for sedition during the 1790s', SH vi (1981), 155–84; Goodwin, Friends of liberty, 307–58; and Alan Wharam, The treason trials, 1794, Leicester 1992.
⁹² Goodwin, Friends of liberty, 329–34.
⁹³ The 'Pop-Gun Plot' was 'Allegedly a scheme devised by some LCS members to assassinate the king by shooting a poisoned arrow through an air gun'. This was not in fact a LCS plot, but a plot of a few anarchic members. Also, during Thomas Hardy's trial, controversy developed over connections between the LCS and 'the arming societies'. This was a question only of the LCS being guilty by association, on the grounds that Franklow's society in London and Watt's in Edinburgh had planned to arm. See discussion in Thale, LCS selections, 220, 232.
⁹⁴ See, for example, LCS, Address, 1793, in Claeys, Political writings, iv. 61.
⁹⁵ LCS, Resolutions and address, 134.
⁹⁶ British Convention, The address, 89.
⁹⁷ Stevenson, 'Popular radicalism', 73.
⁹⁸ Paine argued that the Bill of Rights allowed government to divide amongst itself all powers and profits. The nation was merely left with the right of petitioning, which was an insult: Rights of man, part 2, 193.

first printed in 1793, listed twenty-two peers who would sign and add weight to a proposed petition.[99] And it is striking that in the same year the LCS, a society which had previously promoted Paine's *Rights of man*, resolved that the duke of Richmond's letter to Colonel Sharman, originally dated 1783, be published and bound up with its regulations and a copy be given to every new member if finances allowed.[100] This letter incorporated the duke's reform plan which, whilst radical for 1783, was hardly so in 1795.[101]

Thus radical political activism was still entrenched in the limited discourse of reform, a discourse in many ways less radical than that promoted by the radical pamphleteers during the years 1791–2. Indeed some of the language and focus of criticisms made by the societies and some individual radicals reflected those of the reform movement of the 1780s and earlier. There was once again radical condemnation of rotten borough-mongers, corrupt courtiers, cabinet intrigue, party and faction.[102] Hence whilst radical pamphlets of 1791–2 maintained the focus on aristocracy, the radical political campaigns of 1793–6 reverted in some respects to the practices and language of the reform movement of the 1780s. The effect of this was to dilute the emphasis upon aristocracy, to make it more abstract and less a matter of immediate politics.

It is true that some radicals may have identified themselves as Painite republicans, as Jenny Graham has argued.[103] But that did not mean that they promoted republicanism in their published pamphlets.[104] Iain Hampsher-Monk has suggested that Thelwall 'privately admitted to republican sympathies'.[105] Yet this book shows that Thelwall's published works proposed only reform. Similarly many more radicals may have wanted to abolish their hereditary aristocracy than actually proposed it. Revolution was the only tried and tested route to so drastic a change to government, as the French had illustrated. But concrete proposals for initiating revolution are notably absent from either radical pamphlets or the public documents of the societies.

It is perhaps surprising that there were not more proposals for the introduction of an elective House of Lords, along the lines of the American

---

[99] See Gerrald, *A convention*, 210, and Claeys, *Political writings*, iv. 161, for biographical details of Gerrald.

[100] LCS, *Address*, 29 June 1795, 254–5.

[101] Richmond proposed a reform of government, the most radical element of which was his proposal for 'universal suffrage' as he termed manhood suffrage with a few limitations.

[102] Thelwall, *Peaceful discussion*, 392 and *Sober reflections*, 380–1; Cartwright, *Commonwealth in danger*, 119; LCS, *Address*, 57–8, 63–4; British Convention, *The address*, 92; Yorke, *Reason urged against precedent*, 69; Gerrald, *A convention*, 161–2; Frend, *Peace and union*, 108.

[103] Graham, *The nation, the law and the king*, 25.

[104] It should be noted that Graham rarely refers to the political pamphlets but largely relies on different primary sources, including much private correspondence published subsequently.

[105] However, he provides no source for this: Iain Hampsher-Monk, 'John Thelwall and the eighteenth-century radical response to political economy', *HJ* xxiv (1991), 4.

senate. Although America was commonly held up as an example of free government, proposals for introducing a similar system into England were not made during this period.[106] Indeed Frend argued that America was too different to be used as any kind of example.[107] Consequently the attack on aristocracy had nowhere to go. As John Cartwright recognised, the people 'can effect no change of system, but by their collective force and by actual violence'.[108] Ultimately calls for peaceful reform rather than violent revolution were almost universal. The pamphlets clearly indicated that one reason that the majority of radicals did not want a revolution was that they still supported some version of the English constitution. As a broadside claimed, reform was needed to 'reinstate the Constitution in its original purity'. This could only be obtained by 'a true Representation of the People'.[109]

This still leaves the historian questioning the purpose of anti-aristocratic rhetoric. Was it a genuine out-pouring of the hatred and resentment felt by an oppressed people against their oppressors, a mechanism to mobilise the people, or merely an adoption of French rhetorical tools to add novelty and bite to an otherwise familiar and hitherto unsuccessful movement for political reform? The answer is probably a mixture of all three, for individual 'radicals' clearly had different agendas. Radicals shared a rhetoric in their representations, which did not necessarily reflect the 'reality' of a shared political intent or ideology. What this rhetoric does reflect, however, is that the representations of aristocracy were at the very heart of radicalism in providing a potent enemy to be attacked, with words, if not by direct action.

Inequalities

It was within the campaign for reform, the demands for equality of political rights by means of increased representation and universal suffrage that the most concrete challenge to aristocratic hegemony was made, albeit indirectly. Here radicals continued to attack the political model of a propertied and enfranchised versus a propertyless and disenfranchised society, as defended by loyalists. Paine said that it was 'dangerous and impolitic, sometimes ridiculous, and always unjust to make property the criterion of the right of voting'.[110] Bentley attacked members of the Association:

> whose *pretence* is to preserve liberty and property – but whose *real* aim seems to be to persuade the Nation, that if the government make laws which allow

---

106 [Vaughan], *Catechism of man*, 225; Dyer, *Complaints of the poor*, 2.
107 Frend, *Peace and union*, 106.
108 Cartwright, *Commonwealth in danger*, pp. lxxvii–xxviii, 44.
109 John Hampden, *To the inhabitants of Nottingham*, 1793, in *Political broadsides*, fo. 81.
110 Thomas Paine, *Dissertation on first principles of government*, 1795, in Foot and Kramnick, *Thomas Paine reader*, 460.

honest, labouring men to have only *half so much* food and raiment as their forefathers had, they ought to be contented and happy with it – in order that the Associators may have *double the quantity* that *their* ancestors had![111]

Most radicals justified universal suffrage on the grounds that the people performed the labour that made the country its wealth and thus were entitled to an equal voice in politics. As Paine emphasised, it was 'the cultivator and the manufacturer' who were 'the primary means of all the wealth that exists in the world'.[112] Cartwright declared that giving the people a vote was not arming them with weapons and he asked: 'what would be the condition of political society if the husbandman and the artizan were not members of it? ... tell me whether he who weaves or he who wears the broad-cloth, is the most useful member of political society'.[113] The British Convention at Edinburgh argued that value was in 'the honest hands that bring forth the fruits of industry', and not 'the useless mouths which consume them'.[114] Lovett stated that the idle rich man was 'a useless being on earth' and concluded that the rich should work for there could be 'thousands more of useful industrious people employed' and this would make them more happy.[115]

Thus radicals broadened the political meaning of 'property' to define not merely land and wealth but also the means of acquiring them. To Thelwall 'Property is nothing but human labour. The most inestimable of all property is the sweat of the poor man's brow.'[116] Gerrald concurred: '[the] manual labour of the peasant, the ingenuity of the artist, the talents of the scholar, are the property of each'. He continued: 'He who enjoys a comfortable income from the earnings of his industry, is equally a man of property, with him who, by the partial regulations of society, inherits it from his ancestors.'[117] Stuart argued that 'Dr. Smith, and all profound political oeconomists, affirm, every Artizan, Manufacturer, and Labourer' to be as 'valuable to the state as acres of land'. Indeed the principles and practice of the constitution recognised 'all who were of CONSIDERATION' whether by 'Landed Property' or 'Manufactures or Commerce' and, as the latter 'now are of much more importance to the kingdom than its land', the franchise should be extended accordingly.[118] In an inversion of Burke the British Convention at Edinburgh claimed that it was 'those useful and laborious occupations of life, which, while they contribute to the ease and comfort of the rich, are the solid pillars which support the great fabric of society'.[119]

---

[111] Thomas Bentley, *The poor man's answer to the rich associators*, 1793, 1.
[112] Ibid. 461–2.
[113] Cartwright, *Commonwealth in danger*, 90.
[114] British Convention, *The address*, 92.
[115] Lovett, *Citizen of the world*, 4–7.
[116] Thelwall, *Natural and constitutional rights*, 31.
[117] Gerrald, *A convention*, 204–6.
[118] Stuart, *Peace and reform*, 303, 314.
[119] British Convention, *The address*, 92.

Ultimately Thelwall called on 'Ye artificers, ye mechanics, ye manufacturers of the land! ye genuine props and pillars of the nation', to agitate once more for reform.[120] Hence radicals argued that value, both economic and moral, was in the making and not the wearing, with the producer and not the consumer. Here radicals drew upon the ideas of theorists such as John Locke and Adam Smith. Whilst Locke's labour theory implied property rights in labour, Smith confirmed that 'the produce of labour constitutes the natural recompense or wages of labour', but in capitalist systems, the labourer 'must share it with the owner of the stock which employs him'.[121] Thus, in their campaign for political equality, radicals constantly reinterpreted the political meaning of property to encompass not just land but all, even the most esoteric, forms of property. They challenged the traditional source of power in English politics, land. And the clear implication of this challenge was that the aristocracy's link with land, its ownership of great estates, no longer justified its political dominance. Discourse about the political significance of land perhaps constituted the most important attack on aristocracy in real terms.

Moreover economic equality also remained at the top of the agenda in radical pamphlets. Radicals were united in their belief that the war with France was responsible for the increased poverty and hardship suffered by the people.[122] As the LCS put it in July 1793:

> British gold now subsidizes armies of Continental Slaves, and the blood of half Europe is pledged for the destruction of France! Supplies of every kind are sent from hence! Commerce is nearly stopped! Failures innumerable take place! Manufacturers are ruined! Artizans are starving! Provisions rise in price! the Revenue decreases, and fresh Taxes are wanting! for fresh supplies of blood, the Liberties of our Country are invaded! The Seaman is forcibly torn from his family! The Peasant kidnapped from the plough! and the starving Labourer is compelled to sell his Life and his Liberty for Bread. – If such, O much oppressed Britons! are the effects of a four months' War, what are you to expect when it shall have lasted as many years?[123]

The British Convention at Edinburgh agreed that the 'present situation of

---

[120] Thelwall, *Rights of nature*, 404.
[121] Adam Smith, *The wealth of nations*, ed. E. B. Bax, London 1905, i. 48, 65, as quoted in Perkin, *Origins*, 233.
[122] For studies on the war with France see Clive Elmsley, *British society and the French wars, 1793–1815*, London 1979, and his 'Revolution, war and the nation state: the British and French experiences, 1789–1801', in Philp, *French revolution*, 99–117; Wells, 'English society and revolutionary politics', and *Wretched faces: famine in wartime England, 1793–1801*, Gloucester 1988; C. K. Harley, 'British industrialisation before 1841: evidence of lower growth during the Industrial Revolution', *Journal of Economic History* xcii (1982), 267–89; and J. E. Cookson, 'Political arithmetic and war in Britain, 1793–1815', *War and Society* i (1983), 37–60, and 'The English volunteer movement of the French wars, 1793–1815: some contexts', *HJ* xxxii (1989), 867–91.
[123] LCS, *Address*, in Claeys, *Political writings*, iv. 63.

the people is awful and alarming to a degree hitherto unparalleled'.[124] The Birmingham SCI in March 1793 complained that, due to the war and corruption, 'the working part of the nation are grievously oppressed, by an enormous public debt of *Two Hundred and Seventy Millions*' and 'a dreadful catalogue of Taxes' and 'the dearness of the necessaries of life'.[125] By 1795 the LCS was claiming that as a result of 'the present cruel and disastrous War, gaunt Famine stalks along your streets, and haggard Wretched-ness assails you in every shape', while 'the present Ministry', is 'exporting your food to foreign mercenaries'.[126]

Just as aristocracy was held responsible, partially at least, for the war, it was also the focus of much criticism regarding economic inequality in radical pamphlets of 1793–6. The Painite model of an *ancien régime*, of 'aristocracy and people' was also dominant here. Baxter condemned 'the Pride and Luxury of the Great' who were building 'splendid Houses' and 'even elegant Dog-Kennels', as well as converting arable land 'into Pasturage for the breed of Horses for pleasure', while 'the honest and labouring Poor cannot obtain the necessaries of Life'.[127] One anonymous pamphleteer declared that

> [the] prosperity of a nation does not, according to modern calculation, consist in the improved condition of the people, but in the childish and expensive splendour of courts, in the pride and insolence of an over-grown nobility, pensioned on the public purse, and doubling the necessary taxation; and, above all, in the accumulation of wealth in a few hands.[128]

As Frend pointed out, 'the fault of most governments seems chiefly to consist in this, that they pay the most attention to the maintenance and support of the Corinthian Capitals of society,[129] as some orders have foolishly been called, to the great neglect of the comfort and wellfare of the most numerous and important part of the community'.[130]

Thelwall confirmed that it was the aristocracy, the 'idle class', with its elevation based in the feudal system, which had kept the people in ignorance and poverty. For, 'as accumulation encreases, the comparative ignorance of the multitude increases . . . the incessant labour, to which they are doomed, to support the wasteful luxury and profligate ostentation of the idle class' sinks them lower into a state of ignorance. Indeed it becomes 'a matter of state policy, among these idle classes, to keep the mass of mankind as ignorant as possible: the dull brain, as well as the strong shoulder . . . being

---

124 British Convention, *The address*, 93.
125 Birmingham SCI, *Resolutions*, in *Political broadsides*, fo. 36.
126 LCS, *General meeting*, 29 June 1795, 253–4.
127 Baxter, *Resistance to oppression*, 441.
128 Anon., *Estimate of the value of national opulence to the mass of the people*, in Eaton, *Politics for the people*, pt i, 75.
129 Burke (ed. O'Brien), *Reflections*, 245.
130 Frend, *Peace and union*, 113.

regarded as a necessary ... to bear the heavy yoke'.[131] Yorke also identified aristocracy as at the root of inequality: 'the institution of privileged orders is usurpation, and its continuance criminal' and the 'tendency of every species of public monopoly, whether of honours, distinctions, or traffic, is to perpetuate errors, prejudices, corruptions, dependence, and to enrich and exalt a *few*, by the impoverishment, vassalage, ignorance, and venality of the *many*'.[132] Thus, radicals argued, not only did the aristocracy retain the wealth of the nation for its own it also intentionally kept the people poor and ignorant.

Moreover radicals challenged the loyalist promotion of a commercial and prosperous England where all benefited. Thomas Bentley attacked claims of 'prosperity and happiness, which have been lately so profusely and publicly made'.[133] Lovett declared that it was not the case that the wealth and luxury of the rich brought prosperity for all. For whilst 'the higher orders of people receive the luxuries of life in abundance ... to support these luxuries the poor are robbed'.[134] In any event, he continued, 'The riches of England is not real, but imaginary', it has all 'been spent in foreign wars'.[135] Commerce had in fact only 'sunk the industrious poor into still more abject misery' and this was because 'only the opulent and powerful are represented in Parliament' and so only their interests were served.[136] Baxter declared that the people would not believe 'the Assertion of a corrupt and hypocritical Minister, and his dependants' that commerce was flourishing, when evidence of poverty and hardship as a result of 'this accursed War' was plain to see.[137]

Returning to the fray Thomas Paine mused 'whether that state that is proudly, perhaps erroneously called civilisation, has most promoted or most injured the general happiness, is a question that may be strongly contested'. For 'on one side, the spectator is dazzled by splendid appearances; on the other, he is shocked by extremes of wretchedness'. Paine noted that 'The most affluent and the most miserable ... are to be found in the countries that are called civilised.'[138] Instead radicals argued that it was only America that actually possessed the commercial society that the loyalists had identified in England.[139]

The solutions displayed in pamphlets to such extreme inequality were in general no more radical during 1793–6 than in 1791–2. Few plans for

---

131 Thelwall, *Rights of nature*, 486.
132 Yorke, *Thoughts on civil government*, 258.
133 Thomas Bentley, *The poor man's answer to the rich associators*, 1793, 2.
134 Lovett, *Citizen of the world*, 6.
135 Ibid. 9.
136 Thelwall, *Natural and constitutional rights*, 30–1.
137 Baxter, *Resistance to oppression*, 440–1.
138 Thomas Paine, *Agrarian justice*, 1795, in Foot and Kramnick, *Paine reader*, 474–5. It should be noted, however, that this text is listed elsewhere, including on the BLPC, as first published in 1796 and both Claeys and Godwin identify it as published in 1797: Claeys, *Thomas Paine*, 33; Goodwin, *Friends of liberty*, 581. 1796 appears to be the correct date.
139 Gerrald, *A convention*, 170; Lovett, *Citizen of the world*, 43.

agrarian equality were proposed, although Godwin's *avant-garde* blueprint for a new society with no private ownership of land and an equal distribution of goods was published.[140] Moreover, in the main, radicals still did not focus upon equality of property. In his *Dissertation on first principles of government* (1795), Paine condemned only hereditary property and accepted that 'property will always be unequal', because people differed in talents, ambitions and opportunities.[141] In *Agrarian justice*, Paine again promoted a redistribution of wealth. He argued that private property in 'cultivated' land could, and indeed did, legitimately exist, but that compensation should be paid to the community by landholders for the loss of the land to the people.[142] Thelwall also rejected ideas of 'equality of landed possession', because it would not be commercially practical, and because the introduction of such a concept would inevitably lead to violence and disorder.[143] He claimed, in terms surprisingly similar to those of the loyalists, that rather than being levelled, society should consist of 'imperceptible gradations of rank, where step rises above step' and 'all were connected together by inseparable interests'.[144]

Yet whilst the traditional condemnation of wealth as the source of luxury was still to be found in radical writings during this period, a debate about the inequality of wealth in the workplace was also emerging.[145] Indeed some radicals began to call for a fairer share of wages for the poor labourer and here it was not the aristocracy *per se* that was identified as the perpetrator of such inequality in the workplace.[146] Paine argued that 'the accumulation of personal property is, in many instances, the effect of paying too little for the labour that produced it'. Consequently 'the working hand perishes in old age, and the employer abounds in affluence'.[147] James Parkinson condemned 'the permitting at the same time, the combination of masters and the severe laws against the combination of workmen to exist' as 'infamously unjust, partial and oppressive'. And 'by preventing wages rising beyond a certain point, determined by the masters themselves, and by placing no limits to their

---

[140] Godwin, *Enquiry concerning political justice*. See also Lovett, *Citizen of the world*, 1–3; Oswald, *Government of the people*, 102; and Bentley, *Rights of the poor*, 2. Spence continued to promote primarily the same system of redistribution of land throughout his political writings as in his *Real rights*, 1790.
[141] Thomas Paine, *Dissertation on first principles of government*, 1795, in Foot and Kramnick, *Thomas Paine reader*, 462.
[142] Paine, *Agrarian justice*, 477–8.
[143] Thelwall, *Rights of nature*, 472–3.
[144] Idem, *The tribune*, ii, as quoted in Claeys, *Politics of English Jacobinism*, p. xliii.
[145] Bentley, *Rights of the poor*, 1.
[146] For studies on early trades unionism see Thompson, *Making of the English working class*; John Rule, *The labouring classes in early industrial England, 1750–1850*, London 1986; John Rule (ed.), *British trade unionism, 1750–1850: the formative years*, London 1988; and J. Smail, 'New languages for labour and capital: the transformation of discourse in the early years of the industrial revolution', *SH* xii (1987), 49–71.
[147] Paine, *Agrarian justice*, 485.

depression' little encouragement is 'held out to industry and ingenuity'.[148] It was the 'great disproportion between the rates of wages of labor, and the prices of necessaries, or the expences of living, among the majority of the working-people' that was increasingly causing concern to radicals.[149] Dyer claimed that the 'principal grievance of the poor people of England' was 'the high price of provision' but, if 'the price of labour rose with the price of provision, the people would eventually, on this head, have no cause for complaint'.[150] And here it was 'the employer' or 'the master' who was the focus of radical criticism, rather than the aristocracy.

It was Thelwall who pursued this issue most thoroughly.[151] He, with Paine, was one of the first to seek solutions to poverty in economic terms, in fair wages rather than merely in political rights. In the *Rights of nature* (1796), he declared that much was said about the rights of property, the crown, parliament and the peerage but 'let us, for once, enquire a little into the RIGHTS OF LABOURERS'.[152] Thelwall sought to 'restore the freedom of commerce' by giving to all 'an equal participation of all the necessaries of life, which are the product of their labour'.[153] He commented upon 'the scandalously inadequate price of labour-wages' and 'the unreasonable number of hours through which the labour of the day is protracted'.[154] There was, he argued, an implied compact between employer and labourer, the object of which was 'to promote the accommodation of the whole' of civil society. All the 'abundancies' of life stemmed from labour. The labourer, therefore, has 'a right (as his share of the benefit) to maintain himself, *and a family*, in decency and plenty' and to give his children an education. The landed proprietor 'is only a trustee for the community' and is entitled only to fair compensation for his role.[155]

Thelwall promoted a society, reflecting his vision of America, where 'every hired cultivator is enabled, by tolerance diligence and sobriety, to become, in time, a master and proprietor himself'.[156] Capitalism clearly became attractive to Thelwall as a possible means of achieving the emancipation of the labouring classes.[157] He also perceived the possibility of the labour force forming a powerful political society of its own. As he said, 'every large workshop and manufactory is a sort of political society, which no act of

---

148 [Parkinson], *Knaves acre association*, 15.
149 Bentley, *Rights of the poor*, 3.
150 Dyer, *Complaints of the poor*, 98.
151 For Thelwall see Claeys, *Politics of English Jacobinism*, pp. xiii–lx; Geoffrey Gallop, 'Ideology and the English Jacobins: the case of John Thelwall', *Enlightenment and Dissent* v (1986), 3–20; Hampsher-Monk, 'John Thelwall', 1–20; and E. P. Thompson, 'Hunting the Jacobin Fox', *P&P* cxlii (1994), 94–140.
152 Thelwall, *Rights of nature*, 476.
153 Idem, *The tribune*, i. 67; iii. 290.
154 Idem, *Rights of nature*, 399.
155 Ibid. 477–8.
156 Ibid. 479.
157 Hampsher-Monk, 'John Thelwall', 18.

parliament could silence and no magistrate disperse'.[158] Thelwall recognised that it was a capitalist economic system with an active labour movement, which could potentially deliver both a voice to the people through a united labour force and greater equality to all through fairer wages.

Moreover, in his move towards seeking solutions to inequality through redistribution within a capitalist economic system, Thelwall identified monopolies, both governmental and commercial, rather than aristocracy as the source of economic inequality. It was an 'organized system of monopoly', which, 'in spite of an abundant harvest', denied 'to the craving family of the artificer and the peasant, . . . a plenteous meal'.[159] Such monopolies created 'an artificial scarcity' by destroying produce which 'cannot be sold at an extravagant price', rather than allowing 'the swinish multitude' to enjoy it'.[160] Other radicals also identified different commercial elites in the debate about economic equality. Bentley complained of 'the exclusive privileges, franchises, or charters, possessed by many trades, and corporations'.[161] The LCS stated that high prices were caused partly by the war, but 'chiefly by that pernicious system of monopoly'.[162] Inevitably, in the debate about fairer wages for labourers, an elite of employers or masters began to emerge in radical pamphlets.

Thus, although for Thelwall and the majority of other radicals aristocracy was at the root of the present inequality and corruption, radical representations suggest that a few, at least, were beginning to seek the solutions to inequality in economics rather than politics. The pamphlets reveal that this did not merely mean, as Wahrman has suggested, that radicals had made the simple shift from the political formulation of 'aristocracy and people' to the social formulation of 'rich and poor', which reiterated the same 'oppressive antitheses'.[163] The representations show that radicals, as well as loyalists, were beginning to move away from structuring the social structure upon the Painite dual scheme, as an *ancien régime* of 'aristocracy and people'. In fact the emerging radical focus on capitalist relations in the workplace, in a commercial and industrial environment, came dangerously close to repositioning the country within the competing loyalist commercial model.[164] But with, for radicals, different social implications.

---

[158] Thelwall, Rights of nature, 400. See also Goodwin, Friends of liberty, 473.
[159] Thelwall, Rights of nature, 391–2.
[160] Idem, The tribune, i. 70; Butler, Burke, Paine, Godwin, 208.
[161] Bentley, Rights of the poor, 3.
[162] LCS, Proceedings of a meeting, 326, 318. See also LCS, Account of general meeting, 53–4.
[163] Wahrman, Imagining the middle class, 76.
[164] Hampsher-Monk, 'John Thelwall', 20.

Rhetoric or revolution?

Despite the caustic anti-aristocratic rhetoric vomiting forth from them, radical pamphlets did not reflect a united desire for revolution, republican government or agrarian equality. It was only a few, and a disparate few, that proposed any truly radical action. Since they were campaigning against great odds, most limited their programme to a few key aims. Radical pamphlets show that the majority, and crucially among them the popular societies such as the LCS and SCI, continued to agitate only for the reform of government as it was presently structured. Whilst the accompanying discourse on the incumbent property qualification for political rights did present a concrete but indirect challenge to aristocratic supremacy, such reform would have had little direct effect on the House of Lords. Thus in reality the radical attack on aristocracy was of uncertain application and ultimately had nowhere to go except revolution and by 1793–6 few would even contemplate that. Moreover the shift away from the focus on condemnation of aristocracy *per se*, and towards a broader, commercial elite by the likes of Thelwall, moved radicalism away from the Painite focus upon an *ancien régime* England on the old 'aristocracy and people' model. Unfortunately for radicalism this shift inadvertently brought radicalism closer to loyalist representations of a modern commercial and industrial nation.

Nevertheless the plethora of radical representations of the English aristocracy published between 1791–6, when taken together, must inevitably have altered perceptions amongst the people. It is an important point that, from Paine to Yorke, the most consistently radical representations to be found in radical pamphlets concerned the aristocracy. No doubt such representations were damaging to the aristocracy, not because they were necessarily accurate, but because they identified the aristocracy as both a tyrannical oligarchy and a corrupt, idle, profligate, parasitic elite, a separate caste, similar to the aristocracy of the French *ancien régime*. And with the majority of radicals and reformers still seeking reform within the constitution it was surely their portrayals of aristocracy, rather than their actual proposals for reform, that presented the greatest immediate challenge to aristocratic political and social hegemony.

Furthermore, sedition proceedings brought by the government against radicals increased, particularly in the treason trials of 1794. From 1792 the publication of radical material had become increasingly perilous. Government action thus changed the dynamics of the French Revolution debate. Radicalism was no longer in the position of attacker, but was forced onto the defensive. Increasingly radicalism represented itself only as the 'victim' of, rather than a contender for, power.[165] Events in France also rendered the cause of revolution more opaque. It is significant that it was predominantly in

---

[165] Williams, *Artisans and sans-culottes*, 101.

its vitriolic anti-aristocratic rhetoric that radicalism remained within the context of an attack. Radicalism needed to represent England as an *ancien régime* dominated by a hegemonic aristocracy, like pre-revolutionary France, in order to win the argument. Loyalist writers, by contrast, moved away from the focus upon aristocracy and the image of an *ancien régime* that accompanied it. Thus it was loyalist writers during 1793–6 who took up the cudgel of attack and moved in for the argumentative kill.

5

Loyalist Strategies and Synthesis, 1793–1796

> The question before us is not, whether the British Flag shall maintain honour, or the British Name respect – whether we shall preserve our Commerce or our Colonies, nor even whether we shall continue to enjoy the mild and benign influence of our Laws, Religion, and inimitable form of Government; – but, whether . . . we shall become prey to devouring anarchy, and experience the horrors of which France presents so dreadful a spectacle, and which she endeavours to render universal.[1]

Many of the issues raised in loyalist pamphlets during the years 1791–2 remained important in 1793–6. The reverence for the English constitution and issues concerning leadership and equality were all still frequently raised by loyalists. Within these debates a number of shifts in emphasis can also be detected. These were largely due to changing events in France and their effect on English politics. Above all the fact that the two countries were at war and 'the Terror' in France from September 1793 to July 1794 gave loyalists much ammunition for condemnation of the revolution. Their confidence increased as radicalism became increasingly fragmented. Loyalists therefore took the opportunity to compare a commercial and prosperous England (or Britain – the terms were used interchangeably) under stable government with a starving and anarchic France.

In loyalist representations the focus began to shift away from aristocracy and towards criticism of the increasingly demagogic leadership in France, compared with a broader, open elite in England. Mainstream loyalism developed a stronger commercial emphasis. It was not government and political rights that were the locus of loyalist pamphlets but wealth and prosperity in a commercial and successful nation, with its traditional system of mixed government preserved. Crucially then the aristocracy was moved out of the limelight in the French Revolution debate. Aristocracy no longer required defending at home, but became part of the defence. Nevertheless it was still representations rather than a sociological reality which were dominant in this debate. The English aristocracy may have been manoeuvred out of centre-stage in loyalist representations, but in reality little had changed and the aristocracy was still at the centre of the establishment which the loyalists were defending.

---

1   John Bowles, *Objections to the continuance of the war examined and refuted*, 1794, 56.

During the years 1791–2 a number of 'loyalisms' had emerged in the pamphlets. In particular the conservative reactionary Anglican position identified by historians as the source of the later Tory party was still upheld by those on the far right of the debate. Certainly the longevity of such conservative ideas is illustrated by the publication of loyalist periodicals: the *British Critic* (1793–1843) and the *Anti-Jacobin* (1797–8) and its successor the *Anti-Jacobin Review and Magazine*, published until 1821.[2] Yet, whilst various loyalisms, political and religious, continued to exist during 1793–6, a new unity developed between two significant loyalist groups. In the years 1791–2 as well as the conservative defence of 'Church and State' there developed a new defence. Some loyalists clearly recognised that it was necessary to move away from the model of English society as an *ancien régime* of 'aristocracy and people', promoted by radicals.[3] Consequently, some moderate loyalists developed a new model which defined a commercial and prosperous England benefiting from industrial and colonial expansion with a largely economically gradated society and an open elite.[4] During the years 1793–6, however, this model was promoted by conservative supporters of Pitt's government as well as more moderate loyalists. The fact that the Portland Whigs finally split from the Foxite reform Whigs over war with France in 1794 and formed a coalition with Pitt's government must have added a new, and stronger Whig dimension to conservative loyalism. As a result a synthesis of political conservatism and more liberal commercialism can be seen developing within loyalism. The two-fold loyalism of the conservative political model and the new commercial model were forming an increasingly unitary 'loyalism'. Certainly, mainstream loyalism became increasingly more Whig than Tory, more a defence of the mixed constitution than a 'conservative reaction'.[5] As a result of this greater unity radical issues of political rights and reform of government were brushed aside by a newly confident loyalism.

Moreover during the period 1793–6 one important aim of loyalist writers was gaining the support of the working people. Many pamphlets were written for a popular audience.[6] In particular the Association for the Preservation of Liberty and Property against Republicans and Levellers, which was founded by John Reeves in November 1792, published many such tracts, written by the Association and other loyalists.[7] Fear of revolution at home and invasion from France also prompted loyalists to write pamphlets which attempted to

---

[2] The latter of these publications has been identified by Gunn as promoting a 'High-Tory' position: *Beyond liberty*, 176–7.
[3] Warhman, *Imagining the middle class*, 35–6.
[4] For the rejection of the Painite model and the emergence of the loyalist commercial model see chapter 3 above.
[5] Claeys, *Thomas Paine*, 154–5.
[6] For greater symmetry, the pamphlets aimed at the people, including a few early ones dated 1792, are included in this chapter.
[7] John Reeves is described by Goodwin as 'a monopolist, if there ever was one, of lucrative public offices': *Friends of liberty*, 264

recruit the labouring poor to the loyalist cause. Such fears, together with an abiding fear of French atheism, likewise provoked many Anglican clergymen and evangelical laymen to put pen to paper.[8] Anglican conservative pamphlets, aimed at the people generally, continued to emphasise concepts of political obedience and non-resistance and acceptance of one's place in the social order, as they had in 1791–2. Some pamphlets, however, took a more commercial position and promoted the loyalist commercial model.

Redefining the elite

Language is of importance to the French Revolution debate at this stage as much for what is not said as for what is said. The term 'aristocracy' was not used by loyalists to identify the English nobility during the period 1793–6, and rarely even to identify its role in the House of Lords. It had become even more of a taboo than during 1791–2. A typical attitude among the loyalist pamphleteers was expressed by Charles Patton, who confirmed that 'the word *aristocracy* properly means a government of the nobles or peers' but then argued that it had become 'of so indeterminate a signification' that it should be rejected.[9] 'Aristocracy' had been adopted by English radicals, with all the negative French connotations, as a term of abuse.[10] As the reign of Terror took hold in France, in September 1793, the persecution of *'aristocrates'* – a term loosely used in France to mean anyone opposed to the revolutionary regime – became a function of the Jacobin government.[11] Arthur Young noted that in France 'The cry of aristocrat or traitor is followed by immediate imprisonment or death.'[12] One pamphleteer was not alone in distancing England and its aristocracy from the French; 'the conduct of our nobility and gentry' is 'at least as good a testimony in their favour, as the senseless cry of aristocrat can be against these orders'.[13]

Paradoxically loyalists identified the new French leadership as an 'aristocracy' of a different kind. Loyalists continued to claim that in republics and democracies the leadership inevitably became an 'aristocracy'. The French could not, warned John Somers Cocks, 'curb the aristocracy . . . as we

---

[8] Anglican clergymen and evangelical laymen did, however, present a more conservative position than that taken by the majority of mainstream loyalist writers.
[9] Charles Patton, *An attempt to establish the basis of freedom on simple and unerring principles*, Edinburgh 1793, in Claeys, *Political writings*, vi. 388–9.
[10] See chapter 2 above.
[11] In 1793 the Jacobins, lead by Maximilien de Robespierre, instituted the reign of terror to deal with internal enemies of the French Republic. Robespierre justified the use of terror to defend democracy in his speech of 5 February 1794: Marvin Perry, Joseph R. Peden and Theordore H. Von Laue (eds), *Sources of the western tradition*, Boston, Mass. 1991, ii. 102–3.
[12] Young, *Example of France*, 73.
[13] Anon., *An exposure of the domestic and foreign attempts to destroy the British constitution, upon the doctrines recommended by a member of parliament*, 1793, 39.

Englishmen do now'.[14] Aristocracy, one anonymous pamphleteer confirmed, was rule by those 'Ambitious and aspiring spirits' that existed 'in all communities', who in time would rise to power and 'if not checked will be dangerous to the community'. Such an aristocracy could not be found in mixed government, where there was 'a check to the ambition of the great' but could be found in republican France.[15] Loyalists suggested that France had merely replaced one tyranny with another, absolute monarchy with an aristocracy of demagogues. This was prefigured in Burke's *Reflections*, where he had warned that the leaders of the National Assembly would become demagogues.[16]

Pamphlets aimed at the people relied on their readers' ignorance of the complexities surrounding the term 'aristocracy'. One address, the text written as by a 'poor man', complained that radicals spoke of 'Aristocrates and Democrates, and twenty other hard words which I have never heard of'.[17] Another pamphlet explained, 'YOU have lately heard some folks talk about a thing called Aristocracy ... Now if the Lords were to say, that the King and Members sent by Voters should not help to make Laws that would be Aristocracy.' Such an 'Aristocracy', it was stated, was of no benefit to the people for 'The Lords would begin quarrelling about who should be uppermost'. They would bribe the unruly to get a mob together and the people would be reduced to slaves. For 'in all places where an Aristocracy has been set up ... the People have been always used like slaves'.[18] Thus the term 'aristocracy' was returned to the traditional classical interpretation as a form of tyrannical government of the few, to be found largely in republics. And this was the interpretation adopted by loyalists during 1793-6. For the most part loyalists avoided using the term 'aristocracy' at all to describe the English nobility, or indeed any other formulation of the English elite.

Some loyalists, particularly Anglican clergymen, continued to describe an elite of the 'nobility'. This was generally defined by loyalists in terms of membership of the House of Lords. One writer claimed 'we think an order of nobility' 'necessary both to the maintenance of the crown and the protection of the people'. The 'nobility ... as a body' were suited for this role for they had 'an eminent sense of honour and loyalty, and an hereditary pride in that character'.[19] Yet in general broader definitions of the elite were dominant during this period. Definitions generally complied with the loyalist model of an open elite. As Corfield has noted, by the later eighteenth century

---

[14] John Somers Cocks, *A short treatise on the dreadful tendency of levelling principles*, 1793, in Claeys, *Political writings*, vii. 353-4.
[15] Anon., *A new dialogue between Monsieur Francois and John English on the French Revolution*, c. 1793, in Claeys, *Political writings*, viii. 15.
[16] Burke (ed. O'Brien), *Reflections*, 129-34, 214.
[17] Anon., *Address to the members of the various box-clubs and benefit societies in Great Britain by Strap Bodkin, staymaker*, 1793, in *Association papers*, part 2, no. 6, 13.
[18] Anon., *A parish clerk's advice to the good people, on the present times*, 1793, in *Association papers*, part 2, no. 7, 5.
[19] Anon., *Exposure of the domestic*, 42, 44.

concepts of economic 'class' were in common usage.[20] Yet, as Young illustrated, loyalists preferred not to define too closely a 'class, order or set of men'.[21] Concepts of class were still too close to radical and French identifications of the aristocracy. Loyalist definitions of the elite reflected the commercial and prosperous nation they promoted. A pamphlet addressed to the people defined 'the great' and 'the poor', 'superiors' and 'inferiors' but focused on the 'profits of masters' and 'Journeymen's wages'.[22] One pamphleteer described England's society in economic terms: the 'Master' employs the 'servant', the 'Tradesman' employs 'Journeymen and Apprentices', the 'Farmer' engages 'your Carters, Threshers, Hedgers, and Shepherds', a 'Clothier' employs 'Scribblers, Shearmen, and Burlers', and, 'if you are a Hard-ware maker at Birmingham or Sheffield', you have 'workmen' to work your 'Engines'.[23]

The elite was a broad and vague entity, which incorporated 'Master-Manufacturers, Traders and Others'.[24] In one pamphlet Young used economic categories and differentiated between 'THE LANDED INTEREST' which he defined merely as farmers, 'THE MONIED INTEREST', those with 'portable wealth' and 'THE COMMERCIAL INTEREST' which incorporated 'Traders and manufacturers'.[25] Moreover war with France was an event in which 'Every class – every rank is deeply interested; for it is the welfare of all which has been endangered', the 'Merchant, the Manufacturer, the Peasant, and the Peer – all persons of every description'.[26] Clearly it was no accident that the merchant and manufacturer were listed first here, for the survival of commerce and industry were of primary importance during the war and those who represented it had, loyalists implied, become more significant than the hereditary aristocracy. The economic elite was altogether a broader category from all walks of life, which by 1793 loyalists never described as 'aristocracy' and only rarely as 'nobility' without the addition of other elite groups.

Wahrman has argued that both radicals and loyalists were 'committed to a basic dual social scheme' of aristocracy and people. But whilst for radicals 'it was the abyss between these two social ends which was key', loyalists wanted 'to see the gap bridged'. Consequently loyalists often invoked 'a scheme of numerous social gradations, at small intervals, superimposed as it were on the basic dual paradigm'.[27] Yet the pamphlets reveal that those loyalists who did utilise a simple 'rich and poor' paradigm did so within the context of the graduated commercial economy, not as part of a Painite *ancien régime* society of

---

[20] Corfield, *Power and the professions*, 8.
[21] Young, *Example of France*, 108.
[22] Anon, *Address to the members*, 11–13.
[23] Anon., *Parish clerk's advice*, 6–7.
[24] Association, *Special meeting of the committee of the society*, 6 December 1792, in *Association papers*, part 1, no. 1, 13.
[25] Young, *Example of France*, 108–13.
[26] Bowles, *Objections to the war*, 37–8.
[27] Wahrman, *Imagining the middle class*, 86.

repression. Loyalists represented society as one of economic opportunity and, crucially, with an open elite.

Moreover it is clear that the increasing focus on economic divisions meant that, for loyalists, the 'poor' described primarily 'the honest and industrious poor', the labouring poor.[28] But the economic focus gave no clear definition of 'rich'. In a sense if 'poor' meant the labouring poor then the 'rich' could incorporate anyone and everyone else above that category, including those from the middle ranks, in a way that the definition of 'aristocracy' on the Painite model did not. This enabled loyalists to interpret the 'rich and poor' paradigm in accordance with their commercial model, with its gradated society and open elite.

The loyalist commercial model

England, at the heart of the emergent British empire, was heralded by loyalists as the foremost nation in the world. And during 1793–6 the loyalist commercial model was promoted not just by moderates but also by some conservative loyalists and in pamphlets aimed specifically at the people. The nation was 'happy and thriving in a degree unknown in its own annals and those of other nations'.[29] 'We enjoy all the trade and commerce of the world: in the full tide of success; our liberties secured; our manufacturers employed; our resources increasing.'[30] Arthur Young praised 'the boundless wealth of this kingdom':

> the gigantic fabric reared on the industry of this kingdom: throw into one vast amount, the public funds – the paper circulation of every species – the gold and silver, whether money or plate – the manufacturing establishments that have raised new cities, as it were by enchantment – the capitals invested in roads, canals, and other public works – the shipping, magazines, and mercantile wealth of a thousand kinds, and spread throughout the globe.[31]

Wealth was lauded and not just landed wealth but all wealth, as the above quotation illustrates. The focus was very firmly on commerce and industry as a route for all to social and economic elevation, as justification for war, and also as justification for retaining the constitution and government without reform and as a source of national pride.

Moreover war with France encouraged the loyalist synthesis of commercial economics and traditional politics. Radicals argued that the war damaged manufactures and trade, and increasingly ruined businesses in England. Loyalists, however, defended both the war and the state of English commerce

---

[28] Anon., *A serious caution to the poor*, 1792, in *Association papers*, part 2, no. 8, 13.
[29] Anon., *Exposure of the domestic*, 74.
[30] Anon., *New dialogue*, 15.
[31] Young, *Example of France*, 111–14.

against such radical attack. Here again the pamphlets reveal the French Revolution debate to be an interactive affair in which each side responded to the representations of the other. John Bowles claimed that the 'Gazettes' confirmed that although the war had caused an initial convulsion in the commercial world, the 'late commercial failures' were not due to the war but to problems of credit and circulation, which were a direct result of 'the rapid progress and wonderful extent of the prosperity of the country'. Indeed 'Commerce' had 'been protected by the war' rather than damaged by it, as radicals had claimed.[32] Commercial and industrial success was of paramount importance to the country's defence against France. Another writer commented that the English people set '[a high] value on the superior advantages resulting from our foreign commerce, the encouragement of our internal manufacturers, the expediency of an oeconomical attention to the concerns of finance, and the increase of our public revenue'.[33] For 'France knows', yet another anonymous author confirmed, that England 'is superior to her hitherto in arts, in science and in arms, and possessing as we do, from our industry, a larger portion of the commerce of Europe, she views our pre-eminence with an eye of jealousy'.[34]

Consequently it was further declared that 'If there should be a temporary stagnation in trade', or 'if there should be a check to that amazing and formerly unknown flourishing state in which this Nation has for some years past found itself', it was well known that England owed it 'solely to the boundless ambition, the ferocious tyranny, and the implacable rancour of our constant rival, and almost perpetual enemy', France.[35] Ultimately, Bowles contended, once the war was over the country would be at an advantage in Europe, for its commerce, unlike that of France, would be flourishing. But the 'only way to this summit of prosperity lies through the rugged path of war'.[36] Thus the loyalist stress on commercial power gained a new role and was essential in the defence of the war as well as for the defence of the constitution.

The enduring English constitution

England's mixed constitution was still at the forefront of the French Revolution debate during the years 1793–6. As one anonymous pamphleteer confirmed, in England things were very different from France, for the king

---

32 Bowles, *Objections to the war*, 27 n. 30.
33 [M. Dornford], *The motives and consequences of the present war impartially considered*, 1793, 15.
34 Anon., *Thoughts upon our present situation, with remarks upon the policy of a war with France*, 1793, 57.
35 Anon., *Mr. Justice Buller's charge to the grand jury of the county of York*, 1793, in *Association papers*, part 1, no. 8, 16.
36 Bowles, *Objections to the war*, 31–3.

was free and his powers were limited by law and the balance of the mixed constitution:

> The House of Lords is composed either of an ancient nobility, qualified by rank, education, and property, and inheriting from their ancestors an attachment to the constitution; – or of those selected, from time to time, from the orders of the church and the law, from the professions of the navy and army, or from the rest of the laity, and advanced by the Crown by their piety, their learning, their valour or their services.[37]

It was this form of government, with an open elite, which made England such a 'flourishing manufacturing country'.[38] For loyalists the established constitution continued to be championed as the root of good government, utility, commerce and prosperity. As Moore proclaimed 'The Constitution of this Country, is the glory and pride of every true Briton – the admiration and envy of surrounding Nations – under it we have arrived at such a pitch of power, increase of Trade, Commerce, Manufactures, and Riches, as is unparalleled in History!'[39] As these pamphlets well illustrate, loyalists had reached a synthesis of traditional government with the commercial model. Traditional 'English' virtues were also equated with a united Britain and an emergent British empire.

Robert Bisset was in no doubt that history showed that none were ever so happy as 'the SUBJECTS OF THE BRITISH GOVERNMENT'.[40] Another pamphleteer asked 'what could be more wicked than to attempt to destroy that sacred pedestal of British happiness, which has for so many ages supported the column of our greatness? The Constitution of England'.[41] He argued that in England it was 'the superior industry of the people', so 'cherished by the admirable principles of our constitution', which made it 'the most powerful and wealthy nation in Europe'.[42] Again England's constitution and commerce are represented as mutually beneficial.

France and its government were still a major focus of loyalist attention but by 1793 it was clear that England's mixed constitution was no longer a model that revolutionary France was likely to adopt. Consequently France was roundly condemned by loyalists for the unsuccessful alternatives it had chosen and was compared unfavourably with England. John Reeves argued that the French and American constitutions were 'either an illusion or

---

[37] Anon., *A word in season to the traders and manufacturers of Great Britain*, 1793, in *Association papers*, part 2, no. 1, 10.
[38] Ibid. 6.
[39] Thomas Moore, *An address to the inhabitants of Great Britain on the dangerous and destructive tendency of the French system of liberty and equality*, York 1793, in Claeys, *Political writings*, viii. 44.
[40] Robert Bisset, *Sketch of democracy*, 1796, 352.
[41] It is notable that 'Britain' and 'England' are used together here and are obviously interchangeable terms to this pamphleteer.
[42] Anon., *Thoughts upon our present*, 6–8.

imposture', merely a system of setting down certain 'fundamental principles' in the 'abstract'.[43] In France, an anonymous pamphleteer declared, 'the population alone is represented' and the people are subjected to 'the overpowering influence of the mob, which has banished from their elections the higher orders of society and left the field alone to the veriest dregs of the people'. As a result the French were 'enslaved by an anarchy more grinding than the blackest tyranny recorded in the pages of despotism'.[44]

France was generally condemned for atheism, immorality, violence, bloodshed and anarchy. Moore declared that there was no revolution in history which had been 'attended with such outrageous proceedings, such inhuman, bloody, and deliberate Massacres, Murders, Assassinations ... as the late Revolution in France'.[45] Bowles further argued that France had assumed the 'name of a Republic' and 'renounced all sense of honour and humanity', for 'she is transformed from a polished to a barbarous nation, retaining the arts of civilization only to become dreadfully savage'.[46] Indeed 'this once-polished nation and civilized people degraded by their actions, below the savage tribe' were worse than 'the brute creation'.[47] Somers Cocks confirmed that the French had a 'wild species of republicanism'.[48] Ultimately, one anonymous pamphleteer confirmed, all 'republics, of whatever form, which have yet existed' have become either 'aristocracy, or demagogue tyranny'.[49] Here again 'aristocracy' was connected with republican leadership and republicanism was linked to savagery.

Loyalists also defended the English constitution against republics. Moore proclaimed:

> O thrice-happy Englishmen! Did you but know you own happiness, you whose Lives, Liberty, and Property, the hand of Power cannot touch, and whom no Tyrants dare insult; beloved by your King, protected by your Laws, you have equal Justice done, equal Protection afforded you, with the richest man or greatest Peer in the Kingdom.[50]

The House of Lords was essential in the defence of the constitution for it was 'from the natural spirit of nobility, this house of noblemen, will be apt to reject any thing which leans too much to the republican side'.[51] Loyalists warned that it was the aim of radicals in England to follow the example of

---

43 Reeves, John, *Thoughts on the English government: letter the first*, 1795, in Claeys, *Political writings*, viii. 222.
44 Anon., *Thoughts upon our present*, 12, 22.
45 Moore, *Address to the inhabitants*, 29.
46 Bowles, *Objections to the war*, 50.
47 Moore, *Address to the inhabitants*, 44.
48 Somers Cocks, *Short treatise*, 353.
49 Anon., *An address to the people of Great Britain: containing a comparison between the republican and reforming parties*, Edinburgh 1793, in Claeys, *Political writings*, vii. 308.
50 Moore, *Address to the inhabitants*, 29.
51 Anon., *Address to the people*, 313.

France. But rather than focusing on the possible demise of the aristocracy in such an event, loyalists focused on the potential loss of commerce and prosperity. Revolution at home would, Scott argued, 'put an end to all commerce and to the arts, and bring us back to the primitive state'.[52] Arthur Young concurred that revolution would threaten 'our stocks, our manufactures, and our commerce'.[53] Indeed, Bowles pointed out, 'the actual condition of France displays a faithful representation of the effects of anarchy upon the commercial'.[54] He warned that the French revolutionary leader 'Danton has declared that the people must be excited to vengeance against the Rich . . . the bloodthirsty demagogue has denounced the "Aristocracy of Trade" ' and his colleague 'has avowed it necessary "to convince the *Merchants* that France could do without them" '.[55] Even the relatively 'bourgeois' reaction in France in 1795 under the Directory was not enough to dispel the polemical impact of Terror. Thus crucially the aristocracy was no longer in the spotlight as it had been during the years 1791–2. And for the most part the English aristocracy were no longer directly defended by loyalists but had now become part of the loyalist defence.

Furthermore loyalists represented war with France as a war of defence against a possible French invasion, an invasion by the French people. And it was not just the aristocracy that needed to be defended but the entire nation. As Bowles put it, the war was 'necessary for our own preservation'.[56] War was always 'a national calamity', Moore declared, but now it was necessary to ensure 'the independence of the British Nation' for it was the aim of French 'Assassins' to subjugate the nation under their 'despotic yoke' and to take their land and property.[57] Young confirmed that they 'speak commonly, in the streets of Paris, of conquering Europe'.[58] England's role in this war, the loyalists stressed, was defensive. One anonymous author pointed out that Englishmen had originally supported the French Revolution and that it was not until the French 'degenerated into savage beasts, and threatened to devour you, that you shut the door against them, and stood on the defensive'.[59] The English aristocracy was represented as playing an essential and traditional role in that defence. Another pamphleteer confirmed 'Who ever reads the history of our country will find', that the nobility 'have never, in critical times, neglected the high duties of their station'; they always

[52] A. Scott, *Plain reasons for adopting the plan to the societies calling themselves the Friends of the People*, Edinburgh 1793, in Claeys, *Political writings*, viii. 20.
[53] Young, *Example of France*, 150.
[54] Bowles, *Objections to the war*, 31.
[55] Ibid. 37–8.
[56] Ibid. 36.
[57] Moore, *Address to the inhabitants*, 40–1.
[58] Young, *Example of France*, 67.
[59] Anon., *War with France, the only security of Britain, at the present momentous crisis*, 1794, 3.

protected the crown and the people.⁶⁰ Moreover a number of songs were published which promoted the role of aristocracy as defenders of the state:⁶¹

> Our Nobles, for Liberty freely will bleed,
> Since they planted her first, in the fam'd Runnymead;
> Most sacred our Gentry her boughs will sustain,
> From the blows of vile France, or their engine, Tom Paine.⁶²

This song implies that the aristocracy had fought for the country's liberty and the establishment of the English constitution by the signing of Magna Carta at Runnymede in 1215. The aristocracy, loyalists suggested, now played a similarly essential role in the national war against France.

French demagogues versus English gentlemen

As the main focus of the French Revolution ceased to be the aristocracy, this shift was reflected in loyalist representations of France. Comparisons were now rarely made between the two aristocracies but between the new and broader categories of political leadership. Loyalists portrayed the new leadership of France as republican demagogues and compared them unfavourably to the English leadership. To Bowles the French leaders were 'lawless ruffians', a 'set of usurpers' who had 'formally adopted vice, cruelty, impiety, and perfidy, as their political system'.⁶³ Another pamphleteer stated that the French leadership was attempting to impose its ideas upon its opponents 'by fire and sword, by tortures and the lamp-post'.⁶⁴ And according to the Association, the people of France 'groan under new tyrannies'; they must suffer 'one desperate leader after another' – all 'ruffian Demagogues' – who 'have already surpassed the wildest phrenzies of Fanaticism, Superstition, and Enthusiasm; plundering and murdering at home, and propagating their opinions by the sword in foreign countries'. Whilst 'their philosophy is the idle talk of Schoolboys', their 'actions are the savage ferociousness of wild beasts'.⁶⁵

The Terror in France, led by apparently just such demagogues, reinforced this argument. In France, Moore explained, 'the Jacobin Club' had taken over government and consequently it was composed of 'such villains' as 'all Europe besides could not produce; Men of no Education, Property, Honour or

---

60 Anon., *Exposure of the domestic*, 38.
61 The *Political broadsides* volume contains a number of such songs on the theme of war with France.
62 Anon., *A song to be sung an hundred years hence, to the tune of 'Hearts of Oak'*, 1793, in *Political broadsides*, fo. 60.
63 Bowles, *Objections to the war*, 7, 11.
64 Anon., *Exposure of the domestic*, 11.
65 Association, *Proceedings which reported the resolutions of a meeting at the Crown and Anchor Tavern, 20 November 1792*, in *Association papers*, part 1, no. 1, 4.

Virtue, sworn Enemies to Religion'. Indeed 'MARAT and ROBESPIERRE' were two men 'who are a disgrace to society, whose names cannot be mentioned without horror and detestation'.[66] One loyalist poem condemned several well-known members of the French National Convention:[67]

> Blood-hound Marat,
> Foul-mouth'd Carra,
> And fiend-like Robespiere,
> Half-cut Chabot,
> And false Brissot,
> Petion, to villains dear.[68]

This poem certainly suggests considerable familiarity with French events and leaders among loyalist writers. One tract declared that even English 'children stigmatize the vain and cringing coxcomb by the name of a Frenchman'. 'God forbid that we should have a Marat or Robespierre among us!'[69] Ultimately the people of France, 'like the old French, by flattering and imitating the vices of their princes and nobles, will bow beneath the yoke of tyranny' and France will become 'dependent on, an aristocracy', but here it had become an aristocracy of demagogues.[70]

Loyalists compared leadership in England with that in France. The unscrupulous ambitious demagogue was condemned and the public-spirited and virtuous English gentleman lauded. Reeves claimed that 'the mind and manners of a Frenchman need much purifying'.[71] And William Playfair confirmed that 'Disorder must naturally be prolonged greatly by that corruption of manners which is the consequence of it.'[72] France had lost its manners along with its nobility and was thus doomed to savagery. After all it was always the 'higher ranks' who had 'the greatest influence on the manners of society'.[73] But 'manners' here did not merely denote the behaviour of polite society. Nor did they denote Edmund Burke's traditional 'manners of the age',

---

[66] Moore, *Address to the inhabitants*, 30–2.
[67] Robespierre, leader of the Jacobins and instrumental in the 'terror', was guillotined in 1794. Jean Paul Marat, a Jacobin leader, was murdered in the bath in 1793. Jacques-Pierre de Warville Brissot and Jean Louis Carra were influential Girondin newspaper owners. Brissot was accused of being an enemy agent and guillotined during the 'terror'. Jerome Petion, mayor of Paris from October 1791–3, was also a Girondin. Francois Chabot, a Jacobin appointed a liquidator of the Company of the Indies, became embroiled in the 'economic terror' of 1793–4: Simon Schama, *Citizens: a chronicle of the French Revolution*, London 1989, 588, 714, 736, 756, 803–4, 808–10, 846.
[68] Anon., *Life and character of Mr. Thomas Paine . . . and inscribed to the Society against Levellers and Republicans*, n.d., in *Political broadsides*, fo. 41.
[69] Anon., *An antidote against French politics*, 1793, in *Association papers*, part 2, no. 5, 2.
[70] Somers Cocks, *Short treatise*, 353–4.
[71] [Reeves], *Thoughts on the English government*, 227.
[72] William Playfair, *The history of Jacobinism, its crimes, cruelties and perfidies*, 1796, 28.
[73] John Bowles, *Reflections on the conclusion of war*, 1800, 406.

rooted in the age of chivalry.[74] Rather they described the virtues necessary to the leadership of a civilised, enlightened society in a commercial age.[75] Loyalists were clear: England had a society formed on the loyalist commercial model with an open elite, rather than a purely hereditary one. Loyalists identified the ubiquitous English gentleman as the very embodiment of such manners.[76] George Croft promoted the value of 'commercial gentlemen' in the House of Commons: 'I cannot but think it of infinite service to the community that so many professional men find their way into the House of Commons' for 'Who can judge of commercial questions so well as commercial gentlemen?'[77]

Few men, argued Bisset, possess the 'qualifications', 'knowledge', 'ability' and vigour' to be good statesmen.[78] Indeed erudite political texts could only be understood by 'gentlemen', 'men of taste, literature and knowledge of abstract reasoning'. Such men would despise the vulgar writings produced by radicals. Such radical writings were a tool to convert the 'uninformed multitude' used by 'The demagogue who ... fills their minds with imaginary grievances, who flatters their vanity with ideas of importance, who calls them from industry and useful labour, and contentment', who misleads them in fact, with his representations. The people were only 'deluded by democratic theories, or enamoured of fanciful innovations'.[79] In 1796, in what was clearly a partial snipe at Thelwall, Bisset compared 'wise and able men' (from Aristotle to Hume) to the 'London Corresponding Society, and hireling lecturers'.[80] Thus the gentleman was set against the demagogue or democrat: two opposing examples of leadership, or rather one who leads and the other who misleads. Leadership during this period became an issue concerned with truth and falsehood, representation and reality.

Moreover this comparison between French demagogues and English gentlemen became for loyalists a central issue in the debate about leadership during this period. Loyalists did continue to extol the qualifications and talents of the nobility, the significance of their property ownership and the importance of their influence and independence in government.[81] And to

---

[74] Quoted in anon., *A brief reply to the observations of Ben Bousfield Esq., on Mr Burke's pamphlet*, Dublin 1791, in Claeys, *Political writings*, vii. 56.
[75] Pocock, *Virtue, commerce and history*, 48–9.
[76] See Corfield, 'The rivals'.
[77] George Croft, *Plans of parliamentary reform, proved to be visionary*, Birmingham 1793, 7.
[78] Bisset, *Sketch of democracy*, 18–19.
[79] Ibid. pp. xx–xxii, xxv.
[80] Ibid. 20.
[81] See, for examples, anon., *Thoughts upon our present*, 12, 14, 17, for government by the few of superior wisdom and character; anon., *The earl of Radnor's charge to the grand jury of the county of Berks, 15 January 1793*, in *Association papers*, part 1, no. 9, 6–7; Croft, *Plans of parliamentary reform*, 4–5, for promotion of a property owning leadership; Young, *Example of France*, 94; and Moore, *Address to the inhabitants*, 42–3, on patronage and influence. See also chapter 3 above. It is significant that, during this period, leisure was no longer widely promoted by loyalists as a necessary requirement for leadership.

loyalists property ownership was still the only acceptable qualification for political rights. As in 1791–2 titles were still interpreted as rewards for merit and services to the state, rather than a hereditary entity in their own right. But such issues did not dominate loyalist pamphlets as they had done during the years 1791–2. The country that loyalists promoted in their pamphlets of 1793–6 had an open elite, in which wealth and talents were at least as important as rank.

A number of loyalists promoted wealth over rank. One writer claimed that 'it is not titles which render a man of power and of consequence in the state, but wealth, abilities, and honour', and mostly wealth it seems.[82] For 'a poor, weak dishonourable duke, is very near of as little say in a state, as contemptible and as useless, as a poor, weak, and dishonourable commoner'.[83] It was 'the wealthy family' that all the poorer families in the neighbourhood will look up to as 'naturally higher'. And 'Take all the higher families' of wealth 'in a nation', and you have a nobility fairly formed by nature'. Such a 'natural nobility' was, he claimed, to be found in the 'British House of Peers'.[84] The earl of Radnor stated that not all may support 'Distinctions of Rank' 'but with respect to that of Fortune, all the members of every great community whatever are likewise interested', for it is the source of 'happiness'.[85] Charles Patton agreed that 'upon wealth, influence and power must necessarily attend'.[86] Evidently, the influence of the loyalist commercial model, with its economic focus and open elite, was far-reaching.

Thus loyalist writers implied that in a modern and commercial society the political leadership as well as the economic elite was broader than an exclusive caste of nobility. There may still have been superior and inferior ranks but, and this is of some significance, loyalist representations suggested that these 'top people' were not imposed from above but had emerged as the natural result of either a meritocracy or a plutocracy. There was no power-wielding oligarchy imposing itself as a definitive class upon the rest of society, in the loyalist view. Land, wealth and titles may in reality, as Corfield has claimed,[87] have constituted the three overlapping claims to social authority, but loyalists did not necessarily represent them as such.

---

[82] Langford identified the late eighteenth-century elite as 'a plutocracy': *Polite and commercial people*, 5.
[83] Anon., *Address to the people*, 311.
[84] Ibid. 312–13.
[85] Anon., *Radnor's charge*, 6.
[86] Patton, *Attempt to establish*, 385.
[87] Corfield, *Power and the professions*, 8.

Equality of opportunity

The issue of inequality was again constantly raised in pamphlets during this period. Radical calls for equality of political rights continued to be misrepresented by loyalists as calls for equality of property. France was constantly held up as an example of the results of applying systems of equality. Young said of France

> [the] quarrel now raging in that once flourishing kingdom, is not between liberty and tyranny, or between protecting and oppressive systems of government; it is ... collected to a single point – it is alone a question of property; it is a trial at arms, whether those who have *nothing*, shall not seize and possess the property of those who have *something*.

It can never end, Young asserted, 'but in the equal and universal ruin of all'. In France 'a gigantic and devouring despotism has levelled in the dust all security to those whose properties raise them above the mob'.[88] And Bowles concurred: 'The French Revolution began by attacking the Monarch, the Nobles, and the Clergy ... But the danger was by no means peculiar to them', for 'We now see property of every species, public and private pillaged with as little ceremony as that of the Church and Nobility, at first.'[89] Bisset pointed out that all attempts at introducing democracy in England, including during the seventeenth-century English civil war, were an attempt at 'general equalization of rank and property'.[90] Equality could only exist in 'a savage state' where there can be no 'security of property'.[91] Inequality, confirmed Somers Cocks, was 'a necessary consequence' of the security of property. It was also naturally inborn in men. 'Various in all respects are the qualifications of mind and body which fall to the lot of different human creatures.' From inequality of property arises 'inequality of station' and under 'this beneficial order of things the rich furnish the means of industrious livelihood to the poor'. Thus, crucially, it was the rich who enabled the poor to earn their living and, with the recent increase in 'the opulence of the rich', had come 'advantageous employment to a greater number of poor than before'.[92]

The loyalist message was clear: all would suffer if 'levelling' was introduced in England. Moore asked: 'Suppose the Nobility were all deprived of their Titles, what advantage would it be to your or me – should we live the better for it? – Not at all.' The 'natural consequences' of equality 'would be, your Commerce, Credit, and Manufactures would be lost; there would be a total stagnation of Trade and famine would result', as had happened in France.[93]

---

88 Young, *Example of France*, 778–9.
89 Bowles, *Objections to the war*, 37–8.
90 Bisset, *Sketch of democracy*, pp. xiv, 343–6.
91 Somers Cocks, *Short treatise*, 347–8.
92 Ibid. 348.
93 Moore, *Address to the inhabitants*, 39.

Again here the aristocracy was part of the loyalist defence, rather than the defended. In a system of equality, there would be no 'Manufacture; no Commerce, no Credit' only 'plunder', 'robbery' and 'all those publick disorders which make life miserable'.[94] Arthur Young warned that levelling would not just affect the great estates but all farmers; it would therefore result in attacks on 'a farm of 200l, a year' as well as 'property of 40,000l. a year'. Property owners were united here against the levelling 'beggar, without a loaf, but with a pike on his shoulder'.[95] One pamphleteer claimed that if radicals should 'raise a mob, the Nobility, Gentry, Yeomanry, including Farmers, Tradesmen, and even Labourers, who have five or six pounds worth of goods to lose, will join together'.[96] Thus, by identifying allegiances between increasingly large and diverse interest-groups, representations of English society were constantly shifting and broadening to depict a cohesive society with an open elite.

Most important, the loyalists claimed that the equality which was prevalent in England was equality of opportunity. Loyalists were making an inclusive argument here. Whilst equality of the type that radicals wanted could never exist in civil society, equality of opportunity was at the root of English society. The elite was only the elite because it had earned its high position. Loyalists continued to argue, as they had in 1791–2, that all could rise through the ranks, politically, socially and economically. As Richard Watson put it: 'Nor is any order of men exclusively entitled to the enjoyment of the lucrative offices of the state. All cannot enjoy them, but all enjoy a capacity of acquiring them. The son of the meanest man in the nation may become a general or an admiral, a lord chancellor or an archbishop.'[97] Moreover William Atkinson stated that 'the lower classes . . . are now rejoicing in the fruits of their industry and are stepping fast forwards into the middle ranks of society'.[98] Indeed, he confirmed, 'the middle ranks' in 'all commercial parts of the country' had 'stepped from the humble shed of poverty'.[99] In one pamphlet the Association argued that 'Men become great, who have greatly distinguished themselves by the application of talents natural or acquired' and 'Men become rich, who have persevered with industry in the application to Trade and Commerce, to Manufactures and other useful employments.'[100]

---

[94] Association, *Proceedings*, 3–4.
[95] Young, *Example of France*, 78.
[96] Anon., *A letter to the people of England, on their present situation*, Egham 1792, in Claeys, *Political writings*, vii. 245.
[97] [Richard Watson], *Appendix to the bishop of Llandaff's sermon*, 1793, in *Association papers*, part 1, no. 7, 7. Although no author is given for this appendix, it is assumed that it is written by Richard Watson, bishop of Llandaff from 1782.
[98] [William Atkinson], *A concise sketch of the intended revolution in England*, 1794, in Claeys, *Political writings*, viii. 194.
[99] Ibid. 193.
[100] Association, *Proceedings*, 1.

Here to be rich and great required different qualifications but both social positions were open to all.

Moreover whilst there might not be equality of property there was, in England, an equality of feeling. Reeves suggested that Englishmen shared a 'constitution of mind', enjoyed by 'the first Nobleman ... in common with the meanest of his tradesmen, his tenants, or his servants', which ensures 'a feeling of a congenial equality among us'.[101] It is significant that in this promotion of equality of opportunity loyalists promoted industry as the route for any man however poor to achieve wealth and status. In a subversion of the radical promotion of personal industry as the source of national wealth, loyalists promoted industry as the source of personal wealth, in a land of equality of opportunity. This can be called the 'industry idiom' and it was particularly prominent in pamphlets for the people.

Pamphlets for the people

Pamphlets aimed at the people are a significant proportion and an important sector of the loyalist primary sources of the period 1792–6. Not all such pamphlets reflected the same aims. In particular there were those with a predominantly moral and religious theme and those with a political one. It is also notable that, although the majority of pamphlets for the people were written by the more conservative loyalists, many of the political works promote the loyalist commercial mode, in part at least. Although in some instances these pamphlets presented or appeared to represent the same message, there are subtle nuances that are significant for understanding the spectrum of loyalist views.

Anglican clergymen continued to support loyalism during 1793–6, but such support often remained a conservative reactionary defence of the Church and State and did not reflect the dominant more moderate loyalist message. The priority of clergymen was generally moral reform and defence of the Church against invading atheism. Robert Hole notes that the Association published a number of the loyalist tracts that were written by clergymen.[102] Samuel Hayes dedicated a sermon to the Association in 1793 and supported loyalist maxims with the weight of Christianity.[103] He claimed that 'Divine Providence' had distinguished England 'by signal marks of favour and protection'. France, on the other hand, was 'the polluted spot' of 'infidelity and atheism', where the 'scenes of confiscation, rapine and massacre' would 'disgrace even hordes of savages'.[104] The loyalist clergyman Thomas Hardy

---

101 [Reeves], *Thoughts on the English government*, 222.
102 Hole, 'English sermons', 32–3.
103 See Samuel Hayes, *A sermon preached in St. Margaret's Church, Westminster, on Sunday 27 January 1793*, 1793.
104 Ibid. 2, 3, 10, 12–15.

(not to be confused with his radical namesake) also argued that France was now destroyed because 'The Catholic Church . . . fell in the first shock', and hence France had lost 'two main pillars of strength'.[105]

Moreover the defence of the establishment necessarily invoked defence of the aristocracy. Hardy claimed that the 'moral prosperity' of the country could only be 'secured and advanced by the conduct of men of rank and property. The importance of these men is great in the system of this country, both in a civil and religious view'. For the peers were not just political leaders in the House of Lords but also 'the leaders of society' and as such were 'morally responsible, for the principles of the people'.[106] Indeed Hardy argued that not even men of property and honour could be virtuous leaders without the support of religion.[107] For such conservative churchmen the aristocracy was still an essential pillar of the crucial Church/State alliance.[108] Anglican loyalism thus clearly invoked the Painite model of an *ancien régime* England, long discarded by more mainstream loyalists in favour of the loyalist commercial model with its broader, open elite.

By contrast, as far as the Association was concerned its main aim was not to achieve moral reform but to win over the lower ranks to the loyalist cause in order to ensure the stability of the state in the face of the danger from radicalism and the French. John Reeves had expressed anxiety that '*Reformers* are all among the classes of society, with which we have necessarily too little intercourse. Artificers and handicraftsmen, journeymen and apprentices in great manufacturing towns.'[109] Clearly these were the people loyalists had to reach. The Association stated that it was the aim of radicals to 'overthrow' the 'present System of Government and Society, by infusing into the minds of ignorant men causes of discontent adapted to their various stations'.[110] And it was the main aim of the Association to combat such opinions and to quiet any potential unrest. As Hannah More so succinctly put it, 'A dinner of herbs, says the wise man, with quiet,/ Is better than beef and discord and riot.'[111] In its attempts to reach the people, the Association published pamphlets that invoke the loyalist commercial model and promote the vision of a prosperous, commercial England, rather than Anglican morality. The fact that a number of historians have identified an element of government control in the publications of the loyalist Association reinforces the sugges-

---

[105] Thomas Hardy, *The importance of religion to national prosperity, a sermon*, Edinburgh 1794, 20–1. For the other Thomas Hardy, the radical founder and secretary of the LCS, see Goodwin, *Friends of liberty*, 332–52.
[106] Hardy, *Importance of religion*, 24–5.
[107] Ibid. 15.
[108] See Clark, *English society*, 263.
[109] Reeves, *Thoughts on the English government*, 250.
[110] Association, *Proceedings*, 1.
[111] Anon., *The riot: or, half a loaf is better than no bread, in a dialogue between Jack Anvil and Tom Hod*, in *Political broadsides*, fo. 91.

tion here that there was a synthesis developing between conservative Pittite loyalists and more moderate loyalists.¹¹²

The Association may have used Anglican and evangelical tracts to reinforce its message to the people, but it also addressed the people on wider issues which promoted the loyalist commercial model and used the 'industry idiom'. Evidently, loyalists recognised that what the people wanted was to be rich. As Charles Patton confirmed, inevitably 'poverty desires riches'.¹¹³ Consequently loyalist representations stressed England's prosperity and imperial/commercial expansion. The people were reminded that 'the country to which they belong is revered abroad, and prosperous and opulent'.¹¹⁴ Songs reinforced this message:

> Our commerce is great, manufactors well paid,
> The world our mart, so extensive our trade;
> All, all, have employment, the idle alone
> Have cause of complaint, but the fault is their own.¹¹⁵

Neither England nor its regions were generally represented by loyalists as suffering hardships as a result of the war. 'You've never had it so good' was the dominant message. The French were used to *'Black bread'* and *'Wooden shoes'* whilst the English enjoyed *'white bread, strong leather shoes, and good shirts'*.¹¹⁶ This was, of course, an old comparison commonly invoked in the eighteenth century. Hogarth's print, *O! The Roast Beef of Old England* (1749) depicted the English with abundant roast beef and ale and the French with thin soup and rags.¹¹⁷ But in the 1790s such comparisons were often directly connected to the promotion of the loyalist commercial model. The pamphleteer Thomas Moore declared that 'Labouring men' in England were now better off than one hundred years ago. Consequently 'great and rapid advance of late is owing to the prosperous state of our Manufactories, and the amazing increase of Commerce, which employ such a number of hands' and has resulted in the 'increase of wages to the poor' and 'bread for every man who will work'.¹¹⁸ Another pamphleteer confirmed that 'by reason of the great increase in trade, there is great demand for your labour – and the wages given you are extremely liberal'.¹¹⁹

France was held up as an example to the people of the result of imposing equality. There, loyalists claimed, manufacturers and artisans had lost their

---

112 On this issue see Eastwood, 'Patriotism and the English state', 146–68; Dozier, *King, constitution and country*, 55–75; Mitchell, 'Association movement', 56–77; Duffy, 'William Pitt', 945.
113 Patton, *Attempt to establish*, 386.
114 Anon., *Antidote against French politics*, 9.
115 Anon., *A song*, in *Political broadsides*, fo. 60.
116 Anon., *New dialogue*, 11.
117 Derek Jarrett, *England in the age of Hogarth*, St Albans 1976, 20.
118 Moore, *Address to the inhabitants*, 43.
119 Anon., *Serious caution*, 13.

work, the peasants had lost the land and many were starving. This catastrophe had occurred because of the revolution, but, loyalists stated, more importantly because of the loss of markets for luxury goods and manufactures. 'In one large Town only, there are thirty thousand manufacturers all out of work ... because their Masters are ruined for want of customers, and the workmen are ruined with their Masters.'[120] The people were starving because in France there were no longer any rich and great men who had previously provided them with work and wealth. The message was clear, if implicit; abolition of aristocracy had brought ruin for all. One pamphleteer warned that, in Lyon alone, 'ten thousand persons who lived by making rich dresses for the Courtiers are reduced to absolute beggary'.[121] Another declared that there was almost 'a famine' in urban areas 'amongst the lower classes of people, who were totally dependent on the bounty of the nobility and clergy, maintained in their service, or contributed by their labour to supply their luxuries, and the latter amongst the manufacturers out of employ'.[122] And 'the forlorn deplorable Emigrants from France' were 'thronging every street of London and dependent on your charity for every morsel of bread they eat'.[123]

If a system of equality was introduced in England, loyalists warned, the same would happen here. There would be 'no rich people' and consequently 'of course no fine carriages – no fine manufactures from Manchester – no hardware from Sheffield or Birmingham – no fine broad cloths from Gloucestershire or Wiltshire' and all the labouring people would be reduced to poverty.[124] The commercial and industrial sector, loyalists implied, was reliant on the custom of the rich. One anonymous pamphleteer cautioned: 'Instead of indulging wild notions of equality ... show respect and submission' to your superiors for it is due to 'their superiority' that you earn 'the great wages ... in their employ'.[125] He continued to exhort the people to defend the property of their superiors for 'without their fortunes and capitals, this country would not have risen to the consequence that it has; manufactures could not have reached the perfection that we boast; agriculture would not have received the improvements it has; the wages of the manufacturer and labourer would not be what they are'.[126]

Thus pamphlets for the people suggested that there was an equality of interest and opportunity in the national prosperity which, somewhat

---

[120] Anon., *Parish clerk's advice*, 7.
[121] Anon., *A dialogue between a labourer and a gentleman*, 1793, in *Association papers*, part 2, no. 8, 6–7.
[122] [Dornford], *Motives and consequences*, 57.
[123] John Bull, *French kindness and French humanity*, 1793, in *Association papers*, part 2, no. 6, 15.
[124] Anon., *A country curate's advice to manufacturers*, 1792, in Claeys, *Political writings*, vii. 297.
[125] Anon., *The duties of man in connexion with his rights: or, rights and duties inseparable*, 1793, 21–2.
[126] Ibid. 23.

paradoxically, was reliant on an inequality of wealth and status. The people should not forget that they were reliant on the wealth of the rich and great for the very work that could, in turn, bring the people wealth and status. Here many conservative writers can be identified as promoting the loyalist commercial model. This reinforces the argument that a synthesis developed, during the years 1793–6, between the traditional conservative and the moderate loyalists.

The pamphlets aimed at the people have been described by a number of historians as reinforcing subordination, loyalty and obedience amongst the lower classes.[127] Olivia Smith stated that they reflected 'rigid class divisions'. The class of the writer and of the intended recipient was clearly delineated and a strict social order imposed, with mechanics only writing for other mechanics, farmers for farmers and so on.[128] It is certainly true that a number of pamphlets, particularly those written by Anglican clergymen and evangelicals, did promote such concepts. Yet mainstream loyalists commonly argued that inequality was 'more the result of every man's own exertions, than of any controuling institution of the State', or the will of God.[129]

Moreover, and most significantly, pamphlets aimed at the people also invoked the 'industry idiom' and were at pains to stress that those who were industrious could become rich and rise through the ranks. And clearly to be rich was the aim:

> If by your own industry and honesty you can make yourselves rich, there is no law of this Kingdom which forbids you. You daily see numberless instances of individuals rising very honourably from poverty to great wealth, and you cannot but know that industry and honesty generally meet with great encouragement and success in this Kingdom.[130]

Another writer exhorted: 'My Countrymen, if you have a desire to rise in the world . . . rise by your own virtue and industry.'[131] The Association exclaimed:

> How many persons now of great rank and fortune, who were born without either! How many rich Merchants and Traders who begun their career in the lowest employment of the shop and counting-house . . . It is by the effects of this industry, that the Gentleman is enabled to support his rank and station; and the Merchant and Tradesman to employ his Clerks, Journeymen, and Apprentices.

Indeed 'employment is found for all' and 'there is no place upon earth where

---

[127] Hole, 'English sermons', 35. See also Dickinson 'Popular conservatism', 111.
[128] Smith, *Politics of language*, 75.
[129] Ibid.
[130] Anon., *Serious caution*, 10.
[131] Anon., *A picture of true and false politics: addressed to the understandings and feelings of Britons*, 1793, in *Association papers*, part 2, no. 5, 13.

there are so many ways, in which a man by his talents and industry may raise himself above his equals'. This is a 'pre-eminent happiness' which had been 'encreased of late years in a wonderful degree', by 'the prosperity' it has caused.[132] Even Hardy, who went so far as to complain in one pamphlet that 'the spirit of the commercial system has grinded' the bonds between ranks 'too severely', argued in another tract that 'the path of fortune is safe and open to the genius and exertion of youth'.[133] It is interesting to note, however, that the first of these pamphlets by Hardy was a sermon preached to the General Assembly of the Church of Scotland, whilst the second was a sermon preached to the people.

Correspondingly a number of pamphlets for the people contained stories of poor labourers who rose to wealth and status through hard work. In a typical story, 'Old John', a 'Journeyman Brick-layer', rose to be a 'worthy Lord-Mayor' through honest hard work and 'died dignified with the City's highest honours'.[134] Susan Pedersen has argued that pamphlets such as Hannah More's *Cheap repository of moral and religious tracts* (1795–8) were, as their title suggests, less anti-Jacobin tracts and more an attack on popular culture and chapbook literature and the immorality with which they were imbued. Chapbooks and tracts directed at the poor and illiterate were deemed bawdy and vulgar and many of the songs encouraged drinking, dancing and romance.[135] Pedersen argued that 'the Cheap Repository should be seen less as a specific anti-Jacobin work than as a part of a continuing upper-class endeavor to reform and moralize the poor'.[136]

Yet a number of these tracts did contain the loyalist message and promote the 'industry idiom'. The *Cheap repository* included the tale of 'Tom White', a reformed and hard working postillion, who 'grew rich for one of his station' and was elevated to become 'Farmer White'. It also included the tale of a shoemaker's apprentice, whose master had 'died in a drunken fit at the Greyhound'. The apprentice then, through hard work, 'gained the love and respect of his late master's creditors', who 'set him up in business though he was not worth a shilling of his own'. He became rich and successful.[137] And Hannah More's 'Farmer Furrow', who invested 'an odd 50l.' which he had 'by him' on 'government security', found, when he wanted to give it to his

---

[132] Association, *Proceedings*, 1.
[133] Hardy, *Importance of religion*, 29, and his *Fidelity to the British constitution: the duty and interest of the people, a sermon*, 2nd edn, Edinburgh 1794, 28.
[134] Anon., *Liberty, and property, courage and common sense*, 1793, in *Association papers*, part 2, no. 7, 4.
[135] Susan Pedersen, 'Hannah More meets Simple Simon: tracts, chapbooks, and popular culture in late eighteenth-century England', *JBS* xxv (1986), 84–113, esp. pp. 100–7.
[136] Ibid. 107.
[137] Hannah More, 'The history of Tom White the postillion', in Hannah More, *Cheap repository of moral and religious tracts*, 1795–6, i. 14–15, and 'The apprentice turned master: the second part of the two shoemakers', ibid. ii. 2.

daughter on her marriage a few years later, that it had grown 'almost to a hundred!'[138]

Thus by the mid-1790s loyalism had largely moved on from the Anglican tradition, to promote industry and the loyalist commercial model of the economy and of society. England, loyalists argued, had a mutually dependent, multi-layered society where all may be 'employed' and anyone may rise through the ranks by his talents and industry. Religious piety and virtue may still be the route to greater rewards in the next life but industry was now a route for all to elevation in this one. Moreover, on the basis that industry was the source of wealth and status, loyalists could argue that those with hereditary wealth or position had by their own industry, or by means of the industry of their ancestors, acquired their wealth and position. As one pamphleteer explained, if 'some persons be born to great possessions', that is because 'their fathers or fore-fathers underwent the toil and fatigue of acquiring those possessions, and afterwards left them to be enjoy'd by their descendants'.[139] Another claimed that it was by God's Providence but also, 'their own or the talents and prudence of their ancestors' that the aristocracy were placed in higher stations.[140] Thus loyalists applied the 'industry idiom' to the hereditary aristocracy and argued that their elevated position was merely the result of the past industry of their ancestors. Consequently the aristocracy could be incorporated into the loyalist commercial model as they represented, partially at least, an open elite.

Paradoxically a number of pamphlets for the people contained implicit criticisms in their representation of aristocracy. This suggests a subterranean clash between the Anglican moral position, invoking hostility to luxury, and the loyalist 'industry idiom'. In a dialogue between 'a Tradesman' and his 'Porter', the latter says:

> 'there's a Duke in the county where I was born that they say has thirty thousand a-year: isn't that a shame, Sir?' 'he keeps such a stud of horses, and six or eight carriages, and a matter of forty servants ... It was only last year that he took in his head to grub up a fine wood, which had not been planted above ten years, because he thought it would look better about half a mile off ... Now is it not a shame, Sir to throw away so much money?'

The master replies that 'n this country no man *can* throw money away, for every sort of expence, however idle it may seem, is in the end a public benefit'. Moreover the duke employs many people, who 'derive a great part of their living from his extravagance'.[141] In the same pamphlet, 'John' complains that 'Courtiers ... receive large salaries for doing nothing in the

---

138 Idem, *Village politics: addressed to all mechanics, journeymen, and day labourers in Great Britain*, 4th edn 1793, in Claeys, *Political writings*, viii. 6.
139 Anon., *Serious caution*, 11.
140 Anon., *Duties of man*, 21.
141 Anon., *Dialogue between a labourer and a gentleman*, 4–5.

world'. The master confirms that they, like the duke, keep many labourers, servants and tradesmen in work.[142] In another pamphlet, a 'Gentleman' explains to 'John', a labourer, that 'the Squire' gets 'no pleasure at all' from his 'fine clothes, and houses, and carriages, and servants' and 'good living and idleness bring upon the rich . . . the gout and many other disorders'.[143] Such pamphlets were clearly trying to make the common points that it was not just the great who benefited from their wealth and, conversely, that wealth does not necessarily bring happiness. Nevertheless such criticisms do reflect a common negative representation of the aristocracy as a luxurious, extravagant and idle elite, somewhat reminiscent of Paine's portrayals of aristocracy. It should not be forgotten, moreover, that similar criticisms were common during the eighteenth century from all facets of the political spectrum within the luxury debate. Their inclusion in popular tracts illustrates the range within loyalism; the fact that there were many different 'loyalisms'. It is also a rhetorical device, to admit apparently damaging facts against one's own case, only to defeat or to circumvent them subsequently.

Hannah More's *Village politics* (1793) certainly barely concealed her criticisms of the aristocracy:

> And as to our great folks, . . . I don't pretend to say they are a bit better than they should be: but that's no affair of mine; let them look to that; they'll answer for that in another place. To be sure, I wish they'd set us a better example about going to church, and those things.

Moreover they 'spend too much . . . in feastings and fandangoes' and 'my lady flies about all summer to hot water and cold water, and fresh water and salt water, when she ought to stay at home with Sir John'.[144] Although More went on to stress that the poor benefited from Sir John and his castle in terms of abundant employment and paternalistic benevolence in the form of Sunday schools, the criticisms are plainly there.[145] Yet, as historians have noted, the evangelical Hannah More was unusually vociferous in her condemnation of the manners and morals of the aristocracy.[146] Indeed she went on to play an instrumental role in the reformation of manners movement which flourished in the early nineteenth century, whereas many of the pamphleteers of the mid-1790s subsided once the immediate danger from France was over.

Conversely a number of pamphlets, particularly those for the people, represented an elite with a conspicuous aristocracy as charitable and philan-

---

[142] Ibid. 6–7.
[143] Ibid. 10–11.
[144] More, *Village politics*, 7.
[145] For Hannah More see M. G. Jones, *Hannah More*, Cambridge 1952, and Ann Stott, *Hannah More: the first Victorian*, Oxford 2003.
[146] See Hannah More, *Thoughts on the importance of the manners of the great to general society*, 1788.

thropic towards the poor. An anonymous author in 1793 described 'our nobility', whose 'Private bounty and personal benevolence' made 'the people of England ... attached to this part of the constitution'.[147] One of the *Cheap repository tracts* represented 'Betty', 'the Orange Girl', who 'came into the world before so many good gentlemen and ladies began to concern themselves that the poor might have a little learning'.[148] And Sunday schools as the only source of education for many of the poor were much vaunted by loyalists and Anglican clergy as representations of aristocratic benevolence. Another pamphleteer asked:

> do you not always find your superiors ready to assist you, supplying you with fuel and provisions till you are again able to earn your bread? Are not your children educated at their expence ... What are all our charity and Sunday schools, our hospitals and dispensaries, our numerous and increasing charitable institutions to alleviate every human woe, but so many monuments of the liberality of the rich and great to the lower orders of the people?[149]

Such 'excellent Institutions' were provided to 'bring forth latent merit from obscurity', thus enabling 'the inferior ranks' to participate in 'the Advantages arising from commerce', the 'Offices in Church and State' which 'are equally open to all ranks of people'.[150] It was those of 'superior stations in social life', 'persons of independent fortune and liberality', who possess a 'respect and attachment to Virtue and Religion', who were chiefly responsible for such charity.[151] And Richard Watson praised 'the rich' for providing 'charities', 'immense sums annually ... for the support of hospitals, infirmaries, dispensaries – for the relief of sufferers by fire, tempests, famines, ... great sickness and other misfortunes'.[152]

Such representations celebrated a wealthy, liberal and virtuous elite. This concept could encompass both the paternalistic, patriarchal aristocracy and a new philanthropic elite, its wealth based on commerce and industry. Charity, such descriptions suggested, was adapting to the loyalist commercial model. The paternalist aristocracy was being replaced by a broader philanthropic elite. The issue of representation and reality emerges again here and raises the question how far loyalist portrayals reflected the reality of a philanthropic elite?

---

[147] Anon., *Exposure of the domestic*, 38.
[148] Anon., 'Betty Brown the St. Giles orange girl', in *Cheap repository shorter tracts*, 1798, as quoted in Pedersen, 'Hannah More', 89.
[149] Anon., *Duties of man*, 24–5.
[150] [Eirenophilos], *A discourse on the advantages which accrue to the country from the intimate connexion which subsists between the several ranks and orders in society*, 1793, 17–19.
[151] Ibid. 22–9.
[152] [Watson], *Appendix to the bishop of Llandaff's sermon*, 8.

The commercial model to the fore

It is clear that the loyalist commercial model was fully utilised during this period to promote a prosperous and progressive nation, which was far from the savagery of republican and revolutionary France. Bowles predicted that at the end of war with France:

> Brilliant beyond all experience will then be the situation of this Country: secure of all the benefits which incomparable Constitution, natural and acquired advantages, and increased weight in the political balance can bestow; the emporium of Commerce – the Arbiter of Europe – the object of universal respect and confidence – the pride of nations – the tutelary Guardian of Society – then will the sun of Britain's glory shine forth with meridian splendour.[153]

As this model was constructed by melding the traditional constitution with the new economy and society loyalists in effect masked reality with representations of change.[154]

Loyalist pamphlets were stronger on rhetoric than on historical examples. Moreover it is significant that loyalists did not fully promote the aristocracy as leaders within the new commercial model. Wahrman has identified what he terms a 'landed class idiom', in that 'establishment writers' defined the landed class as 'the repository of all virtues'.[155] This is certainly true of many loyalist pamphlets of the period 1791–2, but it is clear that by 1793–6 loyalists, in the main, were keen to identify an open elite, based on the loyalist commercial model. In this the 'landed class' was not specifically represented as the 'repository of all virtues'. Indeed it was the broader elite of the 'rich', rather than the aristocracy alone, that was identified as providing leadership in commerce and industry, finance and trade. Loyalists tended in their pamphlets to promote the role of the aristocracy primarily in government as members of the House of Lords, to stress the aristocracy's qualifications for that role. John Bowles predicted that after war with France was over the 'Trading Interest will appear with distinguished lustre'.[156] It was thus the 'Trading Interest' which was to take on the 'distinguished lustre' traditionally reserved by Burke and others for the aristocracy. Few pamphleteers during this period defended the aristocracy with the ferocity and enthusiasm of Burke in his *Reflections*. Burke may have heralded the beginning of a flexible conservatism but he also signalled the end of aristocracy as the sole representative of an acceptable gothic elite in an *ancien régime* England.

Ultimately the loyalists manoeuvred the aristocracy out of the spotlight in

---

[153] Bowles, *Objections to the war*, 32–3.
[154] Classic examples of this synthesis are found in the pamphlets of John Bowles, Thomas Moore and the anonymous pamphlet, *Thoughts upon our present situation*.
[155] Wahrman, *Imagining the middle class*, 87–8.
[156] Bowles, *Objections to the war*, 31–3.

the French Revolution debate, where Burke and Paine had placed it and radicalism retained it. By promoting commercial prosperity over hereditary wealth, and industry rather than leisure, the loyalists pushed aristocracy into a specialist niche of merely political influence in the constitution. Sociological reality, of course, was quite different. England retained the mixed government of king, lords and commons and no reforms were enacted during the 1790s. The aristocracy had lost neither wealth, elevated position, nor political influence in government during the years 1790–6.[157] Despite loyalist representations to the contrary, the country was to all intents and purposes still ruled by an aristocratic oligarchy. Loyalists were clearly promoting representations of an elite which may have been developing, but did not as yet truly predominate.

There then arises the question how far the aristocracy needed to adopt middle-class values, as suggested by Paul Langford, and to reform their behaviour and morality, as Linda Colley has claimed, as a result of pressure from below?[158] Radical criticisms of aristocracy may well have changed perceptions of aristocracy in the minds of their fellow countrymen. But radicalism achieved no concrete reforms of government, or society during the years 1790–6.[159] Radical rhetoric was therefore undercut by the loyalist alternative, which depicted the country as one that already had a commercial, progressive and open elite.

These loyalist pamphlets, intended for the people, were largely propaganda, promulgated purely to win the masses back from a dangerous radicalism and to boost support for loyalism. This was recognised by the pamphleteers themselves, as the loyalist clergyman, George Croft, confirmed: 'The laudable attempts which have been used to convince the lower classes of the people that they are happy, have already been more successful than we expected.'[160] As H. T. Dickinson emphasised, loyalism was 'as much a propaganda victory as a success for the forces of law and order'.[161] By successfully masking continuity with change, by promoting the loyalist commercial model, by appealing to the desire for personal and national wealth amongst the people and by giving the people hope that they could achieve such wealth and status, loyalists had found a strong new answer to Paine and to radicalism.

---

[157] See Cannon, *Aristocratic century*, 1–33.
[158] Colley, *Britons*, 149, 152–3; Langford, *Public life*, 510, and *Polite and commercial people*, 565–6.
[159] See chapter 4 above.
[160] Croft, *Plans of parliamentary reform*, 28.
[161] Dickinson, *British radicalism*, 25.

Conclusion

'These are the Times that Try Men's Souls!'

This quotation, taken from Thomas Paine's *The crisis* (1776),[1] was adopted by Henry Redhead York as the title for his pamphlet in 1793. This small interaction illustrates the complexity and intricacy of the pamphlet debates of the early 1790s. The impact of these debates was far-reaching in terms both of the dissemination of political ideas and their influence upon later political debate.

The pamphlet debates

The radical attack on aristocracy during 1790–6 was vehement and vitriolic; the term 'aristocracy' became a term of abuse. More important, 'aristocracy' came to denote a despotic ruling class perceived as opposed to 'the people'. The English aristocracy, then, became in radical writings the enemy of the people. This identification represented a reversal of the common depiction of the aristocracy at the Glorious Revolution of 1688–9. Despite Burke's rhetoric, radical writings all but obliterated the image of a benign and paternalistic aristocracy, the protectors of the people and natural leaders in government. Instead radicals identified an idle, parasitic and corrupt aristocracy similar to that of *ancien régime* France. As government action increasingly forced radicals onto the defensive from 1792 the continuing force of anti-aristocratic rhetoric clearly helped to keep the radical attack alive. As this study has revealed, aristocracy was and remained throughout the years 1790–6 politically and rhetorically central to the radical challenge and, thus, to the French Revolution debate.

Moreover radical representations depicted English society as one of Europe's 'old societies'; *ancien régime* France had been another. John Cannon has argued that 'the discernment of the aristocracy, not as part of the inevitable order of things but as a separate group, pursuing its own interests' provoked the radical challenge of the 1790s.[2] But the pamphlets suggest that in fact it was the other way round. It was the radicals of the 1790s, and foremost among them Thomas Paine, who represented aristocracy as a separate class or caste like the French aristocracy. Radicals also went one step further

---

[1] B. Kucklick (ed.), *Thomas Paine: political writings*, Cambridge 1997, 41.
[2] Cannon, *Aristocratic century*, 178.

and identified England as a society divided on the French, *ancien régime* model of 'aristocracy and people'. The English people, radicals argued, suffered political and economic hardships similar to those of their French counterparts. The source of this hardship in England, as it had been in *ancien régime* France was, predominantly, aristocracy. This portrayal of England as essentially an *ancien régime* directly challenged the assumption, long embedded in the English consciousness, that England had the best and most progressive constitution. As radicals discovered, however, this assumption was hard to shift.

Few in England, even amongst radicals, seriously contemplated a revolution in England. Loyalists took advantage of this fact and depicted the revolution in France as violent and brutal anarchy, a bloody orgy of horror and terror in which no one's life or property was safe from the frenzied mob. Radical demands for equality of political rights were transposed by loyalists into demands for equality of property. Loyalists pointed to France and the spectre of levelling and accused radicals of wanting to level all property in England. This issue was depicted in loyalist pamphlets as affecting all those with property, however little, and this was one significant way in which loyalists appealed to the mass of the people. Loyalists were united in their conviction that political rights should be linked to property ownership. And property ownership remained at the centre of the debate about political rights throughout 1790–6 and for many years thereafter.

The multi-faceted loyalism that emerged during the years 1791–6 proved to be a powerful movement. Loyalism was not merely a conservative defence of 'Church and King' and aristocracy; nor was it entirely a Whig promotion of a commercial and prosperous, but also essentially *ancien régime*, society. Instead loyalism was a multi-faceted movement which shifted and changed in the flexible and fluid channels of the French Revolution debate. And interestingly, in the populous Westminster constituency for which Charles James Fox was MP, this alliance was reflected in voting patterns in the 1790s.[3] Clearly the loyalist focus on commerce and economics, and the promotion of the commercial model of society, contributed greatly to such shifts.

Loyalists certainly defended the aristocracy, restating its integrity and reputation and emphasising its essential role in the English constitution. It was this role, they argued, that differentiated the English aristocracy from its French counterpart. The radicals, including Paine, recognised this distinction. But contrary to Wahrman's suggestions loyalists did not represent the country on the dual paradigm of 'aristocracy and people' with an exclusive elite. Instead they took an essentially Whig position, but developing Whig social theory further, and promoted a new commercial model of society in which the aristocracy constituted only part of an open elite. This ensured

---

3 Corfield, Green and Harvey, 'Westminster man', 168–72.

that during 1793–6 the aristocracy was manoeuvred out of the centre stage in the loyalist argument. Aristocracy no longer needed to be defended; it had become part of the loyalist defence.

Moreover the pamphlet literature shows that during the years 1790–6 the new loyalist commercial model was increasingly promoted. Mainstream loyalism developed a stronger commercial emphasis. Loyalist pamphlets increasingly moved away from the radical focus on political rights and promoted wealth and prosperity in a commercial and successful nation, but with its traditional system of mixed government preserved. Thus a synthesis of political conservatism and more liberal commercialism can be identified as emerging within loyalism. This two-fold 'loyalism' was increasingly converging to create a newly confident loyalism.

In fact radical rhetoric was countered by the new loyalist alternative. With the development and promotion of the new commercial model loyalism did more than merely defend the *status quo*, it went on the attack. Loyalists challenged Painite claims that society should be inclusive in terms of man's political rights by claiming that English society already was inclusive. It was inclusive and equal in terms of opportunity for all could rise in its open society politically, economically and socially. This argument, which equated personal opportunity with national prosperity, was intended to provide an enticing carrot to the mass of the people. Indeed loyalists produced a model of English society which suggested that Englishmen already had what the French revolutionaries had originally demanded. They had liberty under the constitution, equality of opportunity and fraternity within the open commercial society fostered within an industrial and prosperous country.

The English constitution also played a consistently important part for both radicals and loyalists in the French Revolution debate. Loyalists were united in their defence and promotion of the much-acclaimed English constitution, which they argued was at the heart of all that was good about England. The pamphlets suggest that ultimately the majority of radicals also supported the English constitution, albeit ripe for reform. Clearly this enduring support expressed in published pamphlet literature helped to ensure that no revolution took place in England during 1790–6.

At this point it is helpful to consider the effect upon the English aristocracy of the radical attack and of a debate within which aristocracy was for some six years a central focus. Linda Colley has argued that in the face of a radical attack that stretched back intermittently to the American War, the elite within England and Britain as a whole saw the need to reform. It needed to 'repel suggestions that it was an exclusive and over-lavish oligarchy and legitimise its authority anew'. Aristocrats must demonstrate 'that they were authentically and enthusiastically British' and not 'a separate interest in the state'. And, she says, 'they succeeded in doing precisely this'.[4] Yet it should

---

[4] Colley, *Britons*, 155.

CONCLUSION

not be forgotten that in England, unlike in France, the radical attack upon aristocracy was restricted to written representations and that much of the attack took the form of rhetoric and propaganda. Whilst clearly the radical attack changed perceptions of aristocracy amongst the English people, it did not within the years 1790–6, or indeed during the remainder of the decade, achieve any concrete change. No reforms of parliament were enacted and the English aristocracy was not required to relinquish any of the rights and privileges that formed the basis of its political and social hegemony. Moreover loyalist representations increasingly depicted an English aristocracy that was harmoniously integrated, as part of a broader open and commercial elite. Here loyalists portrayed an aristocracy that did not need to reform. In fact loyalists were merely representing continuity masked as change, but the power of such written representations in forming contemporary opinion should not be underestimated. It can be argued, therefore, that by the end of the debate it was loyalism rather than radicalism, that had the most immediate impact upon the status of the aristocracy.

Certainly the pamphleteers themselves questioned the validity of their opponents' representations. The French Revolution debate became increasingly a propaganda battle with each side accusing the other of misrepresentation. Radical writers accused loyalists of providing inaccurate depictions in their pamphlets. In 1794, for example, the radical writer Daniel Stuart accused the loyalists of publishing 'the most violent inflammatory libels' in their 'hand-bills and ballads', which were inciting the people to violence.[5] This was an interesting reversal of the usual accusations made against radicals that they were inflaming the people to violence. Stuart also identified members of the loyalist society, the Association for the Preservation of Liberty and Property against Republicans and Levellers, as 'Tory *Jacobin* Associators'. And he complained that the people were being misled by loyalist publications that stated the French 'had roasted alive, basted with oil, and eaten many . . . Nobles', whilst others had been 'made into pies'.[6] In contrast the radicals claimed that their material reflected reality. The British Convention declared that 'The picture we have drawn is not overcharged . . . not a fiction of the imagination, but a representation of FACTS.'[7] And in 1794 Joseph Gerrald said of his description of England: 'This is not the gaudy picture of a distempered imagination, but the real representation of things which are.'[8]

Loyalists, in turn, condemned radicals for intentionally misleading the people. In 1793 the Association stated that its aim in publishing was 'to counteract the poison that had been disseminated' by radicals and 'to restore the minds of the People to that tone of good sense, which had ever been the

---

5 Stuart, *Peace and reform*, 285.
6 Ibid. 287, 297.
7 British Convention, *The address*, 93.
8 Gerrald, *A convention*, 191.

characteristic of this country'.⁹ Arthur Young claimed that Paine and his followers were 'mad-men and mountebanks' who spouted only 'childish visions and silly theories'. Their 'Clubs and Societies' had exposed 'the Publick Peace' to considerable danger by 'the circulation of mischievous Opinions'.¹⁰ Indeed John Stewart declared that 'the RIGHTS OF MAN has intoxicated the irreflective part of the British community, and poisoned the minds of the plebeian inhabitants of great cities'. Such 'seductive writers', Stewart continued, used the 'artifice of eloquence' and 'blinded the guardian reason that passion, escaping from its prison, might aberrate in the wide field of its unrestrained propensities'.¹¹ The prominent pro-war loyalist, John Bowles, accused the radicals of relying on 'fallacies or misrepresentations' in their attempts to 'prejudice the public opinion against the war'.¹²

In this war of words radicals and loyalists also accused each other of using misleading language, of mis-using language. Burke and Paine were both condemned by their opponents for their inappropriate language. To Mary Wollstonecraft, Burke's *Reflections* was a 'wild declamation'.¹³ John Thelwall complained that:

> [Burke's] mode of writing is at once declamatory and dogmatical in the highest degree. Assertion and metaphor mingle in such splendid confusion; and facts without proofs, and conclusions without arguments, are so accumulated and involved, that it is almost impossible to decide what is to be regarded as premises, and what is illustration.¹⁴

Burke was accused of consecrating in his writings 'the unclassic jargon of lawyers, monks and sophists of the middle ages'.¹⁵ In turn Paine was condemned for displaying a 'giddy discomforting opinion', 'fit only for that wretched banditti of revolutionists, who are ever greedy of political hurricanes'.¹⁶

Indeed it was not just the representations themselves that contributed to the complexity of the debate, but also the language in which they were couched. Burke invoked what has been identified here as an established 'language of aristocracy' and embellished it with gothic idioms. Paine introduced a new language to political debate, which appealed to the people and also adopted French condemnations of aristocracy. The subsequent polarisation of terminology of the two sides is confirmed by Wahrman. He argued

---

⁹ *Association papers*, part 1, p. ii. See also Black, *The association*.
¹⁰ Young, *Example of France*, 58, 85.
¹¹ John Stewart, *Good sense addressed to the British nation, as their pre-eminent and peculiar characteristic, in the present awful crisis: or, war of social existence exhibiting the actual and eventful state of various nations*, 1794, 10–11.
¹² Bowles, *Objections to the war*, 64.
¹³ Wollstonecraft, *Vindication of the rights of men*, 8.
¹⁴ Thelwall, *Rights of nature*, 439.
¹⁵ Christie, *Letters on the revolution*, 157–8.
¹⁶ [Hervey], *New friend*, 75.

that there emerged a radical language of 'undivided inclusiveness' and a 'conservative language' of 'sharp exclusiveness'. That is, after the French Revolution radicals based their 'anti-aristocratic critique' on the Painite language of natural rights, 'whose all inclusive basis guaranteed that no social group was privileged over another'. The 'conservative reaction, on the other hand, emphasized exclusivity, that is the privileged position of the ruling class', Burke's Corinthian Capital of British society.[17] Yet Wahrman did not go far enough in his analysis of loyalist language and the models of society it invoked.

To represent loyalism as comprising only the 'conservative reaction' is to underestimate its extent and variety. The fact that many loyalists rejected Burke's vision of an *ancien régime* England is further illustrated by their rejection of his corresponding aristocratic language. For example, Hearn agreed with Paine that 'the language of passion is seldom that of reason'.[18] Indeed, in response to Paine's use of a plain language for the people, some loyalists recognised the need to adopt a more accessible language. One respondent, whilst condemning Paine's language as 'low and Billingsgate', recognised that he 'writes to the vulgar, to the mob; and the author must meet him on vulgar ground'.[19] Another anonymous writer concurred that, in the battle for the support of the people, political commentary did 'not require the aid of eloquence or rhetoric'.[20] Conversely, in a pamphlet published in 1792, John Gifford accused Paine and his followers of confusing the people with 'dark mazes of abstract theorems' and 'metaphysical disquisitions' rather than using the 'simple language of Common Sense' that he, Gifford, had invoked.[21]

In promoting their commercial model of an inclusive society, loyalists rejected some of the major tenets of 'aristocratic language'. Gone were the gothic idioms and imagery utilised by Burke. Indeed the radical's use of the word 'gothic' as a term of criticism was sometimes adopted by loyalists.[22] On the issue of reform one anonymous writer called for caution in removing 'the Gothic buttress', which was described as 'displeasing to the eye'.[23] Boothby referred to primogeniture as a 'Gothic institution',[24] and Hearn reflected Wollstonecraft's usage, with a reference to 'Gothic darkness' having been 'dispersed by the rays of philosophy'.[25] The concept of honour was invoked by loyalists, but primarily as a moral principle in a meritocratic society. Nor did the majority of loyalist pamphleteers invoke Burke's celebration of aristocratic manners as the source of civilisation. Links with chivalry and a

---

[17] Wahrman, *Imagining the middle class*, 55.
[18] [Hearn], *Short review*, 341–2.
[19] Anon., *Defence of the constitution*, 13.
[20] Anon., *Defence of the rights*, 289.
[21] Gifford, *Plain address*, 6.
[22] See Smith, *Gothic bequest*, 97–131.
[23] Anon., *Cursory remarks*, 129.
[24] Boothby, *Letter to the Rt. Hon. Edmund Burke*, 261.
[25] [Hearn], *Short view*, 322.

romantic medieval past were not generally made.²⁶ Indeed few references to chivalry were found in loyalists' pamphlets. Lewelyn did confirm that chivalry may have had 'a happy effect in humanizing mankind' and introduced 'politeness and good order' but that was in 'the eleventh century'. He went on: 'Chivalry was the offspring of violence' and 'destructive of liberty' but 'necessary and laudable' at that time.²⁷

Ultimately the complex crosscurrents of the debate resulted in even Burke abandoning, albeit temporarily, the language of aristocracy. In his *Letter to a noble lord* Burke appeared to be attacking the very nobility he had defended with such emotion and vigour in *Reflections*. In fact Burke was defending himself and his pension against attacks from two noble members of the reforming Foxite Whigs. Clearly to Burke such noblemen were not behaving as they should, nor did they appreciate the lengths he had gone to on their behalf in *Reflections*. Burke's resentment was great and he expressed it, not in aristocratic language, but in language generally associated with Paine. 'Poor rich man!', he scoffed at the duke of Bedford, in 'his few and idle years ... [he] can hardly know anything of publick industry in its exertions, or can estimate its compensations when its work is done.'²⁸ Here Burke inadvertently illustrates the significance of radical anti-aristocratic rhetoric in changing the way the aristocracy was represented in England. As Burke himself said, 'in the masquerades of the grand carnival of our age, whimsical adventures happen; odd things are said and pass off'.²⁹

As Gregory Claeys has suggested, two opposing languages may be identified in the French Revolution debate. These are not Wahrman's inclusive and exclusive languages. Claeys has pinpointed one radical language of natural rights and another, a loyalist language, not of 'Burkean feudalism' but of 'civilisation, especially in the form of commercial society'.³⁰ Taking Claeys further this book illustrates that the loyalist language of 'civilisation' was the language invoked to promote the loyalist commercial model. This language became, with the development of that model, an inclusive language that reflected the economically gradated society with an open elite that loyalists were promoting. Loyalist language then moved away from Wahrman's exclusive language which emphasised the privileged position of the ruling class. Moreover this shift in loyalist representations also resulted in the consequent demise of the language of aristocracy, which may have been partial and, possibly, temporary but is significant. It suggests that the linguistic hegemony of aristocratic language had to be forfeited in the loyalist campaign in order to attract the support of the people. Consequently loyalist language was shifting ever closer to radical usage.

²⁶ See, for example, anon., *Remarks on Mr. Paine's pamphlet*, 50.
²⁷ Lewelyn, *Appeal to men*, 39–40, 42. See also Bowles, *Protest*, 61.
²⁸ Burke, *Letter to a noble lord*, in Ritchie, *Further reflections*, 284.
²⁹ Ibid. 283.
³⁰ Claeys, 'French Revolution', 74.

In fact, as David Eastwood has suggested, loyalists adopted and redeployed some radical political language.[31] Loyalists promoted the 'real rights of man' and consistently warned that 'the real Rights of Mankind' should not be sacrificed to a radical zeal.[32] It was 'the object of the modern "Rights of Man" ' to create only 'restlessness and dissatisfaction'.[33] 'Liberty', a word fully utilised by radicals in England and France in connection with equality of political rights, was consistently invoked by loyalists to connect political rights firmly to property. As one respondent said, 'I love liberty as much as Mr. Paine, but differ from him in my opinion of what it is.'[34] Another declared that the radical proposals would 'affect directly or indirectly, the liberty and property of every individual in these kingdoms'.[35]

Thus the range of language invoked by loyalists illustrates the different political positions that existed within loyalism. Moreover such use and rejection of language suggests a linguistic interaction between radicals and loyalists. Mark Philp has argued that it is necessary to consider the extent to which radicals and loyalists 'shaped and conditioned each others' objectives and tactics'.[36] He continued: 'we come closer to the realities of the 1790s' if we think of people as 'debating issues and affirming or changing commitments' within the debate, rather than as subscribing to a particular set of radical principles or a particular ideology'.[37] The pamphlets certainly reveal the process of intellectual ferment in action.

The legacies of the debate

The pamphlet debate, having reached its peak in 1792–3, was in serious decline by 1796, as publication figures indicate.[38] This was largely due to Pitt's so-called 'Reign of Terror' of 1794–7. Sedition proceedings against radicals were stepped-up and the treason trials of 1794 saw many prominent radicals prosecuted.[39] Two acts often referred to as the 'Gagging Acts' or the 'Two Acts', which restricted the right of free speech and public meeting, were passed in December 1795.[40] As Gwyn Williams said, by 1796 citizens 'could

---

[31] See Eastwood, 'Patriotism and the English state', 160–1, and Williams, *Artisans and sans-culottes*, p. xix.
[32] [Sewell], *Rejoinder to Mr Paine's pamphlet*, 173.
[33] [Bowles], *Protest*, 44.
[34] Anon., *Remarks on Mr Paine's pamphlet*, 64.
[35] Anon., *Interests of man*, 56.
[36] Philp, 'Fragmented ideology', 56.
[37] Ibid. 66.
[38] For details of this decline in publication figures see Goodrich, 'Peers or parasites?', 217–19.
[39] Many prominent radicals were prosecuted and tried, including John Thelwall, Henry Redhead Yorke, Thomas Hardy, John Horne Tooke, Joseph Gerrald and Daniel Isaac Eaton: Goodwin, *Friends of liberty*, 307–58.
[40] Ibid. 360, 387.

hardly open their mouths in public. The Two Acts were the full stop'.[41] Over the next few years at least government action continued to suppress pamphlet publication. The debate that had focused upon arguments initiated by Burke and Paine was therefore at an end by 1796.

But no history stands alone. Every fragment of historical study, every interpretation, contributes to the ever-shifting base of historiography. Whilst the vast and rich seam of primary sources available and relevant to this book presents a significant fragment, a contribution, in themselves there is also a wider context to be considered. While the pamphlets of the French Revolution debate reveal many connections with the past,[42] the historiography suggests that they also had a long-term impact and influenced political debate into the nineteenth century and beyond.

Whilst in the later 1790s radicalism was forced underground and focused upon militant action rather than written debate,[43] Claeys has argued that Painite radicalism re-emerged in 1817 with the expansion of the reform movement. Such radicalism remained prominent in the debate over the Reform Bill of 1830–2.[44] Moreover a number of historians have remarked on the political legacy left by loyalist representations of 1790–6. For example, Dickinson has stated that a reactionary ruling class 'forged a more coherent conservative ideology', which led in the early nineteenth century to the development of a new Tory party 'committed to the defence of monarchy, the established church and private property'.[45] It seems, however, that loyalists did not only leave a conservative legacy. Analysis of the relevant historiography suggests that, although historians have not generally noted the fact, representations reflecting the new loyalist commercial model of 1790–6 can be identified in debates at least up to and including the debate on the Reform Bill.

The debates about taxation during 1797–9 clearly encompassed a number of issues familiar from the early 1790s. Pitt's triple assessment, and then the introduction of income tax in 1799, provoked considerable debate, both within parliament and outside. Which sectors of society should carry the burden of taxation became the central issue. Arguments about landed versus commercial wealth, about earned and unearned income and about the value of the various sectors of society reappeared. Dror Wahrman has argued that, in the debate on the triple assessment, many of the opposition complained that it would be the middle classes rather than the aristocracy that would bear the brunt of taxation. Here government supporters could be found justifying such a tax by invoking traditional defences of a landed aristocracy and airing old fears about new commercial wealth and the moral issue of 'luxury'

---

[41] Williams, *Artisans and sans-culottes*, 102.
[42] See introduction above.
[43] For example Wells, *Insurrection: the British experience*; Royle, *Revolutionary Britannia?*
[44] Claeys, *Thomas Paine*, 213–14.
[45] Dickinson, 'Popular conservatism', 103.

amongst a newly wealthy middle class. Commercial wealth, they argued, was becoming dominant and adventurers without landed property, manners or independence were destroying the social order.[46]

Yet within a range of government supporters' responses quoted by Wahrman can be found a number invoking concepts of a commercially prosperous Britain. One defender of the tax argued that merchants and manufacturers were now the most affluent members of society whilst those whose income came entirely from land were struggling with increasing debt.[47] A similar focus upon a commercial Britain can also be found amongst those opposed to the tax proposals. One Joseph Cawthorne identified the British as a 'trading people' and manufactures and commerce as the sources of Britain's wealth. He also went on to argue that great property was 'inactive' and, thus, it was the industrious part of society, the 'manufacturing and trading people', who should be protected from increased taxation.[48]

Again historians suggest that the debate over the introduction of income tax found the landed interest pitted against the commercial interest. Landowners opposed the government's imposition of what appeared to be an increased land tax that favoured commercial wealth. Wahrman has identified an almost universal landed social vocabulary dominating this debate within parliament. But clearly this vocabulary incorporated gentry and farmers as well as a landed aristocracy.[49] Country tax-payers of all classes who relied upon an income from the land were united against commercial wealth. This suggests that the traditional battle between old landed wealth and new commercial wealth was being fought out within new parameters. Clearly, during these debates, the ideas and models of society promoted by loyalists during 1790–6 were being invoked once again.

The debate on the Reform Bill in 1830–2 saw a resurgence of issues familiar from the early 1790s. Here the issue of reform was taken up within parliament by the reform Whigs and it was the Whig Earl Grey who eventually piloted the Reform Bill through parliament to enactment in 1832.[50] Yet largely extra-parliamentary radical agitation for parliamentary reform had been building up since Waterloo. Once again pamphleteering became an important part of the debate. William Cobbett, Francis Place, Sir Francis Burdett and the ever-loyal John Cartwright now led radicalism. Whilst most Painite radicals of the 1790s were no longer active, Painite views were revived in the debate over the Reform Bill.[51] Anti-aristocratic rhetoric can again be found in nineteenth-century radical pamphlets engaged in this

---

46 See Wahrman, *Imagining the middle class*, 120–3.
47 Ibid. 115–18.
48 [Joseph Cawthorne], *The injustice and impolicy of the bill to increase the assessed taxes &c. with a commutation*, 1798, 5–6. 27, 57, 74–5, quoted in Wahrman, *Imagining the middle class*, 117–18.
49 Wahrman, *Imagining the middle class*, 141–4.
50 Turner, *British politics*, 23–5, 68–9.
51 Claeys, *Thomas Paine*, 210–12.

debate, and a number of historians have identified a traditional loyalist defence of the aristocracy being invoked.[52]

Nevertheless the fact that the Reform Bill was being promoted in parliament by what amounted to a Whig ministry of 'blue blood and great landowners'[53] must have meant that the anti-aristocratic rhetoric of 1790–6 that focused on aristocracy as a class was no longer dominant in the debate. It became the rhetoric appropriate only to the radical element of those agitating for reform rather than being central to the entire radical/reform cause, as in 1790–6. Thus radicalism was pushed out into the cold once again, but this time by a government of reform Whigs. Inevitably the measures enacted under the legislation fell far short of the demands of Painite radicals, and the radicals who had continued to campaign for so much more were bitterly disappointed. Radicals fought on for political rights for ordinary working men well into the nineteenth century. Yet radicalism was subject to the influences of the day and by 1850 demands for parliamentary reform became increasingly influenced by economic analyses and demands for the rights of labour which, as we have seen, had begun to emerge in the later writings of Paine and Thelwall.[54] The old constitutionalism and concern with aristocratic corruption, which had been the main focus of 1790s radicalism, was gradually surpassed by a preoccupation with capitalist labour relations.[55]

At the other end of the political spectrum historians have argued that the Tory[56] opposition to reform took a traditional stance and expressed the view throughout the debate that the Reform Bill amounted to 'a revolution that will overturn all the natural influence of rank and property'. As in the early 1790s a radical desire for levelling was identified and exploited by the Tories. They also expressed the fear that under the proposed bill political influence would be transferred from the landed areas to the industrial sectors, populated by men of new wealth.[57] Land was pitted against other forms of less stable property, the commercial property Burke had reviled. Property was again at the forefront of the debate about political rights and a Burkean defence of it re-emerged in the Tory opposition to reform. The defence against such radical attack, therefore, necessitated a strong defence of the aristocracy, 'the guardian of all our property and rights – the aristocracy of our land'.[58]

Indeed a number of historians have argued that the long-standing connec-

---

[52] For example, Perkin, *Origins of modern English society*, 310.
[53] Clark, *English society*, 403.
[54] See chapter 4 above.
[55] Claeys, *Political writings*, pp. lii–liii.
[56] Party labels 'Whig' and 'Tory' came into regular use during the early 1800s: Turner, *British politics*, 48.
[57] Briggs, *Age of improvement*, 241–2.
[58] *Blackwood's Edinburgh Magazine*, 1830, xxvii. 717, quoted in Perkin, *Origins of modern English society*, 310.

tion between political rights and property was now more central to the debate than during 1790–6. Radicalism was viewed, not just by Tories but also by the Whig government and its supporters, as primarily representing an attack upon property.[59] The traditional link between liberty and property and the adherence to property as the root of political rights remained the mainstay of Whig as well as Tory political theory. Although under the Reform Act rotten boroughs were abolished and the franchise was extended to include '£10 householders', property still remained the key to both representation and the franchise.[60] Historians have traditionally viewed the Reform Bill as a reluctant but intelligent concession by the aristocracy.[61] Perkin declared that the aristocracy sacrificed one pillar of the aristocratic ideal, patronage, in order to save the other, property.[62] This suggests that, like the loyalists before them, the Whigs had favoured continuity over change and the propertied over the unpropertied.[63]

Nevertheless ideas and language previously invoked by loyalists during 1790–6 in the representations of their new commercial model had not died out.[64] On the contrary, such ideas re-emerged within the debate on the Reform Bill. But here they were adopted by the reform Whigs, and to gain support among the 'middle class' rather than the mass of the working people. Perkin noted that reform Whigs, anxious to win over the middle ground and detach it from the radical extreme, described property in terms that incorporated all property, commercial, financial, moveable, as well as land. Francis Jeffrey declared that 'The real battle is not between Whigs and Tories, Liberals and Illiberals and such gentleman-like denominations, but between property and no-property – Swing and the law.'[65] And according to Wahrman, Michael Sadler, in a speech in the House of Commons, stated that 'Commerce multiplied the wealth of the nation' and consequently 'mingled society into a more indistinguishable mass, infusing through the whole a portion of its own spirit of enterprise and independence'.[66] Pro-reform rhetoric would often use terms such as the 'smaller gentry', 'superior trading men', the 'New Rich' or 'the monied class' to describe the middle class to whom the franchise

---

[59] Perkin, *Origins of modern English society*, 308–13.
[60] Turner, *British politics*, 176–8.
[61] Ibid. pp. 194–5. But Cannon argues that not all Whigs viewed reform as a reluctant concession; some ministers such as Durham and Althorp were genuine reformers and pushed for more radical reforms: *Parliamentary reform*, 252
[62] Perkin, *Origins of modern English society*, 310–11; Clark, *English society*, 403.
[63] Grey, despite his apparent commitment to reform, remained committed to aristocratic government and an aristocratic social order during 1831–2. See Clark, *English society*, 363, and Turner, *British politics*, 175.
[64] *Blackwood's Edinburgh Magazine*, xxvii, quoted in Perkin, *Origins of modern English society*, 310.
[65] Lord Cockburn, *Life of Lord Jeffrey*, 1852, ii. 223, quoted in Perkin, *Origins of modern English society*, 311.
[66] Wahrman, *Imagining the middle class*, 323.

should be extended.⁶⁷ And the Whig politician Henry Brougham declared that 'We don't now live in the days of Barons, thank God . . . we live in the days of Leeds, or Bradford, of Halifax and Huddersfield. We live in the days when men are industrious and desire to be free.'⁶⁸ Wahrman has claimed that by the late 1820s concepts of ' "civilisation" and "progress", embodied in commercialization and industrialization' were already envisaged as inextricably linked with the rise of a 'middle class' and played a crucial role in political debate.⁶⁹ This apparent adoption by reform Whigs of ideas that had been developed by loyalists of the early 1790s illustrates the relevance and flexibility of the loyalist model.⁷⁰ And, perhaps, its enduring popularity with the English people.

The 1790s and 1832

Thus clearly, the political ideas formulated during the early 1790s and expressed in radical and loyalist pamphlets were raised once again within, and had considerable influence upon, the debate over the Reform Bill. The constitution was still open to competing interpretations and the connection between land and political rights remained an issue of debate. 'Old corruption' was still a common accusation in radical anti-aristocratic rhetoric. In particular ideas about political and social supremacy reappeared. Where virtue and merit were most commonly to be found within society was a key feature once again, but in 1832 unlike 1790–6 there was an identified alternative repository of virtue to the aristocracy: the middle class. A hereditary landed aristocracy was pitted against, and then ultimately it allied with, a meritocratic commercial middle class. And they converged upon a basic model of society taken from the loyalist synthesis of 1793–6. The loyalist commercial model, or something near it, was invoked to entice the middle classes to join the Whig aristocracy in promoting moderate reform. In a sense then a reconfiguration of ideas can be seen emerging during the debate on the Reform Bill. Just as the loyalists of 1790–6 had in effect borrowed the radical's clothes in promoting the new commercial model, in 1832 the Whig aristocracy had in turn retrieved Whig social theory in the new guise of the loyalist reinterpretation.

The debate amongst historians about the actual effect of the Reform Act upon aristocratic hegemony rages on.⁷¹ A number of historians have argued

---

67 Ibid. 320.
68 *Leed's Intelligencer*, 29 July 1830, quoted in Briggs, *Age of improvement*, 239.
69 Wahrman, *Imagining the middle class*, 300.
70 How far Whig reformers actually adopted the loyalist commercial model, rather than merely reverting to the Whig social model, can only be clarified by further research.
71 See, for example, John W. Derry, *Politics in the age of Fox, Pitt and Liverpool*, London 1990, 195–7, and Wasson, 'Crisis of the aristocracy', 311, for an outline of this debate. See also E. A. Smith, *The House of Lords, 1815–1911*, London 1991, 4, 118, 139–40; Cannadine, *Decline and fall*, 24–5, 36–40, 168–72; Jupp, 'Landed elite', 76; and others

that as a result of the act, the aristocracy lost its 'power of command in the House of Commons' and hence its political hegemony.[72] Jonathan Clark asserted that the aristocracy lost its cultural hegemony after 1832. The destruction of the Church and State alliance and the introduction of what was in effect a unicameral government meant that the rules of the game had changed. The repeal of the Corn Laws in 1846 was the 'last symbolic defeat'.[73] On the other hand, a number of historical studies have concluded that aristocratic hegemony was not fatally challenged until the latter years of the nineteenth century or even as a result of Great War of 1914–18.[74] Certainly the final blow to aristocratic political power was dealt by the Parliament Act of 1911, which abolished the House of Lords' veto over the House of Commons.

Edward Royle has proposed that the Reform Act caused the ruling aristocracy only to falter and then recover. He claims that the fact that there was no revolution in Britain during the late eighteenth and early nineteenth centuries was partly due to the strength and versatility of the aristocracy. From the 1820s it demonstrated great ability to reform its institutions in order to stay in step with an increasingly commercial and industrial society. To Royle the repeal of the Corn Laws provides another example of the Whig aristocracy reforming its own institutions.[75] He invokes the Chartist, G. J. Holyoake, who claimed that one reason why there was no revolution in 1848 was 'The mixed interest of our commercial nobility and the people'.[76] Moreover Beckett has suggested, at variance to Colley, that aristocratic values remained dominant long after 1832. This was largely because the nineteenth-century middle class proved to be a remarkably conservative force showing little desire to oust the aristocracy from its position of social supremacy. Far from the aristocracy adopting middle-class values the reverse happened, with the middle class accepting aristocratic cultural mores.[77]

Whatever the true effects of the Reform Act on aristocratic power, the English aristocracy did not incur the same fate as the French aristocracy in 1789. Indeed in 1832 the English aristocracy could be seen to be giving concessions in response to the demands of the people, something that the French aristocracy had so fatally refused to do in the Estates-General in 1789. In a sense, then, 1790s radicalism created a repertoire of criticisms that was available for opponents of aristocracy, even while aristocracy itself long survived. Some of the same issues were rehearsed whenever the fate of the

---

quoted in Wasson, 'Crisis of the aristocracy', 297–8; Beckett, *Aristocracy in England*, 4–5, 13–14.
72 Wasson, 'Crisis of the aristocracy', 311.
73 Clark, *English society*, 411.
74 Wasson, 'Crisis of the aristocracy', 298.
75 Royle, *Revolutionary Britannia?*, 170–2.
76 Ibid. 171.
77 Beckett, *Aristocracy in England*, 4–5.

House of Lords was under discussion: in 1911, for example, and even in 1999.[78] This late twentieth-century debate and continuing Labour move to replace hereditary peers with more 'ordinary' people reflects the radical arguments of the 1790s for the selection of the governing leadership on the basis of merit and qualifications rather than birth and blood.[79]

It is clear that the pamphlet war of 1790–6 articulated key issues not just for the 1790s but for future generations. As well as providing an enduring anti-aristocratic rhetoric, 1790s radical representations lived on in later radical movements such as Chartism and, debatably, played an important role in the making of the English working class.[80] It is also significant that the loyalist set of ideas about a commercial and prosperous Britain can be seen re-emerging in later debates, expressed in a rich repertoire of ideas. In particular representations of a commercial and prosperous nation, promoted so strongly by loyalists in 1790–6 and adopted by the Whigs in 1832, remained dominant in Britain's self-representation for generations. Such ideas formed the basis of the promotion of the British empire throughout the nineteenth and into the twentieth century. To Joseph Chamberlain the empire was commerce and, he declared, 'History teaches us that no nation has ever achieved real greatness without the aid of commerce.'[81] Moreover it was Britain's 'superior civilisation' that the empire-builders were exporting in exchange for colonisation. And it was loyalist pamphleteers who had identified Britain's history as one of progress towards the peak of civilisation. In 1793 a pamphleteer confirmed that 'The progress from savage life to citizenship is through a long course of gradual civilization'; it is now completed and 'we behold perfect civilization'.[82] Such ideas were also reflected as historical 'reality' in the later historiography of the eighteenth century in particular in the so-called 'Whig interpretation of history'.[83] These examples illustrate their versatility and enduring efficacy.

The effects of the pamphlet war were subtly different in the short term and in the longer. During 1790–6 the French Revolution debate was a lively war of representations in which both radicalism and loyalism embraced new political ideas and models of society. Set against a backdrop of the French Revolution the arguments were vehement, brilliant, intense. The funda-

---

[78] The Parliament Act 1911 abolished the House of Lords' veto over the House of Commons. In 1999 further legislation deprived hereditary peers of their seats in the House of Lords, replacing them with elected peers.

[79] The following phrase headed a recent newspaper article: 'An Upper House of Placepersons will be the ultimate betrayal of the hopes invested in this Government by reformers': *The Observer*, 2 Feb. 2003, 27.

[80] See, in particular, Thompson, *Making of the English working class*.

[81] Joseph Chamberlain, 'Foreign and colonial speeches, 10 June, 1896', in Perry, Peden and Von Laue, *Sources of the western tradition*, ii. 213.

[82] [Cusack Smith], *Rights of citizens*, 286.

[83] A term first introduced by Herbert Butterfield in his *Whig interpretation of history*, London 1931.

mental structure of government and efficacy of the long-esteemed English mixed constitution were open to scrutiny. The appropriate qualifications for basic political rights and elite political leadership were bitterly contested. Radicals and loyalists fought viciously over political, social and economic equality. Edmund Burke and Thomas Paine pushed aristocracy into the spotlight and thereafter the English people were encouraged to consider rival representations of it:

> The Peerage of England, considered in its Foundation; and from the public Virtues or Abilities, of most of its Members, contributes in a high Degree to the Glory of this Country. – It is an Institution of elevated Rank, which serves as a Stimulus of Emulation, an Inducement to Acts of Heroism, for the general Benefit. If Men possess an eminent Portion of Knowledge or public Virtue; if they exercise these in the Service of the Community; on whom can honorary Rewards, be more properly bestowed?[84]

> The British House of Peers, it is an excrescence growing out of corruption; and there is no more affinity or resemblance between any of the branches of a legislative body originating from the right of the people, and the aforesaid House of Peers, than between a regular member of the human body and an ulcerated wen.[85]

---

[84] Anon., *Loyalty necessary to self-preservation: or, an antidote against the baneful influence of republican doctrines*, Bromley 1798.
[85] Paine, *Dissertation on first principles*, 467.

Bibliography

Printed primary sources

[Place of publication is London unless otherwise specified; pamphlets marked with an asterisk appear in Claeys, *Political writings*]

Radical pamphlets
Anon., *A few words but no lies from Roger Bull to his brother Thomas*, 1792*
Anon., *A political freethinker's thoughts on the present circumstances*, 1795*
Anon., *A report of the proceedings of the Committee of Association presented to a meeting of 19 Dec. 1782*, in Lennox, *Sound reason*
Anon., *A rod for the Burkites: consisting of remonstrative answers to the objections and invectives, of the interested, bigoted, and misguided inhabitants of Stockport by the 'Friends of Universal Peace, and the Rights of Man', by one of the 'swinish multitude'*, 2nd edn c. 1792
Anon., *A speech by a manufacturer at a public meeting in Sheffield on 11 June 1792*, 1792
Anon., *Advertisement to the electors of Westminster, 14 June 1796*, in Hardy, *Moral and political magazine*
Anon., *An address to the Jacobine and other patriotic societies of the French: urging the establishment of a republican form of government. By a native of England and a citizen of the world*, 1792
Anon., *An enquiry into the present alarming state of the nation*, 1793
Anon., *Considerations on the French war*, 1794
Anon., *Estimate of the value of national opulence to the mass of the people*, in Eaton, *Politics for the people*, pt i
Anon., *Extermination: or, an appeal to the people of England, on the present war, with France*, 1793*
Anon., *Meeting of the deputies of all the committees and associations, 20 March 1780*, in Lennox, *Sound reason*
Anon., *More reasons for a reform in parliament*, 1793*
Anon., *Petition of the friends of the people to the Honourable the Commons of Great Britain, in parliament assembled*, 1793*
Anon., *Proceedings relative to the Ulster Assembly of Volunteer Delegates on the subject of more equal representation of the people in the parliament of Ireland to which are annexed letters from the duke of Richmond, Dr Price, Mr Wyvill and others*, 1783
Anon., *Reflexions of a true Briton, continued*, in Eaton, *Politics for the people*, pt i
Anon., *Short observations on the Rt. Hon. Edmund Burke's Reflections*, 1790*
Anon., *Some account of a very seditious book lately found upon Wimbledon Common*, 1794
Anon., *Strictures on the letter of the Rt. Hon. Mr Burke, on the Revolution in France*, 1791*

Anon., *The case of Thomas Spence . . . who was committed to prison for selling Paine's Rights of man*, 1792
Anon., *The confederacy of kings against the freedom of the world*, 1792*
Anon., *The evidence summed up: or, a statement of the apparent causes and objects of the war*, 1794
Anon., *The modern Atlantis: or, the devil in an air balloon*, 1784, in Claeys, *Modern British utopias*, iv
Anon., *The pernicious effects of the art of printing upon society, exposed*, c. 1793
Anon., *The perverse definitions imposed on the word equality*, c. 1792*
Anon., *The political crisis: or, a dissertation on the rights of man*, 1791*
Anon., *War*, 1792, in *Political broadsides*, fo. 26.
Barbauld, Anna-Laetitia, *Civic sermons to the people*, 1792
Barlow, Joel, *Advice to the privileged orders: in the several states of Europe resulting form the necessity and propriety of a general revolution in the principle of government part 1*, 1792; *part 2*, 1793*
────── *A letter to the National Convention of France*, 1792, in Barlow, *Political writings*
Baxter, John, *Resistance to oppression: the constitutional rights of Britons asserted in a lecture delivered before section 2 of the Society of the Friends of Liberty . . . 9 November*, 1795*
Beddoes, Thomas, *Where would be the harm of a speedy peace?*, 1795
Bentley, Thomas, *The rights of the poor*, 1791*
────── *A few queries to the Methodists in general and especially to the teachers amongst the people*, 1792, in *Political broadsides*, fo. 5
────── *The poor man's answer to the rich associators*, 1793
────── *A warning to Britons of all ranks: especially the king, the parliament, and the clergy*, 1794
Birmingham SCI, *Resolutions, 4 March 1793*, 1793, in *Political broadsides*, fo. 36
[Boothby, Sir Brooke,], *A letter to the Rt. Hon. Edmund Burke*, 2nd edn 1791*
Bousfield, Benjamin, *Observations on the Rt. Hon. Edmund Burke's pamphlet on the subject of the French Revolution*, 1791*
British Convention, *The address of the British Convention, assembled at Edinburgh*, 1793*
Burgh, James, *Political disquisitions*, 1774–5
Butler, John, *Brief reflections upon the liberty of the British subject*, Canterbury, c.1792*
Cartwright, John, *Take your choice*, 1776
────── *A letter to the duke of Newcastle: together with some remarks touching the French Revolution, a reform of parliament in Great Britain and the royal proclamation of 21 May 1792*, 1792
────── *The commonwealth in danger*, 1795
────── *The constitutional defence of England*, 1796
Christie, Thomas, *Letters on the revolution of France and on the new constitution established by the National Assembly: occasioned by the publications of the Rt. Hon. Edmund Burke, M.P. and Alexander de Calonne, late minister of state*, 1791*
Cooper, Thomas, *A reply to Mr Burke's invective against Mr Cooper and Mr Watt*, 1792
Cuninghame, William, *The rights of kings*, 2nd edn 1791*
Dalrymple, Alexander, *The poor man's friend*, Edinburgh 1793

Damm, Benjamin, *An address to the public, on true representation and the unity of man*, Sheffield 1792
Depont, M., *Answer to the reflections of the Rt. Hon. Edmund Burke*, 1791*
[du Fresnoy], *An address to the National Assembly of France: containing strictures on Mr Burke's Reflections on the revolution in France*, 1791*
Dyer, G., *The complaints of the poor people of England*, 1793
Frend, William, *Peace and union recommended to the associated bodies of republicans and anti-republicans*, 1793*
Gerrald, Joseph, *A convention the only means of saving us from ruin*, 1793, 3rd edn 1794*
―――― *The defence of Joseph Gerrald on a charge of sedition*, 1794
Godwin, William, *Enquiry concerning political justice: and its influence on modern morals and happiness*, 1793, 3rd edn 1798, ed. Isaac Kramnick, London 1985
Hampden, John, *To the inhabitants of Nottingham*, 1793, in *Political broadsides*, fo. 81
Hardy, Thomas (ed.), *Moral and political magazine of the London Corresponding Society*, 1796
Holcroft, Thomas, *A letter to the Rt. Hon. William Windham, on the intemperance and dangerous tendency of his public conduct*, 1795
Hughes, William, *Justice to a judge: an answer to the judges's appeal to justice*, 2nd edn 1793*
Knox, Vicesimus, *Personal nobility: or, letters to a young nobleman, on the conduct of his studies, and the dignity of the peerage*, 1793
LCS, *The address to the French National Convention, 27 September 1792*, in Thale, *LCS selections*
―――― *Address*, 1793*
―――― *Address to the nation, July 1793*, in Thale, *LCS selections*
―――― *Circular letter to other reform societies, c. 1 March 1794*, in Thale, *LCS selections*
―――― *Resolutions and address at a general meeting, 14 April 1794*, in Thale, *LCS selections*
―――― *Account of general meeting, 29 June 1795*, in Thale, *LCS selections*
―――― *Address to the nation, 29 June 1795*, in Thale, *LCS selections*
―――― *Proceedings of a general meeting, 26 Oct. 1795*, in Thale, *LCS selections*
Lennox, Charles, 3rd duke of Richmond, *Sound reason and solid argument for a reform in parliament*, c. 1795
Light, Launcelot, *A sketch of the rights of boys and girls, part 1*, 1792
Lofft, Capel, *Remarks on the letter of the Rt. Hon. Edmund Burke, concerning the revolution in France and on the proceedings in certain societies in London, relative to that event*, 1790, 2nd edn 1791*
Lovett, John, *The citizen of the world*, 1793
[Macaulay, Catherine], *Observations on the reflection of the Rt. Hon. Edmund Burke, on the revolution in France: in a letter to the Rt. Hon. the earl of Stanhope*, 1790*
Mackintosh, James, *Vindiciae gallicae: defence of the French Revolution and its English admirers against the accusations of the Rt. Hon. Edmund Burke*, 1791*
Oswald, John, *A review of the constitution of Great Britain: being the substance of a speech delivered in a numerous assembly on the following questions: 'Is the petition of Mr Horne Tooke a libel on the House of Commons, or a just statement of public*

grievances arising from an unfair representation of the people?', 1791, 3rd edn Paris*

—— *The government of the people: or, a sketch of a constitution for the universal common-wealth*, Paris 1793*

Paine, Thomas, *The rights of man*, London 1791–2, ed. E. Foner, Harmondsworth 1985

—— *Letter addressed to the addressers on the late proclamation*, 1792, in Foot and Kramnick, *Thomas Paine reader*

—— *Agrarian justice*, 1795, in Foot and Kramnick, *Thomas Paine reader*

—— *Dissertation on first principles of government*, 1795, in Foot and Kramnick, *Thomas Paine reader*

[Parkinson, James], *An address to the Hon. Edmund Burke from the swinish multitude*, 1793*

—— *Knaves acre association: resolutions adopted at a meeting of placemen, pensioners, &c. held at the Sign of the Crown Knaves Acre, for the purpose of forwarding the designs of the place and pension club lately instituted in London*, 1793*

Patton, Charles, *An attempt to establish the basis of freedom on simple and unerring principles*, Edinburgh 1793*

Pigott, Charles, *Strictures on the new political tenets of the Rt. Hon. Edmund Burke*, 1791*

—— *The Jockey Club: or, a sketch of the manners of the age*, 1792

—— *A political dictionary: explaining the true meanings of words*, 1795

Price, Richard, *Observations on the nature of civil liberty*, 1776, in Thomas, *Richard Price*

—— *Observations on the importance of the American Revolution*, 1785, in Thomas, *Richard Price*

Priestley, Joseph, *Letters to the Rt. Hon. Edmund Burke: occasioned by his Reflections on the revolution in France &c.*, 1791*

—— *A political dialogue on the general principles of government*, 1791

[Citizen Randol, of Ostend], *A political catechism of man*, 1795

Revolution Society, *The correspondence of the Revolution Society in London, with the National Assembly and with various societies of the friends of liberty in France and England*, 1792

Rous, George, *Thoughts on government: occasioned by Mr Burke's Reflections, &c., in a letter to a friend to which is added a postscript, in reply to Mr Burke's Reflections*, 4th edn 1791*

SCI, *Second address to the public from the Society for Constitutional Information*, n.d., in Wyvill, *Political papers*, ii

[Scott, John], *A letter to the Rt. Hon. Edmund Burke: in reply to his 'Reflections on the revolution in France', &c. by a member of the Revolution Society*, Dublin 1791*

Sharpe, J., *A rhapsody to E***** B**** Esq.*, Sheffield 1792

Sieyès, abbé Emmanuel, *An essay on privileges, and particularly on hereditary nobility*, trans. 1792

Spence, Thomas *The real rights of man*, 1790, in Dickinson, *Political works*

—— *The end of oppression*, 2nd edn 1795, in Dickinson, *Political works*

—— *The rights of infants*, 1796, in Dickinson, *Political works*

Stanhope, Charles, *A letter from the earl Stanhope to the Rt. Hon. Edmund Burke:*

containing a short answer to his late speech on the French Revolution, 3rd edn 1790*

Stuart, Daniel, *Peace and reform, against war and corruption*, 2nd edn 1794*

Thelwall, John, *Peaceful discussion and not tumultuary violence, the means of redressing national grievance: the speech of John Thelwall at the general meeting of the friends of parliamentary reform, called by the London Corresponding Society*, 1795*

────── *The natural and constitutional rights of Britons to annual parliaments, universal suffrage, and the freedom of popular association*, 1795, in Claeys, *Politics of English Jacobinism*

────── *The tribune*, i, 1795–6, in Claeys, *Politics of English Jacobinism*

────── *Miscellaneous subjects, 7 June 1796*, 1796, in Hardy, *Moral and political magazine*

────── *Sober reflections on the seditious and inflammatory letter of the Rt. Hon. Edmund Burke to a noble lord*, 1796, in Claeys, *Politics of English Jacobinism*

────── *The rights of nature against the usurpations of establishments*, 1796, in Claeys, *Politics of English Jacobinism*

Towers, Joseph, *Thoughts on the commencement of a new parliament: with an appendix containing remarks on the letter of the Rt. Hon. Edmund Burke on the revolution in France*, 1790*

[Vaughan, William], *The catechism of man, pointing out from sound principles, and acknowledged facts, the rights and duties of every rational being*, 1794*

Williams, David, *Letters on political liberty*, 1782

Wollstonecraft, Mary, *A vindication of the rights of men*, 1790, in Todd, *Wollstonecraft*

────── *A vindication of the rights of woman*, 1792, in Todd, *Wollstonecraft*

Wyvill, Christopher, *A state of the representation of the people of England, on the principles of Mr Pitt in 1785*, 1793

Yorke, Henry Redhead, *Reason urged against precedent: in a letter to the people of Derby*, 1793*

────── *These are the times that try men's souls!*, 1793

────── *Thoughts on civil government addressed to the disenfranchised citizens of Sheffield*, 1794*

Loyalist pamphlets

Anon., *A brief reply to the observations of Ben Bousfield Esq., on Mr Burke's pamphlet*, Dublin 1791*

Anon., *A candid inquiry into the nature of government, and the right of representation*, 1792

Anon., *A country curate's advice to manufacturers*, 1792*

Anon., *A dialogue between a labourer and a gentleman*, 1793, in *Association papers*, part 2, no. 8

Anon., *A defence of the constitution of England against the libels that have been lately published on it: particularly in Paine's pamphlet on the Rights of man*, 1791*

Anon., *A few minutes advice to the people of Great Britain on republics*, 1792

Anon., *A letter to a friend in the country: wherein Mr Paine's letter to Mr Dundas is particularly considered*, 1792

Anon., *A letter to Mr Paine, on his late publication*, 1792*

Anon., *A letter to the people of England, on their present situation*, Egham 1792*

Anon., *A new dialogue between Monsieur Francois and John English on the French Revolution*, c. 1793*

Anon., *A parish clerk's advice to the good people, on the present times*, 1793, in *Association papers*, part 2, no. 7

Anon., *A picture of true and false politics: addressed to the understandings and feelings of Britons*, 1793, in *Association papers*, part 2, no. 5

Anon., *A rod in brine: or, a tickler for Tom Paine, in answer to his first pamphlet, entitled the Rights of man*, Canterbury 1792*

Anon., *A serious caution to the poor*, 1792, in *Association papers*, part 2, no. 8

Anon., *A song to be sung an hundred years hence, to the tune of 'Hearts of Oak'*, 1793, in *Political broadsides*, fo. 60

Anon., *A whipper for levelling Tommy*, 1793*

Anon., *A word in season to the traders and manufacturers of Great Britain*, 1793, in *Association papers*, part 2, no. 1

Anon., *Address to the members of the various box-clubs and benefit societies in Great Britain by Strap Bodkin, staymaker*, 1793, in *Association papers*, part 2, no. 6

Anon., *An address to the people of Great Britain: containing a comparison between the republican and reforming parties*, Edinburgh 1793*

Anon., *An antidote against French politics*, 1793, in *Association papers*, part 2, no. 5

Anon., *An exposure of the domestic and foreign attempts to destroy the British constitution, upon the doctrines recommended by a member of parliament*, 1793

Anon., *An humble address to the most high, most mighty, and most puissant the sovereign people*, 1793

Anon., *Considerations on Mr Paine's pamphlet on the rights of man*, Edinburgh 1791*

Anon., *Constitutional letters, in answer to Mr Paine's Rights of man*, 1792*

Anon., *Defence of the rights of man; being a discussion of the conclusions drawn from those rights by Mr Paine*, 1791*

Anon., *Letters to a friend, on the late revolution in France*, 1792

Anon., *Letters to a friend on the Test Laws containing reasons for not repealing them, and a defence of the parliamentary speeches of . . . the earl of Guilford and . . . Mr Pitt with cursory remarks in a pamphlet published against these speeches, by an Oxford master of arts, also strictures on Mr Paine's Rights of man*, 1791

Anon., *Letters to Thomas Paine: in answer to his late publication on the rights of man*, 1791

Anon., *Liberty, and property, courage and common sense*, 1793, in *Association papers*, part 2, no. 7

Anon., *Life and character of Mr. Thomas Paine . . . and inscribed to the Society against Levellers and Republicans*, n.d., in *Political broadsides*, fo. 41

Anon., *Loyalty necessary to self-preservation: or, an antidote against the baneful influence of republican doctrines*, Bromley 1798

Anon., *Mr Justice Buller's charge to the grand jury of the county of York*, 1793, in *Association papers*, part 1, no. 8

Anon., *Remarks on Mr Paine's pamphlet*, 1791*

Anon., *Rights upon rights with observations upon observations*, 1791

Anon., *The duties of man in connexion with his rights: or, rights and duties inseparable*, 1793

Anon., *The earl of Radnor's charge to the grand jury of the county of Berks, 15 January 1793*, in *Association papers*, part 1, no. 9

Anon., *The interests of man in opposition to the rights of man*, Edinburgh 1793

Anon., *The riot: or, half a loaf is better than no bread, in a dialogue between Jack Anvil and Tom Hod*, in *Political broadsides*, fo. 91

Anon., *Thoughts upon our present situation, with remarks upon the policy of a war with France*, 1793

Anon., *Tom the bodice maker*, c. 1792, in *Political broadsides*, fo. 42

Anon., *War with France, the only security of Britain, at the present momentous crisis*, 1794

Ashurst, Sir William Henry, *Mr. Justice Ashurst's charge to the grand jury for the county of Middlesex*, 1792*

Association, *Proceedings which reported the resolutions of a meeting at the Crown and Anchor Tavern, 20 November 1792*, in *Association papers*, part 1, no. 1

——— *Special meeting of the committee of the society, 6 December 1792*, in *Association papers*, part 1, no. 1

[Atkinson, William], *A concise sketch of the intended revolution in England*, 1794*

Barwis, Jackson, *A fourth dialogue concerning liberty, containing an exposition of the falsity of the first and leading principles of the present revolutionists in Europe*, 1793*

Bisset, Robert, *Sketch of democracy*, 1796

[Strap Bodkin], *An address to the members of various box-clubs and benefit societies in Great Britain*, in *Association papers*, part 2, no. 6

Boothby, Sir Brooke, *Observations on the appeal from the new to the old Whigs, and on Mr Paine's Rights of man*, 1792*

[Bowles, John], *A protest against T. Paine's 'Rights of man'*, 5th edn 1792*

——— *Dialogues on the rights of Britons: between a farmer, a sailor and a manufacturer*, 1792–3*

Bowles, John, *Objections to the continuance of the war examined and refuted*, 1794

——— *Reflections on the conclusion of war*, 1800

Brown, James, *The importance of preserving unviolated the system of government in every state: with the dreadful consequences of the violation of it [a sermon] . . . to which is added an appendix containing some strictures on the writings of Mr Paine*, 1793

Bull, John, *French kindness and French humanity*, 1793, in *Association papers*, part 2, no. 6

Burke, Edmund, *A vindication of natural society*, 1757, in Harris, *Burke: pre-revolutionary writings*

——— *Thoughts on the cause of the present discontents*, 1770, in Harris, *Burke: pre-revolutionary writings*

——— *Reflections on the revolution in France: and on the proceedings in certain societies in London relative to that event*, 1790, ed. Conor Cruise O'Brien, London 1986

——— *Reflections on the revolution in France: and on the proceedings in certain societies in London relative to that event*, 1790, ed. J. G. A. Pocock, Indianapolis 1987

——— *Substance of the speech of the Right Honourable Edmund Burke, in the debate on the army estimates, in the House of Commons, 9 February 1790*, 3rd edn 1790, in Harris, *Burke: pre-revolutionary writings*

——— *A letter to a member of the National Assembly*, 1791, in Langford, *Writings of Edmund Burke*, iii

————— *An appeal from the new to the old Whigs*, 1791, in Ritchie, *Further reflections*
————— *Speech on the Quebec government bill, 11 May 1791*, in Burke, *Speeches*, iv. 36
————— *Fourth letter on a regicide peace*, 1795, in Langford, *Writings of Edmund Burke*, x
————— *A letter from the Rt. Hon. Edmund Burke to a noble lord, on the attacks made upon him and his pension in the House of Lords, by the duke of Bedford and the earl of Lauderdale*, 1796, in Langford, *Writings of Edmund Burke*, x
Croft, George, *Plans of parliamentary reform, proved to be visionary*, Birmingham 1793
[Dalrymple, Alexander], *Parliamentary reform: as it is called, improper in the present state of this country*, 1792*
Dalrymple, Alexander, *The poor man's friend: an address to the industrious and manufacturing part of Great Britain*, Edinburgh 1793
[Dornford, M.], *The motives and consequences of the present war impartially considered*, 1793
[Eirenophilos], *A discourse on the advantages which accrue to the country from the intimate connexion which subsists between the several ranks and orders in society*, 1793
Elliot, Charles Harrington, *The republican refuted: in a series of biographical, critical and political strictures on Thomas Paine's Rights of man*, 1791*
Erskine, John, *The fatal consequences, and the general sources of anarchy*, Edinburgh 1793
[Gifford, John], *A plain address to the common sense of the people of England*, 1792
[Green, Thomas], *Slight observations upon Paine's pamphlet*, 1791*
Hardy, Thomas, *Fidelity to the British constitution: the duty and interest of the people, a sermon*, 2nd edn Edinburgh 1794
————— *The importance of religion to national prosperity, a sermon*, Edinburgh 1794
Hawtrey, Charles, *Various opinions of the philosophical reformers considered; particularly Pain's Rights of man*, 1792*
Hayes, Samuel, *A sermon preached in St. Margaret's Church, Westminster on Sunday 27 January 1793*, 1793
[Hearn, Thomas], *A short review of the rise and progress of freedom in modern Europe, as connected with causes which led to the French Revolution . . . with a vindication of the English constitution . . . in answer to the calumnies of Thomas Paine*, 1792*
[Hervey, Frederick], *A new friend on an old subject*, 1791*
————— *An answer to the second part of Rights of man*, 1792*
Hey, Richard, *Happiness and rights: a dissertation upon several subjects relative to the rights of man and his happiness*, 1792
Hunt, Isaac, *Rights of Englishmen: an antidote to the poison now vending by the transatlantic republican Thomas Paine*, 1791
Hurdis, James, *Equality: a sermon to which is added a sermon preached on Friday 28 February 1794, the day appointed for the general fast*, 1794*
[Jephson, Graham], *Letters to Thomas Payne: in answer to his late publication on the rights of man*, 1792*
[Jones, John], *The reason of man: with strictures on Rights of man, and others of Mr Paine's works*, Canterbury 1792*
Lewelyn, William, *An appeal to men against Paine's Rights of man*, 1793

Maitland, James, eighth earl of Lauderdale, *Letters to the peers of Scotland*, 1794
[Mason, George], *A British freeholder's address to his countrymen, on Thomas Paine's Rights of man*, 1791*
Molloy, Tobias, *An appeal from man in a state of civil society to man in a state of nature: or, an inquiry into the origin and organization of those political incorporations most productive of human happiness . . . and which also includes strictures on Mr Paine's Rights of man; and points out the true origin of the hereditary monarchy*, Dublin 1792
Moore, Thomas, *An address to the inhabitants of Great Britain on the dangerous and destructive tendency of the French system of liberty and equality*, York 1793*
More, Hannah, *Thoughts on the importance of the manners of the great to general society*, 1788
—— *Village politics: addressed to all mechanics, journeymen, and day labourers in Great Britain*, 4th edn 1793*
—— *The history of Tom White the postillion*, in More, *Cheap repository tracts*, i, 1795
—— *The apprentice turned master: the second part of the two shoemakers*, in More, *Cheap repository tracts*, ii, 1796
Paley, William, *Reasons for contentment, addressed to the labouring part of the British public*, 1792
Patton, Charles, *An attempt to establish the basis of freedom on simple and unerring principles*, Edinburgh 1793*
Peter, Alexander, *Strictures on the character and principles of Thomas Paine*, Portsmouth 1792*
Playfair, William, *The history of Jacobinism, its crimes, cruelties and perfidities: comprising an inquiry into the manner of disseminating, under the appearance of philosophy and virtue, principles which are equally subversive of order, virtue, religion, liberty and happiness*, 1796
Reeves, John, *Thoughts on the English government: letter the first*, 1795*
[Rivers, D.], *Cursory remarks on Paine's Rights of man*, 1792*
[Saint John, John], *A letter from a magistrate to Mr William Rose*, 1791*
Scott, A., *Plain reasons for adopting the plan to the societies calling themselves the Friends of the People and their convention of delegates, as copied from the works of Mr Thos. Paine: in a serious address to the people of Edinburgh. By A. Scott, citizen and hairdresser*, Edinburgh 1793*
Scurlock, Revd David, *Thoughts on the influence of religion on civil government*, 1792
[Sewell, William], *A rejoinder to Mr Paine's pamphlet, entitled, Rights of man*, 1791*
Smith, Adam, *The theory of moral sentiments*, 5th edn 1781
[Smith, William Cusack], *Rights of citizens: being an examination of Mr Paine's principles, touching government*, Dublin 1791*
Somers Cocks, John, *Patriotism and the love of liberty defended*, 1791*
—— *A short treatise on the dreadful tendency of levelling principles*, 1793*
Somerville, Thomas, *Effects of the French Revolution*, Edinburgh 1793
Stewart, John, *Good sense addressed to the British nation, as their pre-eminent and peculiar characteristic, in the present awful crisis: or, war of social existence exhibiting the actual and eventful state of various nations*, 1794
Tatham, Edward, *Letters to the Rt. Hon. Edmund Burke on politics*, 1791
—— *A sermon suitable to the times*, 1792

[Watson, Richard], *Appendix to the bishop of Llandaff's sermon*, 1793, in *Association papers, part 1*, no. 7

Young, Arthur, *The example of France a warning to Britain*, 1793, 4th edn 1794*

Collected papers etc

Association for Preserving Liberty and Property against Republicans and Levellers, *Association papers*, I: *Publications printed by special order of the Society for Preserving Liberty and Property Against Republicans and Levellers, at the Crown and Anchor, in the Strand*; II: *A collection of tracts, printed at the expense of that society, to which are prefixed, a preface, and the proceedings of the society*, 1793 [BLPC, shelfmark, 1141.d.6]

Barlow, Joel, *The political writings of Joel Barlow*, New York 1796

Burke, Edmund, *The works of the Right Honourable Edmund Burke*, London 1808

────── *The speeches of the Right Honourable Edmund Burke in the House of Commons and in Westminster Hall*, London 1816

Claeys, Gregory (ed.), *Utopias of the British enlightenment*, Cambridge 1994

────── (ed.), *Political writings of the 1790s: French Revolution debate in Britain*, London 1995

────── (ed.), *The politics of English Jacobinism: writings of John Thelwall*, University Park, PA 1995

────── (ed.), *Modern British utopias, 1700–1850*, London 1997

Copeland T. W. and others (eds), *The correspondence of Edmund Burke*, Cambridge 1958–78

Corfield, Penelope J. and Chris Evans (eds), *Youth and revolution in the 1790s: letters of William Pattisson, Thomas Amyot and Henry Crabb Robinson*, Stroud 1996

Dickinson, H. T. (ed.), *The political works of Thomas Spence*, Newcastle-upon-Tyne 1982

Eaton, Daniel Isaac (ed.), *Politics for the people: or, a salmagundy for swine*, London 1794

Foner, Eric (ed.), *The complete writings of Thomas Paine*, New York 1945

Foot, M. and I. Kramnick (eds), *The Thomas Paine reader*, London 1987

Hardy, T. (ed.), *Moral and political magazine of the London Corresponding Society*, London 1796

Harris, Ian (ed.), *Burke: pre-revolutionary writings*, Cambridge 1993

Johnson, Dr Samuel, *Dictionary of the English language*, 2nd edn, London 1760

Kucklick, B. (ed.), *Thomas Paine: political writings*, Cambridge 1997

Langford, Paul and others (eds), *The writings and speeches of Edmund Burke*, Oxford 1913–91

LCS, *The correspondence of the London Corresponding Society*, London 1795

More, Hannah, *Cheap repository of moral and religious tracts*, London 1795–6

────── *The works of Hannah More*, London 1853

Political broadsides, British Library bound collection of tracts, broadsides, poems, songs and other similar material, n.d. [BLPC, shelfmark, 648.c.26]

Ritchie, Daniel, (ed.), *Further reflections on the revolution in France*, Indianapolis 1992

Thale, Mary (ed.), *Selections from the papers of the London Corresponding Society, 1792–9*, Cambridge 1983

The parliamentary register; or history of the proceedings and debates of the House of

Commons (and the House of Lords) containing the most interesting speeches etc., 1775–1813, 1784, xxx–xxxi

Thomas, D. O. (ed.), *Richard Price: political writings*, London 1991

Todd, Janet (ed.), *Mary Wollstonecraft: political writings*, Oxford 1994

Wyvill, Christopher, *The correspondence of the Revd C. Wyvill with Rt. Hon. William Pitt, concerning parliamentary reform*, 2nd edn, 2 pts, Newcastle-upon-Tyne 1796

—— *Political papers*, York 1794–1804

Secondary sources

Adonis, Andrew, *Making aristocracy work: the peerage and the political system, 1884–1914*, Oxford 1993

Aldridge, A. O., *Man of reason: the life of Thomas Paine*, London 1960

Alger, J. G., *Englishmen in the French Revolution*, London 1889

Amussen, S., *An ordered society: class and gender in early modern England*, Oxford 1988

Anderson, J. L., 'A measure of the effect of public finance, 1793–1815', *Economic History Review* 2nd ser. xxviii (1974), 610–19

Andrew, Donna, 'The code of honour and its critics: the opposition to duelling in England, 1700–1850', *SH* v (1980), 409–34

Appleby Joyce, 'Modernization theory and the formation of modern social theories in England and America', *Comparative Studies in Society and History* xx (1978), 259–85

Aspinall, A., *Politics and the press, 1780–1850*, London 1949

Ayer, A. J., *Thomas Paine*, London 1988

Aylmer, G. E. (ed.), *The Levellers in the English Revolution*, London 1975

Baker, K. M., *Inventing the French Revolution: essays on French political culture in the eighteenth century*, Cambridge 1990

Barker, H. and E. Chalus (eds), *Gender in eighteenth-century England: roles, representations and responsibilities*, London 1997

Barry, J., 'Consumers' passions: the middle class in eighteenth-century England', *HJ* xxxiv (1991), 207–16

Beckett, J. V., *The aristocracy in England, 1660–1914*, Oxford 1986

Best, Geoffrey, *War and society in revolutionary Europe, 1770–1870*, London 1982

Bewley, C. and D. Bewley, *Gentleman radical: a life of John Horne Tooke, 1736–1812*, London 1998

Bindman, David, *The shadow of the guillotine: Britain and the French Revolution*, London 1989

Black, Eugene C., *The Association: British extraparliamentary political organization, 1769–93*, Cambridge, Mass. 1963

Blakemore, Steven, *Burke and the fall of language: the French Revolution as linguistic event*, Hanover, NH 1988

Booth, Alan, 'Popular loyalism and public violence in the north-west of England, 1790–1800', *SH* viii (1983), 295–313

Botein, S., J. R. Censer and H. Ritvo, 'The periodical press in eighteenth-century English and French society: a cross-cultural approach', *Comparative Studies in Society and History* xxiii (1981), 464–90

Boulton, J. T., *The language of politics in the age of Wilkes and Burke*, London 1963
Brent, Richard, *Liberal Anglican politics: Whiggery, religion and reform, 1830–1841*, Oxford 1987
Brewer, J., 'Rockingham, Burke and Whig political argument', *HJ* xviii (1975), 188–201
—— *Party ideology and popular politics at the accession of George III*, Cambridge 1976
—— *The sinews of power: war, money and the English state, 1688–1783*, New York 1989
—— *The pleasures of the imagination: English culture in the eighteenth century*, London 1997
—— and John Styles (eds), *An ungovernable people: the English and their law in the seventeenth and eighteenth centuries*, London 1980
Briggs, Asa, *The age of improvement, 1783–1867*, London 1959
Bromwich, David, 'Wollstonecraft as a critic of Burke', *PT* xxiii (1995), 617–34
—— *On empire, liberty and reform: speeches and letters: Edmund Burke*, New Haven, Conn. 2000
Brown, F. K., *Fathers of the Victorians: the age of Wilberforce*, Cambridge 1961
Brown, P. A., *The French Revolution in English history* (1918), repr. London 1965
Bush, M. L., *The English aristocracy: a comparative synthesis*, Manchester 1984
—— (ed.), *Social orders and social classes in Europe since 1500: studies in social stratification*, London 1992
Butler, Marilyn (ed.), *Burke, Paine, Godwin, and the revolution controversy*, Cambridge 1984
Butterfield, Herbert, *Whig interpretation of history*, London 1931
—— *George III, Lord North and the people, 1779–80*, London 1949
Canavan, Francis P., *The political reason of Edmund Burke*, Durham, NC 1960
—— 'The Burke–Paine controversy', *Political Science Review* vi (1976), 389–420
Cannadine, David, *The decline and fall of the British aristocracy*, New Haven, Conn. 1990
Cannon, John, *The Fox–North coalition: crisis of the constitution, 1782–1784*, Cambridge 1969
—— *Parliamentary reform, 1640–1832*, Cambridge 1973
—— *Aristocratic century: the peerage of eighteenth-century England*, Cambridge 1984
Capp, B., *The fifth monarchy men: a study in seventeenth-century English millenarianism*, London 1972
Cartwright, F. D., *Life and correspondence of Major Cartwright*, London 1826
Cestre, C., *John Thelwall: a pioneer of democracy and social reform in England during the French Revolution*, London 1906
Chase, M., *'The people's farm': English radical agrarianism, 1775–1840*, Oxford 1988
Christie, Ian R., 'The Yorkshire Association, 1780–4: a study in political organization', *HJ* iii (1960), 144–61
—— *Wilkes, Wyvill and reform: the parliamentary reform movement in British politics, 1760–85*, London 1962
—— *Myth and reality in late eighteenth-century British politics*, London 1970
—— *Stress and stability in eighteenth-century Britain*, Oxford 1986

Claeys, Gregory, 'The effects of property on Godwin's theory of justice', *Journal of the History of Philosophy* xxii (1984), 81–101
——— *Thomas Paine: social and political thought*, Boston 1989
——— 'The French Revolution debate and British political thought', *HPT* xi (1990), 59–80
——— 'Republicanism and commerce in Britain, 1796–1805', *Journal of Modern History* lxvi (1994), 249–90
Clark, J. C. D., *English society, 1688–1832: ideology, social structure and political practice during the ancien regime*, Cambridge 1985
Cobban, Alfred, *Edmund Burke and the revolt against the eighteenth century*, London 1929
Coleman, D. C., 'Proto-industrialization: a concept too many', *Economic History Review* 2nd ser. xxxvi (1983), 435–48
Colley, Linda, 'The apotheosis of George III: loyalty, royalty and the British nation, 1760–1820', *P&P* cii (1984), 94–129
——— 'Whose nation? Class and national consciousness in Britain, 1750–1830', *P&P* cxiii (1986), 97–117
——— *Britons: forging the nation, 1707–1837*, London 1992
Collini, Stefan, Richard Whatmore and Brian Young (eds), *Economy, polity, and society: British intellectual history, 1750–1950*, Cambridge 2000
——— *History, religion, and culture: British intellectual history, 1750–1950*, Cambridge 2000
Cone, Carl, *Burke and the nature of politics*, Lexington, Ky 1957
——— *The English Jacobins: reformers in late eighteenth-century England*, New York 1968
Cookson, J. E, *The friends of peace: anti-war liberalism in England, 1793–1815*, Cambridge 1982
——— 'Political arithmetic and war in Britain, 1793–1815', *War and Society* i (1983), 37–60
——— 'The English volunteer movement of the French wars, 1793–1815: some contexts', *HJ* xxxii (1989), 867–91
Corfield, Penelope J., 'Class by name and number in eighteenth-century Britain', *History* lxxii (1987), 38–61
——— *Power and the professions in Britain, 1700–1850*, London 1995
——— 'The rivals: landed and other gentleman', in Harte and Quinault, *Land and society in Britain*, 1–33
——— Edmund M. Green and Charles Harvey, 'Westminster man: Charles James Fox and his electorate, 1780–1806', *Parliamentary History* xx (2001), 168–72
——— (ed.), *Language, history and class*, Oxford 1991
Crossley, C. and I. Small (eds), *The French Revolution and British culture*, Oxford 1989
Cunningham, H., 'The language of patriotism, 1750–1914', *History Workshop* xii (1981), 8–33
Dann, Otto and John Dinwiddy (eds), *Nationalism in the age of the French Revolution*, London 1988
Davidoff, L. and C. Hall, *Family fortunes: men and women of the English middle class, 1780–1850*, London 1987

Denvir, B., *The eighteenth century: art, design and society, 1689–1789*, London 1983
Derry, John W., *Politics in the age of Fox, Pitt and Liverpool*, London 1990
Deutsch, Phyllis, 'Moral trespass in Georgian London: gaming, gender and electoral politics in the age of George III', HJ xxxix (1996), 637–56
Dickinson, H. T., *Liberty and property: political ideology in eighteenth-century Britain*, London 1977
—— *British radicalism and the French Revolution, 1789–1815*, Oxford 1985
—— *Caricatures and the constitution, 1760–1832*, Cambridge 1986
—— 'Popular loyalism in Britain in the 1790s', in Hellmuth, *Transformation of political culture*, 503–34
—— 'Popular conservatism and militant loyalism, 1789–1815', in Dickinson, *Britain and the French Revolution*, 103–26
—— (ed.), *Britain and the French Revolution, 1789–1815*, London 1994
Dinwiddy, John, 'Christopher Wyvill and reform, 1790–1820', *Borthwick Papers* xxxix (1971), 1–32
—— 'Conceptions of revolution in the English radicalism of the 1790s', in Hellmuth, *Transformation of political culture*, 535–60
—— 'Interpretations of anti-Jacobinism', in Philp, *French Revolution*, 38–49
Donnelly, F. K., 'The Levellers and early nineteenth-century radicalism', *Bulletin of the Society for the Study of Labour History* xlix (1984), 24–8
Doyle, William, *The ancien régime*, London 1986
—— *Officers, nobles and revolutionaries: essays on eighteenth century France*, London 1995
Dozier, Robert, *For king, constitution and country: the English loyalists and the French Revolution*, Lexington, Ky 1983
Dreyer, Frederick, 'Burke's religion', *Studies in Burke and his time*, xvii, London 1976, 199–212
—— *Burke's politics: a study in Whig orthodoxy*, Waterloo, Ont. 1979
Duffy, Michael, 'William Pitt and the origins of the loyalist Association Movement of 1792', HJ xxxix (1996), 943–62
Eastwood, David, 'Patriotism and the English state in the 1790s', in Philp, *French Revolution*, 146–68
Eger, Elizabeth and others, *Women writing and the public sphere, 1700–1830*, Cambridge 2001
Elias, Norbert, *The court society*, Oxford 1983
Elliott, M., *Partners in revolution: the United Irishmen and France*, London 1982
Elmsley, Clive, *British society and the French wars, 1793–1815*, London 1979
—— 'An aspect of Pitt's "Terror": prosecutions for sedition during the 1790s', SH vi (1981), 155–84
—— *War and society in revolutionary Europe, 1770–1870*, London 1982
—— 'Repression, "Terror" and the rule of law in England during the decade of the French Revolution', EHR c (1985), 801–25
—— 'Revolution, war and the nation state: the British and French experiences, 1789–1801', in Philp, *French Revolution*, 99–117
Epstein, James A., *Radical expression: political language, ritual and symbol in England, 1790–1850*, Oxford 1994
Erdman, David V., *Commerce des lumières: John Oswald and the British in Paris, 1790–3*, Columbia, Mo 1986

Flinn, M. W. and T. C. Smout (eds), *Essays in social history*, Oxford 1974
Foreman, Amanda, *Georgiana duchess of Devonshire*, London 1998
Forrest, Alan, *The French Revolution*, Oxford 1999
Freeman, Michael, *Edmund Burke and the critique of political radicalism*, Oxford 1980
Gallop, Geoffrey, 'Ideology and the English Jacobins: the case of John Thelwall', *Enlightenment and Dissent* v (1986), 3–20
Gash, N., *Aristocracy and people: Britain, 1815–65*, London 1979
George, Dorothy M., *English political caricature, 1793–1832*, Oxford 1959
Ginter, Donald, 'The loyalist Association Movement of 1792–3 and British public opinion', *HJ* ix (1966), 179–90
Girouard, Mark, *The return to Camelot: chivalry and the English gentleman*, New Haven, Conn. 1981
Graham, Jenny, *The nation, the law and the king: reform politics in England, 1789–1799*, Washington, DC 2000
Greene, Jack P., 'Paine, America and the "modernization" of political consciousness', *Political Science Quarterly* xciii (1978), 73–92
Goodwin, Albert, *The european nobility in the eighteenth century*, London 1953
—— *The friends of liberty: the English democratic movement in the age of the French Revolution*, London 1979
Gunn, J. A. W., *Beyond liberty and property: the process of self-recognition in eighteenth-century political thought*, Montreal 1983
Habermas, J., *The structural transformation of the public sphere: an inquiry into a category of bourgeois society*, Cambridge, Mass. 1989
Hampsher-Monk, Ian, 'Civic humanism and parliamentary reform: the case of the Society of the Friends of the People', *JBS* xviii (1979), 70–89
—— 'John Thelwall and the eighteenth-century radical response to political economy', *HJ* xxxiv (1991), 1–20
Harley, C. K., 'British industrialisation before 1841: evidence of lower growth during the Industrial Revolution', *Journal of Economic History* xcii (1982), 267–89
Harte, Negley and Roland Quinault (eds), *Land and society in Britain, 1700–1914*, Manchester 1996
Hay, C., 'The making of a radical: the case of James Burgh', *JBS* xviii (1979), 90–117
Heavner, Eric K., 'Malthus and the secularization of political ideology', *HPT* xvii (1996), 409–30
Hellmuth, Eckhart (ed.), *The transformation of political culture: England and Germany in the late eighteenth century*, Oxford 1990
Hill, Christopher, 'The Norman yoke', in Hill, *Puritanism and revolution*, 50–122
—— *Puritanism and revolution: studies in interpretation of the English Revolution of the seventeenth century*, London 1958
—— *The world turned upside down: radical ideas during the English Revolution*, London 1991
Hole, Robert, *Pulpits, politics and public order in England, 1760–1832*, Cambridge 1989
—— 'English sermons and tracts as media of debate on the French Revolution, 1789–1799', in Philp, *French Revolution*, 18–37

Hollingsworth, T. H., 'The demography of the British peerage', *Population Studies Supplement* xviii (1965), 1–108

Hone, J. A., *For the cause of truth: radicalism in London, 1796–1821*, Oxford 1982

Howell, D. W., *Patriarchs and parasites: the gentry of south-west Wales in the eighteenth century*, Cardiff 1986

Hunt, Linda, *Politics, culture and class in the French Revolution*, Berkeley, Ca. 1984

Innes, Joanna, 'Politics and morals: the reformation of manners movement in later eighteenth-century England', in Hellmuth, *Transformation of political culture*, 59–118

Jacob, Margaret and James Jacob (eds), *The origins of Anglo-American radicalism*, London 1984

Jacobsen, Susan, L., '"The tinsel of the times": Smollett's argument against conspicuous consumption in Humphrey Clinker', *Eighteenth-Century Fiction* ix (1996), 71–88

Jarrett, Derek, *The begetters of revolution*, London 1973

—— *England in the age of Hogarth*, St Albans 1974

Jenkins, P., *The making of a ruling class: the Glamorgan gentry, 1640–1790*, Cambridge 1983

Jewson, C. B., *The Jacobin city: a portrait of Norwich in its reaction to the French Revolution, 1788–1802*, Glasgow 1975

Jones, C. (ed.), *Britain and revolutionary France: conflict, subversion and propaganda*, Exeter 1983

Jones, M. G., *Hannah More*, Cambridge 1952

Jones, Peter (ed.), *The French Revolution: in social & political perspective*, London 1996

Jupp, P. J., 'The landed elite and political authority', *JBS* xxix (1990), 53–79

Kates, G., 'From liberalism to radicalism: Tom Paine's *Rights of man*', *JHI* i (1989), 569–87

Keane, Angela, *Women writers and the English nation in the 1790s*, Cambridge 2001

Keen, Maurice, *Chivalry*, New Haven, Conn. 1984

Kelley, Donald R., *The descent of ideas: the history of intellectual history*, Aldershot 2002

Kiernan, V. G., 'Evangelicalism and the French Revolution', *P&P* vii (1952), 44–56

—— *The duel in European history: honour and the reign of aristocracy*, New York 1988

Kramnick, Isaac, *The rage of Edmund Burke: the conscience of an ambivalent Conservative*, New York 1977

—— 'Religion and radicalism: English political theory in the age of revolution', *PT* v (1977), 505–34

—— 'English middle-class radicalism in the eighteenth century', *Literature of Liberty* iii (1980), 5–48

—— 'Republic revisionism revisited', *American Political Science Review* lxxxvii (1982), 629–64

Langford, Paul, *A polite and commercial people: England, 1727–1783*, Oxford 1989

—— *Public life and the propertied Englishman, 1689–1798*, Oxford 1991

Laslett, Peter, *The world we have lost*, London 1965

—— *The world we have lost, further explored*, London 1983

Lecky, W. E. D. H., *A history of England in the eighteenth century*, London 1892

Lieven, D., *The aristocracy in Europe, 1815–1914*, London 1992
Lincoln, Anthony, *Some political and social ideas of English dissent, 1763–1800*, Cambridge 1938
Lockitt, C. H., *The relations of English and French society, 1763–1793*, London 1920
Looser, D., *British women writers and the writing of history, 1670–1820*, Baltimore, MD 2000
McCahill, M. W., 'Peers, patronage and the Industrial Revolution', *JBS* xvi (1976), 84–107
—— *Order and equipoise: the peerage and the House of Lords, 1783–1806*, London 1978
—— 'Peerage creations and the changing character of the British nobility, 1750–1830', *EHR* xcvi (1981), 259–84
McCalman, Iain, *Radical underworld: prophets, revolutionaries, and pornographers in London, 1795–1840*, Oxford 1988
McGovern, Trevor, 'Conservative ideology in Britain in the 1790s', *History* lxxiii (1988), 238–47
McKendrick, N., J. Brewer, and J. H. Plumb, *The birth of a consumer society: the commercialization of eighteenth-century England*, London 1982
McKenzie, Lionel A., 'The French Revolution and English parliamentary reform: James Mackintosh and the *Vindiciae gallicae*', *ECS* xiv (1980), 264–82
McNally, David, 'Political economy to the fore: Burke, Malthus and the Whig response to popular radicalism in the age of the French Revolution', *HPT* xxi (2000), 427–47
MacPherson, C. B., *The political theory of possessive individualism: Hobbes to Locke*, Oxford 1962
Mandler, Peter, *Aristocratic government in the age of reform; Whigs and Liberals, 1830–52*, Oxford 1990
Marshall, D., *Industrial England, 1776–1851*, London 1982
Mason, Philip, *The English gentleman: the rise and fall of an ideal*, New York 1982
Mathias, Peter, *The transformation of England: essays in the economic and social history of England in the eighteenth century*, London 1979
Mingay, G. E., *English landed society in the eighteenth century*, London 1963
—— *The gentry: the rise and fall of a ruling class*, London 1976
Mitchell, Austin, 'The Association movement of 1792–1793', *HJ* iv (1961), 56–77
Mitchell, Leslie G., *Charles James Fox and the disintegration of the Whig party, 1782–1784*, Oxford 1971
—— *Charles James Fox*, London 1992
Moore, D. C., 'Concesssion or cure: the sociological premises of the first Reform Act', *HJ* ix (1966), 35–59
Morris, R. J., *Class and class consciousness in the Industrial Revolution, 1780–1850*, London 1979
Murray, William J., *The right-wing press in the French Revolution, 1789–1792*, Woodbridge 1985
Namier, L. and J. Brooke, *History of parliament: the House of Commons, 1754–1790*, London 1964
Neale, R. S., *Class in English history, 1680–1850*, Oxford 1981

Newman, Gerald, *The rise of English nationalism: a cultural history, 1740–1830*, New York 1987
O'Brien, Conor Cruise, *The great melody: a thematic biography of Edmund Burke*, London 1992
O'Gorman, Frank, *The Whig party and the French Revolution*, London 1967
—— *Edmund Burke: his political philosophy*, London 1973
—— *The rise of party in England: the Rockingham Whigs, 1760–1782*, London 1975
—— 'Fifty years after Namier: the eighteenth century in British historical writing', ECS xx (1979), 99–120
—— *Voters, patrons, and parties: the unreformed electorate in Hanoverian England, 1734–1832*, Oxford 1989
Olson, A. G., *The radical duke: career and correspondence of Charles Lennox, third duke of Richmond*, Oxford 1961
Osborne, J. W., *John Cartwright*, Cambridge 1972
Owen, John B., *The eighteenth century, 1714–1815*, London 1974
Pagden, Anthony (ed.), *The languages of political theory in early modern Europe*, Cambridge 1987
Paulson, R., *Representations of revolution, 1789–1820*, New Haven, Conn. 1983
Pawson, E., *The early Industrial Revolution: Britain in the eighteenth century*, New York 1979
Payne, Harry C., 'Elite versus popular mentality in the eighteenth century', *Studies in Eighteenth-Century Culture* viii (1979), 3–32
Pedersen, Susan, 'Hannah More meets Simple Simon: tracts, chapbooks and popular culture in late eighteenth-century England', JBS xxv (1986), 84–113
Pendleton, Gayle Trusdel, 'Three score identifications of anonymous British pamphlets of the 1790s', *Notes and Queries* xxvi (1976), 208–17
—— 'Towards a bibliography of the *Reflections* and *Rights of man* controversy', *Bulletin of Research in the Humanities* lxxxv (1982), 65–103
Perkin, Harold, *The origins of modern English society, 1780–1880*, London 1969
Perry, Marvin, Joseph R. Peden and Theordore H. Von Laue (eds), *Sources of the western tradition*, Boston, Mass. 1991
Phillips, J. A., 'Popular politics in unreformed England', *Journal of Modern History* lii (1980), 601–23
Philp, Mark, *Godwin's political justice*, Ithaca, NY 1986
—— *Paine*, Oxford 1989
—— 'The fragmented ideology of reform', in Philp, *French Revolution*, 38–49
—— 'Vulgar conservatism, 1792–3', EHR cx (1995), 42–69
—— 'English republicanism in the 1790s', *Journal of Political Philosophy* vi (1998), 235–62
—— (ed.), *The French Revolution and British popular politics*, Cambridge 1991
Plumb, J. H. *The birth of a consumer society*, Bloomington, Ind. 1982
Pocock, J. G. A., 'Burke and the ancient constitution: a problem in the history of ideas', in Pocock, *Politics, language and time*, 202–32
—— *Politics, language and time: essays on political thought and history*, New York 1971
—— *The Machiavellian moment: Florentine political thought and the Atlantic republican tradition*, Princeton, NJ 1975

—— 'Radical criticisms of the Whig order in the age between revolutions', in Jacob and Jacob, *Anglo-American radicalism*, 33–57
—— *Virtue, commerce and history: essays on political thought and history, chiefly in the eighteenth century*, Cambridge 1995
Powell, David, *Tom Paine: the greatest exile*, New York 1985
Quinlan, Maurice, *Victorian prelude: a history of English manners, 1700–1830*, New York 1941
Raven, James, *Judging new wealth: popular publishing and responses to commerce in England, 1750–1800*, Oxford 1992
Reddy, William, *Money and liberty in modern Europe: a critique of historical understanding*, Cambridge 1987
Reynolds, Susan, *Fiefs and vassals: the medieval evidence reinterpreted*, London 1994
Ritchie, Daniel (ed.), *Edmund Burke: appraisals and applications*, Princeton, NJ 1990
Robbins, Caroline, *The eighteenth-century commonwealthman*, Cambridge, Mass. 1959
Robinson, Nicholas K., *Edmund Burke: a life in caricature*, New Haven, Conn. 1996
Royle, Edward, *Revolutionary Britannia? Reflections on the threat of revolution in Britain, 1789–1848*, Manchester 2000
Rudé, George, *Wilkes and liberty*, Oxford 1962
Rule, John, *The labouring classes in early industrial England, 1750–1850*, London 1986
—— *The vital century: England's developing economy, 1714–1815*, London 1992
—— (ed.), *British trade unionism, 1750–1850: the formative years*, London 1988
Schama, Simon, *Citizens: a chronicle of the French Revolution*, London 1989
Schofield, Thomas P., 'Conservative political thought in Britain in response to the French Revolution', *HJ* xxix (1986), 601–22
Sekora, J., *Luxury: the concept in western thought: Eden to Smollet*, Baltimore 1977
Sewell, William, *Work and revolution in France: the language of labour from the old regime to 1848*, Cambridge 1981
Skinner, Q. R. D., *The foundations of modern political thought*, Cambridge 1978
Smail, J., 'New languages for labour and capital: the transformation of discourse in the early years of the Industrial Revolution', *SH* xii (1987), 49–71
—— *The origins of middle-class culture: Halifax, Yorkshire, 1660–1780*, Ithaca, NY 1994
Smith, E. A., *Whig principles and party politics: Earl Fitzwilliam and the Whig party, 1748–1833*, Manchester 1975
—— *The House of Lords, 1815–1911*, London 1992
Smith, Olivia, *The politics of language, 1791–1818*, Oxford 1984
Smith, Roger J., *The gothic bequest: medieval institutions in British thought, 1688–1863*, Cambridge 1987
Smythe-Palmer, A., *The ideal of a gentleman*, London 1909
Soloway, Richard, 'Reform or ruin: English moral thought during the first French republic', *Review of Politics* xxv (1963), 110–28
—— *Prelates and people: ecclesiastical social thought in England, 1783–1852*, London 1969
Spring, D. and E. Spring, 'Social mobility and the English landed elite', *Canadian Journal of History* xxi (1986), 333–51

Stanlis, Peter, *Edmund Burke and the natural law*, Michigan 1958
Stedman Jones, Gareth, *Languages of class: studies in English working class history, 1832–1982*, Cambridge 1983
Stevenson, John, 'Popular radicalism and popular protest, 1789–1815', in Dickinson, *Britain and the French Revolution*, 61–82
Stone, Lawrence, *The family, sex and marriage in England, 1500–1800*, London 1979
—— and Jeanne C. Fawtier Stone, *An open elite? England, 1540–1880*, Oxford 1984
Stott, Ann, *Hannah More: the first Victorian*, Oxford 2003
Sutherland, L. S., *The East India Company in eighteenth-century politics*, Oxford 1952
Thale, Mary, 'London debating societies in the 1790s', *HJ* xxxii (1989), 57–86
Thirsk, J., *Economic policy and projects: the development of a consumer society in early modern England*, Oxford 1978
Thomas, Peter D. G., *The House of Commons in the eighteenth century*, Oxford 1971
Thompson, E. P., 'The moral economy of the English crowd in the eighteenth century', *P&P* l (1971), 76–136
—— 'Patrician society, plebeian culture', *Journal of Social History* vii (1974), 382–405
—— 'Eighteenth-century English society: class struggle without class?', *SH* iii (1978), 133–65
—— 'The peculiarities of the English', in E. P. Thompson, *The poverty of theory and other essays*, New York 1978
—— *Customs in common*, London 1991
—— *The making of the English working class*, London 1991
—— *Witness against the beast: William Blake and the moral law*, Cambridge 1993
—— 'Hunting the Jacobin Fox', *P&P* cxlii (1994), 94–140
Thompson, F. M. L., *English landed society in the nineteenth century*, London 1971
Tosh, John, *The pursuit of history: aims, methods and new directions in the study of modern history*, 2nd edn, London 1991
Tuck, Richard, *Natural rights theories, their origin and development*, Cambridge 1979
Turberville, A. S., *The House of Lords in the eighteenth century*, Oxford 1927
—— *The House of Lords in the age of reform, 1784–1832: with an epilogue on aristocracy and the advent of democracy, 1837–67*, London 1958
Turner, Michael J., *British politics in the age of reform*, Manchester 1999
Vickery, Amanda, *The gentleman's daughter: women's lives in Georgian England*, New Haven, Conn. 1998
Veitch, George, *The genesis of parliamentary reform*, London 1913
Villiers, M., *The grand Whiggery*, London 1939
Vincent, Emma, 'John Bowles and the French revolutionary wars, 1792–1802', *History* lxxviii (1993), 394–420
Wahrman, Dror, 'National society, communal culture: an argument about the recent historiography of eighteenth-century Britain', *SH* xvii (1992), 43–72
—— 'Virtual representation: parliamentary reporting and languages of class in the 1790s', *P&P* cxxxvi (1992), 83–113

—— *Imagining the middle class: the political representation of class in Britain, c. 1780–1840*, Cambridge 1995
Wallach, S., ' "Class versus rank": the transformation of eighteenth-century English social terms and theories of production', *JHI* xlvii (1986), 409–31
Ward, W. R., *Religion and society in England, 1790–1850*, London 1972
Wasson, Ellis Archer, 'The crisis of the aristocracy: parliamentary reform, the peerage and the House of Commons, 1750–1914', *Parliamentary History* xiii (1994), 297–311
Watts, Michael, *The Dissenters: from the Reformation to the French Revolution*, Oxford 1978
Wells, Roger, *Insurrection: the British experience, 1795–1803*, Gloucester 1983
—— *Wretched faces: famine in wartime England, 1793–1801*, Gloucester 1988
—— 'English society and revolutionary politics in the 1790s: the case for insurrection', in Philp, *French Revolution*, 188–277
Western, J. R., 'The Volunteer Movement as an anti-revolutionary force, 1793–1802', *EHR* lxxi (1965), 603–14
Wharam, Alan, *The treason trials, 1794*, Leicester 1992
Whatmore, Richard, ' "A gigantic manliness": Paine's republicanism in the 1790s', in Collini, Whatmore and Young, *Economy, polity and society*, 135–57
Wilkins, Burleigh, *The problem of Burke's political philosophy*, Oxford 1967
Williams, Gwyn, *Artisans and sans-culottes: popular movements in France and Britain during the French Revolution*, London 1981
Williamson, Audrey, *Thomas Paine: his life, work and times*, London 1973
Winch, Donald, *Adam Smith's politics*, Cambridge 1978
Wood, E. M., *The pristine culture of capitalism: a historical essay on old regimes and modern states*, London 1991
Wood, Gordon, *The creation of the American republic, 1776–87*, Chapel Hill, NC 1969
Wood, Marcus, *Radical satire and print culture, 1790–1822*, Oxford 1994

Unpublished theses

Booth, Alan, 'Reform, repression and revolution: radicalism and loyalism in the north-west of England, 1789–1830', PhD diss. Lancaster 1979
Goodrich, Amanda, 'Peers or parasites? Debating the English aristocracy in the 1790s, PhD diss. London 2001
Greig, Hannah, 'The *beau monde* and fashionable life in eighteenth-century London, 1688–1800', PhD diss. London 2003
Morris, Marilyn, 'Attitudes to monarchy in the 1790s', PhD diss. London 1998
Murray, Nancy U., 'The influence of the French Revolution on the Church of England and its rivals, 1789–1802', DPhil. diss. Oxford 1975

Index

Note: Titles of pamphlets are indexed under the author's name; for anonymous titles readers are referred to the bibliography.

absolutism, French 5, 88; in Paine, 57–8, 60
Adams, Daniel, 127
America: and commercial society, 64, 133; republicanism, 6, 93–4, 98, 124; and senate, 82, 128–9
American War of Independence, 17, 23–5, 42, 168
ancien régime, English: in Burke, 9, 13, 31, 41–6, 90–1, 171; and loyalism, 156; in Paine, 6, 9, 57, 62–4, 84, 90, 120, 132; and radicalism, 21–2, 25, 113, 118, 137–8, 166–7; in Wollstonecraft, 47–8
ancien régime, French, 21, 25, 35, 137, 166; in Burke, 41, 43; and loyalism, 95, 104; in Paine, 57, 60, 62; in responses to Burke, 48–9, 52
Anglicanism: and aristocracy, 67–8, 142; and Church and State, 15, 30, 34, 48, 54, 85–8, 140, 155–6, 179; and conservative loyalism, 9, 15, 85–8, 110, 140–1, 155–6, 161; evangelical, 8, 28, 87, 156, 141, 160–1, 162, 163; high church, 85–6; high Tory, 86–7; and inequality, 106; and reformation of manners, 28, 162
Anti-Jacobin, 140
Anti-Jacobin Review and Magazine, 140
aristocracy, English: abolition, 6, 57, 58–9, 61–2, 79, 82, 123–4, 126, 128; *ancien régime*, 9, 13, 21–2, 25, 31; in Burke, 1, 5–7, 9, 13, 22, 29–41, 60, 73, 166, 171, 181; as class, 15, 17, 19, in Burke, 32–3, in loyalism, 96, 143, in Paine, 6, 58, 60, 166, in radicalism, 65, 84, 115, 176; and constitutional reform, 12, 25–6, 129, 176–7; definitions, 15–22, 31–4, 141–4; and display, 71, 104–5; earlier criticisms, 22–5; economic and social value, 108–11; and education, 48, 73, 100–3; and effeminacy, 8, 48, 51, 95; and glamour, 104–5; and idleness, 57, 61, 73–4, 77, 132, 137, 166; and independence, 54, 72, 95, 100, 151; landed, 33, 36, 38–40, 41, 61, 64, 68–9, 84, 98–100, 131; loyalist defence, 30, 94–7, 139, 141–4, 148–9, 156, 162–3, 164, 167–8, 176; monied, 33, 36, 38; natural, 5, 30, 33–4, 101; nobility as, 15–20, 33, 45, 58–60, 84, 141–2; in Paine, 5–7, 8, 9, 13, 57, 58–62, 64–5; in Painite radicalism, 65–74, 79–84, 115–38; as peerage, 20–1, 31–2; and placemen, 59, 77, 117–18; political role (*see* government; oligarchy); and Reform Bill, 178–9; Whig, 16–17, 20, 24, 26–8, 30, 32, 51, 179. *See also* commercialism; feudalism; government; heredity; leadership; pamphlet debate; titles
aristocracy, French, 6–7, 17–19, 57–8, 94–5, 179; abolition, 5, 10, 11, 37, 54, 58–9, 66, 82, 90, 126, 158; in Burke, 31, 32–3, 34–8, 44; in early responses to Burke, 48–9, 51–3, 55; in loyalist writings, 141–2; in Paine, 6, 77–8, 167; in radical writings, 113, 137
aristocracy and people model: in loyalism, 9, 143, 167; in Paine, 17–18, 62, 65, 68, 84, 106, 111, 120; in radicalism, 9, 43, 78–9, 90, 115, 120, 132, 136, 137, 143, 166–7
arming societies, 127
Association for the Preservation of Liberty and Property against Republicans and Levellers, 118, 129, 140, 149, 155, 156–7, 159–60, 169–70
Atkinson, William, *Concise sketch of the intended revolution*, 154

Barbauld, Anna-Laetitia, 74; *Civic sermons*, 75
Barlow, Joel: *Advice to the privileged orders*, 1, 66, 69–70, 74, 76, 79, 80; *A letter to the National Convention*, 74

Baxter, John: *Resistance to oppression*, 119, 125–6, 132, 133
Beckett, J. V., 179
Bedford, Francis Russell, 5th duke of, *see* Russell, Francis
behaviour, aristocratic, 71–2
Bentinck, William Henry Cavendish, 4th duke of Portland, 9, 56, 114, 140
Bentley, Thomas: *A few queries to the Methodists*, 79; *Poor man's answer*, 129–30, 133; *Rights of the poor*, 77, 136
Birmingham Society for Constitutional Information, 132
birth, *see* aristocracy; heredity
Bisset, Robert, *Sketch of democracy*, 146, 151, 153
Boothby, Sir Brooke: *Letter to . . . Burke*, 51, 53, 54, 171; *Observations on the appeal*, 19, 89, 92, 93–4, 98, 102, 104–5
Bousfield, Benjamin, *Observations on ... Burke's pamphlet*, 50
Bowles, John, 89; *Objections to the war*, 139, 143, 145, 147–8, 149, 153, 164, 170; *A protest against T. Paine*, 92, 100, 104, 108, 173; *Reflections*, 150
Brissot, Jacques-Pierre de Warville, 150
British Convention, 118, 127, 130, 131–2, 169
British Critic, 140
Bromwich, David, 30 n. 9, 35
Brougham, Henry, 178
Brown, James, *Importance of preserving*, 109
Burdett, Sir Francis, 175
Burke, Edmund: and Anglicanism, 87; *Appeal from the new to the old Whigs*, 30, 32–3; and aristocracy, 1, 6–7, 22, 29–41, 60, 73, 166, 181, ambivalence, 29–30, *ancien régime*, 13, 31,171, definitions, 31–4, natural, 5, 30, 33–4; cartoon, *frontispiece*; and commercial society, 41, 45; early responses to, 46–54, 55; and England as *ancien regime*, 9, 13, 31, 41–6, 90–1, 171; and Fox ,30; inheritance v. merit, 38–40; and land ownership, 98; and landed v. monied interests, 33, 36, 38–40, 41–2; and language, 13, 170–1; *Letter to a member of the National Assembly*, 37; *Letter to a noble lord*, 32, 40, 55, 126, 172, and medievalism, 13, 31, 43–4, 49–52, 55, 90, 170, 172; and Paine, 57; and pamphlet war, 14, 29, 120–1, 170; *Reflections on the revolution in France*, 5, 7, 13, 19, 23, 29–55, 142, 170; and representative assemblies, 38–9; and 'swinish multitude', 43, 77–8, 120–1, 136; as Whig, 26, 30, 31, 41
Butler, John, *Brief reflections*, 65–6, 77
Byron, F. G., 'The Knight of the Woeful Countenance', *frontispiece*

The Cabinet, 114
Cannon, John, 20, 166, 177 n.61
capitalism, and value of labour, 131, 135–6, 176
Carra, Jean Louis, 150
Cartwright, John, 67, 175; *Commonwealth in danger*, 120, 125, 129, 130; *Letter to the duke of Newcastle*, 70, 73, 82
Cawthorne, Joseph, *Injustice and impolicy*, 175
Chabot, François, 150
Chamberlain, Joseph, 180
charity, and wealth, 108, 109–10, 162–3
Chartism, 23, 180
chivalry: in Burke, 13, 43–5, 49–50, 52, 90, 151, 171–2; in Paine, 62
Christie, Thomas, *Letters on the revolution* 49, 170
Church and State: in England, 48, 54, 85–8, 187; in France, 42; loyalist defence, 15, 30, 34, 85–7, 140, 155–6
civil war, 23, 153
civilisation: and aristocracy, 45–6, 171; and commercial society, 133, 172, 178, 180
Claeys, Gregory, 10, 14, 46, 91, 93, 113, 172, 174
Clark, J. C. D., 9, 22, 29, 30 n. 9, 31 n.11, 85–8, 179
class, aristocracy as, 15, 17, 19; in Burke, 32–3; in loyalism, 96, 143; in Paine, 6, 58, 60, 166; in pamphlet war, 159; in radicalism, 65, 84, 115, 176. *See also* middle class; working class
Cobbett, William, 175
Colley, Linda, 12, 165, 168, 179
commerce: and loyalism, 10–11, 45, 79, 85, 89–91, 92, 98, 100, 107–11
commercialism, loyalist, 85, 107, 139–41, 144–5, 164–5, 167–8; and aristocracy, 10, 19, 45, 89–91, 92, 98, 100, 108–11, 152, 164–5, 171, 179; and broadening elite, 10–11, 18, 137, 140, 151, 160; in Burke, 41, 45; and constitutional reform, 151, 174; and empire, 146; in later debates, 180; and the people,

156–7, 159–61; and radicalism, 64, 133, 136, 137; and war with France, 144–5; and Whigs, 10, 41, 79, 91, 111, 167, 177–8, 178–9, 180
conservatism, 9, 11; Anglican, 9, 15, 85–8, 110, 140–2, 155–6; and Burke, 5, 23, 31, 41–3, 171; and commercial model, 144, 159, 168; and pamphlets for the people, 155–63
constitution, English: and balance, 4, 26, 31, 88, 93–4, 146; in Burke, 4–5, 47, 49; in loyalism, 53, 88, 90, 91–4, 111, 139, 145–9, 168–9; in Paine, 6, 63; in radicalism, 49, 80–2, 113, 124–9, 167, 168. *See also* reform, constitutional
constitution, French, 36–8, 49, 61, 63, 125
Cooper, Thomas: and agrarian reform, 75; and equality, 83; *A reply to Mr Burke's invective*, 69, 72, 73–4, 78; and republicanism, 80
Corfield, Penelope J., 16, 19, 83, 142–3, 152
Corn Laws, repeal (1836), 179
corruption, 25–7, 48; and American War of Independence, 23; and loyalism, 96–7, 99; and luxury, 27–8, 43; in Paine, 59–60, 63; and primogeniture, 59, 78; and radicalism, 20, 67, 76–8, 83, 84, 115, 117–23, 136, 137, 166, 176
country ideology, 15
county movement, 24–6
Croft, George, *Plans of parliamentary reform*, 151, 165
crown, influence on government, 25–6, 30, 31, 87

Dalrymple, Alexander, *Poor man's friend*, 19, 108–9
Damm, Benjamin, *Address to the public*, 70–1, 74, 76, 77, 81
Danton, Georges, 148
demagoguery, 139, 142, 149–52
democracy: and Burke, 30, 32–3, 35; direct, 124–5; in pamphlet debates, 22, 49, 153
Depont, M., *Answer to the reflections*, 52
Dickinson, H. T., 11, 83, 85 n. 3, 91, 127, 165, 174
Dinwiddy, John, 81
Dissenters: French, 34; and loyalism, 87–8; and radicalism, 15, 34, 74
Dornford, M., *Motives and consequences of the present war*, 145
Dozier, Robert, 9, 85, 88 n. 20, 111

Du Fresnoy, *Address to the National Assembly*, 51–2, 53
Dyer, George, *Complaints of the poor*, 116, 124, 135

East India debate (1783–4), 23, 26–7
Eastwood, David, 173
Eaton, Daniel Isaac: arrest and trial, 173 n. 39; *Politics for the people*, 121–3
education, and aristocracy, 48, 73, 100–3
effeminacy, and aristocracy, 8, 48, 51, 95
elite: commercial, 19, 136, 137, 143, 151–2; open: in Burke, 38–9, and demagogues, 151–2, and equality of opportunity, 153–5, loyalist model 10, 19, 91, 94–5, 102–3, 112, 139, 140, 141–4, 146, 167–9, 172, and new peerages, 20–1, 102, 146, and radicalism 105; philanthropic 162–3
Elliot, Charles Harrington, *Republican refuted*, 99, 101
émigrés, support for, 7
empire, in loyalist thought, 146, 180
employers: in loyalism, 143; in radicalism, 134–6
Epstein, James A., 79
equality: in loyalism, 105–8; of opportunity, 153–5, 168. *See also* inequality

feudalism: and Burke, 49–50, 94; and loyalism, 104, 172; and Paine, 60; and radical critique, 52, 69, 117, 121, 126, 132
Filmer, Sir Robert, 87
foppery: and aristocracy, 8
Fox, Charles James, 30, 114, 167; and East India Company, 26–7; support for French Revolution, 4, 56
Foxite Whigs 4, 27, 32, 98, 140, 172
France: Church and State, 42; and commercial society, 41–2; in loyalist writings, 146–7; in Paine, 58–9. *See also ancien régime*, French; aristocracy, French; National Assembly
franchise, extension, 26, 99, 123, 130, 177–8
French Revolution: abolition of aristocracy, 5, 10, 11, 37, 54, 58–9, 66, 82; in Burke, 29–55; and effeminacy, 8, 51; and loyalism, 7, 10–11, 45–6, 86, 88, 105, 139, 145–52, 156–7, 167; and manners, 8, 45–6, 150–1; in Paine, 58–9, 62; in pamphet debate, 3–4,

207

14–15, 22–8, 48–53, 55, 113–14, 180–1; and perceptions of aristocracy 1–3, 7; and radicalism, 3–4, 79–84, 113; and Terror, 7, 112, 113, 139, 141, 148, 149–50; and Whig support 4, 30, 32, 56, 148

French Revolutionary Wars, 15, 113–14, 123–9; and aristocracy, 7, 120, 148–9; and Church and State, 86; and loyalism, 139, 143, 144–5, 157, 170; and poverty, 7, 116, 118, 131–3, 157; and Whigs, 140

Frend, William, *Peace and union*, 125–6, 129, 132

Friends of the People, 11 n. 49, 118

Gagging Acts (1795), 173–4
game laws, 48, 58, 68, 89, 115
gender, and attitudes to France, 7–8
gentlemen: in Burke, 33–4, in loyalism, 151
gentry, 19–20, 26, 33, 100, 175
Gerrald, Joseph: arrest and trial, 127, 173 n. 39; *A convention*, 116, 118–19, 124–5, 127–8, 130, 169
Gifford, John, *Plain address*, 85, 93, 103, 105, 171
glamour, rationale, 104–5
Glorious Revolution, 22, 88, 166; in Burke, 34, 35, 44; and Fox, 56; in Paine, 63
Godwin, William, 13; *Enquiry concerning political justice*, 117, 119, 124, 134
Goodwin, Albert, 140 n. 7
gothic/gothic revival, 6, 49, 171–2
government: and aristocracy, 4, 16–17, 19, 23–5, 179, in Burke 31, 42, 49, 60, 166, in loyalist thought 93, 141–2, 151–2, in Paine 57–60, 63–4, in radical thought 5, 49, 52–4, 72–3, 118–20; mixed: in Burke, 34, 42, in loyalism, 90, 91–4, 111, 139, 142, 145–9, 165, 168, 181, in Paine, 57–8, 63, in popular belief, 4, 16, in radicalism, 49, 82, 84, 123–4, 181; and monarchy, 25–6, 30, 31
Graham, Jenny, 46 n.109, 58 n. 13, 80, 128
Green, Thomas, *Slight observations*, 95, 99, 101
Grey, Charles Grey, 2nd earl, 56, 175, 177 n. 63
Gunn, J. A. W., 86–7, 140 n .2

Hampsher-Monk, Iain, 128

happiness, and industry, 108, 130
Hardy, Thomas (loyalist), *Importance of religion*, 155–6, 160
Hardy, Thomas (radical), 127, 173 n. 39
Hawtrey, Charles, *Various opinions*, 86
Hayes, Samuel, *A sermon*, 155
Hearn, Thomas, *Short review*, 95, 101, 109, 171
heredity: and leadership, 33, 95–6, 98, 101–2, 110, 115, 121; and merit, 38–40, 54, 59–61, 68–9, 72–5, 82, 100
Hervey, Frederick: *Answer to the second part*, 18, 92, 98–9, 108; *New friend*, 96, 97, 170
Hey, Richard, *Happiness and rights*, 101, 108
Hill, Christopher, 57, 62
historiography, of aristocracy, 2
history, Whig interpretation of, 180
Hogarth, William, 157
Hole, Robert, 155
Holyoake, G. J., 179
honour, and aristocracy, 69–70, 73, 120, 142, 171
Horne, George, 85–6, 110
House of Commons: and aristocratic control, 179; in Burke, 39–40; and corruption, 97; and loyalism, 151; in Paine, 63; and radicalism, 54, 73, 75, 123
House of Lords, 15–17, 179–80; in Burke, 1, 40, 181; creation of peers, 20–1, 102, 146; elected, 82; in loyalism, 95–6, 98, 99–100, 142, 146–8; in Paine, 60–1, 181; in radicalism, 66, 82, 123, 128–9, 137
Hughes, William, *Justice to a judge*, 113
Hunt, Isaac, *Rights of Englishmen*, 99, 102, 103, 104, 111

idleness, aristocratic, 77, 132, 137, 166; in loyalism, 107–8; in radicalism, 57, 61, 73–4
income tax, 174–5
independence, aristocratic, 54, 72, 95, 100, 151
industry, in loyalism, 108, 155, 157, 159–61
inequality: economic, 10, 18, 57, 78–9, 115, 131–6, 144; in loyalism, 86, 103, 105–8, 110–11, 181; and opportunity, 153–5, 168; in radicalism, 57, 75–9, 115–17, 129–36, 153, 181; in workplace, 134–6

INDEX

influence: of aristocracy, 97; of crown, 25–6, 30, 31, 87
interests *see* commercialism; land; money

Jacobin Club/Jacobins, 113, 124, 141, 149–50
Jeffrey, Francis, 177
Jephson, Graham, *Letters to Thomas Paine* 96, 104
Jones, John, *Reason of man*, 92, 107, 111
Jones, William, 85–6, 110

labour: as property, 75, 130–1, 134; as source of happiness, 108, 130; as source of wealth, 130–1, 134–6
land: in loyalism, 98–100, 164; and monied interest, 33, 36, 38–40, 41–2, 99, 143, 174–8; in Paine, 61, 64; in radicalism, 68–9, 84, 123, 130–1, 134, 137; redistribution, 48, 75–6, 83, 106, 123–4, 134; and stability, 42
Langford, Paul, 12, 17, 165
language, in French Revolution debates, 12–13, 63, 84, 90–1, 141, 170–3
Lauderdale, James Maitland, 8th earl, *see* Maitland, James
law: and inequality, 68, 115
LCS, *see* London Corresponding Society
leadership: in Burke, 38–40, 166; and French Revolution, 5; in loyalism, 54, 97–103, 105, 141–4, 149–52, 156; in Paine, 59–61; in radicalism, 68, 72–5, 82, 123–4, 179–80. *See also* government
Lennox, Charles, 3rd duke of Richmond, 26, 81, 128
Leslie, Charles, 87
Levellers, Levelling, 23, 76, 90, 106–8, 153–4, 167, 176
Lewellyn, William, *Appeal to men*, 102, 172
liberty: and constitution, 92–3; and property, 31, 39, 47, 106, 173, 177
Locke, John, 26, 88, 131
Lofft, Capel, 46 n.109; *Remarks on the letter*, 54
London Corresponding Society (LCS), 80, 127–8, 131–2, 136, 137, 151
Louis XVI of France, 7, 57, 60, 113
Lovett, John, *Citizen of the world*, 130, 133
loyalism: and *ancien régime*, 22, 41; and Anglicanism, 9, 15, 85–8, 140–2, 155; and aristocracy, 2–3, 6, 8, 11–13, defence, 94–7, 139, 141–4, 148–9, 156, 162–3, 164, 167, 176, definitions, 18–20, economic and social value, 108–11, as hereditary, 95–6, 98, 101–2, 110, and new peerages, 21, role in government, 53, 90–1, 169; as broad coalition, 9; and Church and State, 15, 30, 34, 85–8, 140, 155–6, 171; and constitution, 53, 88, 90, 91–4, 111, 139, 145–9, 168; diversity in, 9, 88–9, 102, 110, 111–12, 140, 167; France and England compared, 139, 149–52; and leadership, 54, 97–103, 105, 141–4, 149–52, 156; and masculinity, 8; and modernity, 91–2, 97, 112; and monarchy, 85, 87; and pamphlet debate, 9, 11, 86–105, 139–65, 180; and pamphlets for the people, 111, 155–63, 165; and prevention of revolution, 10–11; and property, 87, 88, 96, 98–101, 106–8, 153, 167; and prosperity, 92–3, 107–8, 109, 114, 133, 164; and redefinition of the elite, 139, 141–4, 146; response to Paine, 85–112; sources, 85–6; strategies, 139–65; support for French Revolution, 88, 148; and Terror, 7, 112, 139, 141, 148, 149–50; and titles, 47, 103–5, 152; and universal inheritance, 40; Whig, 88–9, 93, 140; and working class, 140–1. *See also* Burke, Edmund; commercialism
luxury debate, 23, 25, 47–8, 74, 87, 134; and corruption, 27–8, 43; and industry, 109, 162; and manners and morals, 8, 15, 27–8; and poverty, 110, 116, 132–3

Macaulay, Catherine, 8, 46 n. 109; *Observations on the reflection*, 50, 53
McCahill, M. W., 21 n. 99
Mackintosh, James, *Vindiciae gallicae*, 48, 50, 51–2, 53, 54
McNally, David, 43, 78
Maitland, James, 8th earl of Lauderdale, 32
manners: in Burke, 43–5, 49–50, 52, 150; in loyalism, 150–1, 162; in Paine, 62–3; in radicalism, 71, 74; reformation, 28, 162; in Wollstonecraft, 48
Marat, Jean Paul, 150
Marie Antoinette, queen of France, 44, 47, 50
masculinity, and war with France, 8

Mason, George, *A British freeholder's address*, 93
medievalism, in Burke, 13, 31, 43–4, 49–52, 55, 90, 170, 172
meritocracy: and Burke, 33, 38–9; in loyalism, 102–5, 107, 110–11, 152, 171; and middle class, 178; in Paine, 58; in radicalism, 72–5, 82, 116, 180; and Wollstonecraft, 48
Methodism: and loyalism, 87
middle class: and conservatism, 179; and equality of opportunity, 154–5; and franchise, 99, 177–8; and taxation, 174–5
Molloy, Tobias, *Appeal from man*, 100–1
monarchy: British, 4, 49, 145–6; and Burke, 30, 33, 34, 38; French 5, 35, 51–2, 60; influence on government, 25–6, 30, 31, 87; and loyalism, 85, 87–8; and Paine, 60
money, and landed interest 33, 36, 38–40, 41–2, 64, 99, 143, 174–8
monopoly, and economic inequality, 133, 136
Moore, Thomas, *Address to the inhabitants*, 146, 147, 148, 149–50, 153, 157
More, Hannah, 8, 87, 156; *Cheap repository*, 160, 163; *Thoughts on the importance of manners*, 28; *Village politics*, 160–1, 162

National Assembly (France): and abolition of aristocracy, 5, 62; and Burke, 34, 36–9, 54, 142; and corruption, 59; and Paine, 62–3; in radicalism, 74
National Convention 1792 (France), 80, 150
nobility: as aristocracy, 15–20, 33, 45, 58–60, 84, 141–2; and wealth, 152
noblesse, French, 5–6, 17; in Burke, 32–3, 37, 43; in Paine, 58; radical criticisms, 51, 68, 82
Norman Conquest, and aristocracy, 22, 57, 62–3, 69

obedience, as obligation, 15, 86–7, 94, 141, 159
Ogilvie, William, *Essay on the right of property in land*, 75
O'Gorman, Frank, 30 n. 9, 41, 42
oligarchy, 4, 165; and Fox, 27; and Paine, 90; and radicalism, 5, 66, 93, 119, 137; revolutionary, 41–2

Oswald, John: *Government of the people* 119, 124; *Review of the constitution*, 66, 69, 70, 71, 72–4, 75, 78–9, 80, 82, 84

Paine, Thomas: *Agrarian justice*,124, 133–41; and aristocracy, 5, 9, 58–62, 105, 167, 181, abolition, 6, 57, 58–9, 61–2, 79, as class, 17, 19–20, 33, 58, 60, 84, 166, and effeminacy, 8, 95; *The Crisis*,166; *Dissertation on first principles of government*,134; and England as *ancien régime*, 6, 9, 57, 62–4, 84, 90, 113, 132; and labour and wealth, 130; and language, 13, 170–1, 172; *Letter on the late proclamation*,78; loyalist responses to, 85–112; and pamphlet debate, 14, 170; and property, 61, 76, 105–6, 129, 134; and radicalism, 56, 64–84, 115; and republicanism, 6, 57, 64–5, 125; and revolution 10, 84; *Rights of man*, 3 n.11, 5, 6–7, 10, 34, 56, 57–8, 77, 123–4, distribution, 64, 81, 128, responses to, 83, 86; and taxation,77–8. *See also* aristocracy and people model
Paley, William, *Reasons for contentment*, 86
pamphlet, definition, 14 n.61
pamphlet debate, 166–73, 180–1; and Burke, 14, 29, 46–54; decline, 173; and definitions of aristocracy, 17–19; and French Revolution, 3, 13–15, 22–8, 48–53, 55, 80–1, 114, 180–1; as interactive, 169–73; and language, 12–13, 63, 84, 141, 170–3; legacies, 173–8; and loyalism, 9, 11, 86–105, 139–65, 180; pamphlets for the people, 111, 155–63, 165; and radicalism, 56, 65–84, 171, 174; and representation and reality, 11; and representations of aristocracy, 1–4, 5, 11–15, 48–53, 65–72, 115–23, 181; and republicanism, 6; and suppression of radicalism, 3–4, 173–4
Parkinson, James: *Address to the Hon. Edmund Burke*,120–1; *Knaves acre association*, 115, 134–5
parliament: annual, 81, 125, 127; and corruption, 48, 76–7, 96–7, 115, 117–20; petitions to, 11, 118, 125–6, 127–8. *See also* House of Commons; House of Lords; reform, constitutional; representation, parliamentary
Parliament Act (1911), 179–80
Patton, Charles, *An attempt to establish*, 141, 152, 157

Pedersen, Susan, 160
Pendleton, Gayle Trusdel, 11 n. 47, 14
periodicals: conservative, 140; radical, 114
Perkin, Harold, 177
Peter, Alexander, *Strictures on the character*, 92, 106, 110
Petion, Jerome, 150
petitions to parliament, 11, 118, 125–6, 127–8
Petty, William, 2nd earl of Shelburne, 26
philosophes, and French Revolution, 36, 42
Philp, Mark, 3, 8, 83, 113–14, 124 n. 68, 173
Piggot, Charles, *The Jockey Club*, 67, 72, 81–2
Pitt, William (younger): coalition government, 9, 114, 140; and commercialism, 140; and East India Company, 27; and peerage, 20–1; suppression of radicalism, 3, 113, 115, 118, 123, 173; and taxation, 174
Place, Francis, 175
placemen, 59, 77, 89, 117–18
Playfair, William, *History of Jacobinism*, 150
Pleydell-Bouverie, William, 3rd earl of Radnor, 152
Pocock, J. G. A., 10, 16, 26; on Burke, 29–30, 31, 40, 41
politics: landed v. monied interest, 33, 38–40, 41–2, 143, 174–8; and religion, 15. *See also* pamphlet debate
poor laws, 110
Pop-Gun Plot, 127
Portland, William Henry Cavendish Bentinck, 4th duke of, *see* Bentinck, William
poverty: and American War of Independence, 25; and French Revolutionary war, 7, 114, 116, 118, 131–3, 157; in loyalism, 93, 109–10, 144, 153, 157; in Paine, 78; in radicalism, 75, 116, 122, 132–5
Presbyterianism, and loyalism, 87
Price, Richard, 14; *A discourse on the love of our country*, 3, 34
Priestley, Joseph, 46 n.109; *Letters to .. Burke*, 50, 53–4
primogeniture: in loyalism, 96, 110, 171; in Paine, 59, 76, 78; in radicalism, 68, 121; in Wollstonecraft, 48
progress: in loyalism, 92, 180; and Wollstonecroft, 48

property: in Burke, 39–40, 42, 47, 48, 176; equality of, 75–7, 105–8, 115, 153–5, 167; and heredity, 96, 98, 101–2, 134; labour as, 75, 130–1, 134; and liberty, 31, 39, 47, 106, 173, 177; and loyalism, 87, 88, 96, 98–101, 106–8, 139, 167; in Paine, 61, 76, 105–6, 129; and political rights, 82, 84, 98–9, 129, 137, 152, 167, 176–7, 178, 181; and radicalism, 54, 75–6, 82–3, 129–34, 137, 176–7; and representation, 54
prosperity: and aristocracy, 107–8, 109, 132; and constitution, 91, 92–3; effects of war on, 114, 133, 157; in radicalism, 74, 114, 132–3

radicalism: activist, 4, 113–14, 174; and aristocracy, 2–3, 5–6, 8, 11–12, 165, 166, 179, abolition, 6, 79, 82, 123–4, 126, 128, definitions, 17–20, and new peerages, 21, Painite criticisms, 65–72, 79–84, rhetoric, 66, 113, 114, 115–23, 126–9, 137–8, 166, 168–9, 172, 175–6, 180; civil war, 23; and Dissenters, 15, 34, 74; diversity, 8–9, 113–38; and effeminacy, 8, 48, 51; and French Revolution, 4–5, 79–84, 113, 123–9; and inequality, 57, 75–9, 84, 105–6, 115–17, 129–36, 153, 181; and language, 13, 63, 84; and loyalist commercial model, 133; loyalist response, 85–112; and merit v. heredity, 59–60, 68–9, 72–5, 82, 115–16, 121; Painite, 56, 64–72, 114, 171, 174, 175–6; and republicanism, 80–1, 128, 137; and responses to Burke, 46–54, 55; revolution v. reformism, 8–9, 12, 79–84, 123–9, 130–1; suppression, 3–4, 10, 83, 112, 113–14, 118, 137, 173–4. *See also* aristocracy and people model; Paine, Thomas; rhetoric
Radnor, William Pleydell-Bouverie, 3rd earl of, *see* Pleydell-Bouverie, William
Randol, Citizen: *Political catechism of man*, 124, 125
rank: abolition, 57, 58–9, 61–2, 79, 123–4, 126, 128; acceptance, 86, 110–11, 134, 141, 143
Reeves, John, 87, 88, 118, 140; *Thoughts on the English government*, 146–7, 150, 155, 156
reform, agrarian, 48, 75–6, 83, 106, 124, 134, 137

Reform Bill (1832), 3, 174, 175–7; and aristocratic hegemony, 23, 178–9
reform, constitutional, 8–9, 12, 88, 169; and Burke, 42–3; and Fox, 114, 140; and radicalism, 65, 81–2, 114–15, 123–31, 137, 168, 175–6; and Whigs, 4, 10, 25–6, 30–1, 34, 42, 56, 140, 175–8
reform, economic, 26, 30, 83
reformism, and radicalism, 8, 79–84, 123–9
Regency Crisis (1788–9), 23, 26–7
religion, and politics, 15. See also Church and State
representation: loyalist, 10, 85–112; in pamphlet debates, 14–15, 180–1; and politics, 1–3; radical, 57, 58–62, 64–84, 114–23, 129, 137–8; and reality, 3, 11–12, 151
representation, parliamentary, 39, 81, 124–5, 133; and property, 54, 177
republicanism: democratic, 6; and loyalism, 93–4, 98, 107, 147; in Paine, 6, 57, 64–5, 125, 128; revolutionary, 80–1, 137
revolution, and reformism, 8–9, 12, 79–84, 123–9
rhetoric, radical, 66, 83–4, 113, 115–23, 126–9, 137–8, 166, 168–9, 172, 180
Richmond, Charles Lennox, 3rd duke of, *see* Lennox, Charles
rights: equality of, 105–6, 167; inequality, 57, 75–9, 84, 105–6, 115–17, 129, 153, 181; and property, 82, 84, 98–9, 129, 137, 152, 167, 176–7, 178, 181
Robespierre, Maximilien de, 141 n.11, 150
Rockingham, Charles Watson Wentworth, marquis of, *see* Wentworth, Charles
Rockingham Whigs, 26, 31
Rous, George: *Thoughts on government*, 50–1, 52, 53
Royal Proclamation on sedition (1792), 3 n. 12, 85
Royle, Edward, 179
Russell, Francis, 5th duke of Bedford, 30, 32, 172

Sadler, Michael, 177
Saint John, John: *Letter from a magistrate*, 96, 97, 101, 106, 107–8
Schofield, Thomas P., 9, 106
SCI, *see* Society for Constitutional Information
Scott, A., *Plain reasons*, 148

Scott, John, *A letter to Burke*, 54
sedition laws, 3, 85, 114, 118, 127, 137, 173
Sewell, William, *A rejoinder*, 86
Sheffield Society for Constitutional Information, 80 n. 181, 127
Shelburne, William Petty, 2nd earl of, *see* Petty, William
Sieyès, *abbé* Emmanuel, *Essay on privileges*, 66, 67–8 and n. 77, 69, 71, 73
Smith, Adam, 130–1; *Theory of Moral Sentiments*, 44; *Wealth of Nations*, 131
Smith, Olivia, 55, 63, 159
Smith, Roger J., 29, 44 n. 91, 49
Smith, William Cusack: *Rights of citizens*, 92, 106, 110, 180
societies, radical, 80–1, 83, 114, 126–8, 132, 137
society, commercial, *see* commercialism, loyalist
Society for Constitutional Information, 127, 137; Birmingham, 132; Sheffield, 80 n. 181
Somers Cocks, John, *Short treatise*, 141–2, 147, 150, 153
sovereignty, popular, 6
Spence, Thomas: *End of oppression*, 120, 123–4; *Real rights of man*, 75–6, 134 n.140; *The rights of infants*, 121, 124
Stanhope, Charles, 3rd earl Stanhope: *Letter from the earl Stanhope*, 52
Stevenson, John, 127
Stewart, John, *Good sense*, 170
Stone, Jeanne, 12
Stone, Lawrence, 12
Stuart, Daniel, *Peace and reform*, 126, 130, 169
subordination: in loyalism, 15, 86, 94, 105, 110–11, 159; in radicalism, 68
suffrage, universal male: duke of Richmond's proposals, 26, 81, 128; in Paine, 61; in radicalism, 82, 99, 119, 125, 127, 129–30

taxation: and commerce, 174–5; and inequality, 77–8, 115, 117, 132; and loyalism, 93
Terror, 7, 112, 113, 139, 141, 148, 149–50
Thelwall, John, 13, 18, 47, 137, 151; arrest and trial, 127, 173 n. 39; *Natural and constitutional rights*, 21, 130; *Peaceful discussion*, 12, 125; *The peripatetic*, 122; and republicanism, 128; *Rights of nature*, 29, 131, 132–3, 134, 135–6,

INDEX

170; *Sober reflections*, 126; *The tribune*, 134 n.144, 135, 136
Thompson, E. P., 23, 65 n. 56
titles, hereditary: in loyalism, 47, 103–5, 152–3; in Paine, 58–9; in radicalism, 53, 66, 68, 70–2, 115
toleration, religious, 34
Tooke, John Horne, 80 n. 181, 127, 137 n. 39
Tories, and conservative loyalism, 87, 96, 140, 174, 176
Tosh, John, 14
Towers, Joseph, 46 n.109; *Thoughts on the commencement*, 50, 52
treason trials (1794), 137, 173
Turberville, A. S., 20–1
Two Acts (1795), 3, 173–4
tyranny, aristocratic, 66, 69, 71, 119, 122, 137, 142

Vaughan, William, *Catechism of man*, 17–18, 116, 117, 119
Vincent, Emma, 89 n. 28

wages, 134–6, 157
Wahrman, Dror, 11, 12, 65 n. 57; and aristocracy and people model, 9, 18, 111, 136, 143, 167; and commercial wealth, 174–5, 177–8; and landed class idiom,164; and language in pamphlet debates,170–1, 172
war: and aristocracy, 69–70. *See also* French Revolutionary wars
Watson, Richard, *Appendix*, 154, 162
wealth: and commerce, 144, 165, 174–5, 177; economic and social value, 108–11, 130–1, 158–9, 162; and heredity, 96, 152; and inequality, 78–9, 132–4, 153; landed v. monied, 19, 33, 36, 38–40, 41–2, 64, 174–7; redistribution, 77, 83, 134–6; and status, 20, 72–3
Wentworth, Charles Watson, marquis of Rockingham, 30, 31
Whatmore, Richard, 58 n. 13
Whigs: and aristocracy, 16–17, 20, 24, 26–8, 30, 32, 51, 179; and commercial model, 10, 41, 79, 91, 111, 140, 167, 177–8, 178–9, 180; and constitutional reform, 4, 10, 25–6, 30–1, 34, 42, 56, 140, 175–8; Foxite, 4, 27, 32, 98, 140, 172; and French Revolution, 4, 9, 30, 32; and loyalism, 88–9, 93, 140; and property and liberty, 177; Rockingham, 26, 31
Wilberforce, William, 28
Williams, David, *Letters on political liberty*, 24, 63
Williams, Gwyn, 83, 123, 173–4
Wollstonecraft, Mary, 8, 64, 76; and medievalism, 49, 50; *Vindication of the rights of men*, 46–9, 170; *A vindication of the rights of woman*, 56, 73, 74
working class: and loyalism, 108–9, 140–1; and radicalism, 180
working hours, 135
workplace, inequalities in, 134–6
Wyvill, Christopher, 24–5

Yorke, Henry Redhead: arrest and trial, 127, 173 n. 39; *Thoughts on civil government*, 18, 115–16, 117, 120, 124–5, 133, 166
Yorkshire Association, 24, 127
Young, Arthur, *Example of France*, 17, 141, 143, 144, 148, 153–4, 170

www.ingramcontent.com/pod-product-compliance
Ingram Content Group UK Ltd.
Pitfield, Milton Keynes, MK11 3LW, UK
UKHW021319180426
11947UKWH00015B/1321